GOOD ENOUGH MOTHERS

Fertility, Reproduction and Sexuality

GENERAL EDITORS:
Soraya Tremayne, Founding Director, Fertility and Reproduction Studies Group and Research Associate, Institute of Social and Cultural Anthropology, University of Oxford.
Marcia C. Inhorn, William K. Lanman, Jr. Professor of Anthropology and International Affairs, Yale University.
Philip Kreager, Director, Fertility and Reproduction Studies Group, and Research Associate, Institute of Social and Cultural Anthropology and Institute of Human Sciences, University of Oxford

Understanding the complex and multifaceted issue of human reproduction has been, and remains, of great interest both to academics and practitioners. This series includes studies by specialists in the field of social, cultural, medical and biological anthropology, medical demography, psychology and development studies. Current debates and issues of global relevance on the changing dynamics of fertility, human reproduction and sexuality are addressed.

Recent volumes:

Volume 49
Good Enough Mothers: Practicing Nurture and Motherhood in Chiapas, Mexico
J.M. López

Volume 48
How Is a Man Supposed to Be a Man? Male Childlessness – a Life Course Disrupted
Robin A. Hadley

Volume 47
Waithood: Gender, Education, and Global Delays in Marriage and Childbearing
Edited by Marcia C. Inhorn and Nancy J. Smith-Hefner

Volume 46
Abortion in Post-revolutionary Tunisia: Politics, Medicine and Morality
Irene Maffi

Volume 45
Navigating Miscarriage: Social, Medical and Conceptual Perspectives
Edited by Susie Kilshaw and Katie Borg

Volume 44
Privileges of Birth: Constellations of Care, Myth and Race in South Africa
Jennifer J.M. Rogerson

Volume 43
Access to Assisted Reproductive Technologies: The Case of France and Belgium
Edited by Jennifer Merchant

Volume 42
Making Bodies Kosher: The Politics of Reproduction among Haredi Jews in England
Ben Kasstan

Volume 41
Elite Malay Polygamy: Wives, Wealth and Woes in Malaysia
Miriam Koktvedgaard Zeitzen

Volume 40
Being a Sperm Donor: Masculinity, Sexuality, and Biosociality in Denmark
Sebastian Mohr

For a full volume listing, please see the series page on our website:
http://www.berghahnbooks.com/series/fertility-reproduction-and-sexuality

GOOD ENOUGH MOTHERS
PRACTICING NURTURE AND MOTHERHOOD IN CHIAPAS, MEXICO

J.M. López

berghahn
NEW YORK • OXFORD
www.berghahnbooks.com

First published in 2022 by
Berghahn Books
www.berghahnbooks.com

© 2022, 2026 J.M. López
First paperback edition published in 2026

All rights reserved. Except for the quotation of short passages
for the purposes of criticism and review, no part of this book
may be reproduced in any form or by any means, electronic or
mechanical, including photocopying, recording, or any information
storage and retrieval system now known or to be invented,
without written permission of the publisher.

Library of Congress Cataloging-in-Publication Data
Names: López, J.M., author.
Title: Good Enough Mothers: Practicing Nurture and Motherhood in
 Chiapas, Mexico / J.M. López.
Description: New York: Berghahn Books, 2022. | Series: Fertility,
 Reproduction and Sexuality; volume 49 | Includes bibliographical
 references and index.
Identifiers: LCCN 2021038458 (print) | LCCN 2021038459 (ebook) |
 ISBN 9781800732520 (hardback) | ISBN 9781800732537 (ebook)
Subjects: LCSH: Motherhood—Mexico—Chiapas. | Mothers—Services
 for—Mexico—Chiapas. | Maternal health services—Mexico—
 Chiapas. | Discrimination in medical care—Mexico—Chiapas. |
 Family services—Mexico—Chiapas.
Classification: LCC HV700.M4 L67 2022 (print) |
 LCC HV700.M4 (ebook) | DDC 306.874/3097275—dc23
LC record available at https://lccn.loc.gov/2021038458
LC ebook record available at https://lccn.loc.gov/2021038459

British Library Cataloguing in Publication Data
A catalogue record for this book is available from the British Library

EU GPSR Authorized Representative
LOGOS EUROPE, 9 rue Nicolas Poussin, 17000, LA ROCHELLE, France
Email: Contact@logoseurope.eu

ISBN 978-1-80073-252-0 hardback
ISBN 978-1-83695-407-1 paperback
ISBN 978-1-83695-408-8 epub
ISBN 978-1-80073-253-7 web pdf

https://doi.org/10.3167/9781800732520

For my mum and dad,
my children Emilia, Issac, Frida and Diego

Contents

List of Illustrations   viii
Acknowledgements   ix

Introduction   1

Part I. Contexts

Chapter 1. La Orilla: Coletas and Coloniality   13

Part II. Childbearing Politics

Chapter 2. Bety and Rosa   33

Chapter 3. Bridging the Gap: Barrio Midwives   63

Chapter 4. Cris, Sofi and Esme: The Birth Centre   85

Part III. Nurture Work

Chapter 5. Lupita and Carlita   117

Chapter 6. Sara, Bania and Lila: Good Enough Mothers   143

Conclusion. Translating a Local-Global Maternal Health   169

Appendix. On Doing Fieldwork with Children   173
References   177
Index   189

Illustrations

Maps

0.1. Mexico (source: public domain, https://commons .wikimedia.org/w/index.php?curid=4786068) xiii
0.2. Los Altos region, Chiapas, Mexico (source: CC BY-SA 4.0, https://commons.wikimedia.org/w/index.php ?curid=88810811) xiii

Figures

1.1. Main Street, la Orilla, Mexico, 2013 © J.M. López 16
1.2. Callejon, la Orilla, Mexico, 2013 © J.M. López 17
3.1. and 3.2 Examples of walk-in clinics, Mexico, 2013 © J.M. López 74
4.1. The lilac façade of the birth centre, Mexico, 2015 © J.M. López 84

Acknowledgements

This book is the product of a decade's worth of life transitions, relationships, family making, births, time spent between two countries and my personal development as anthropologist and researcher. Naming myself as sole author almost feels like a charade. No ethnography is ever made from one individual. The stories are provided by the generous people who share their lives and intimate thoughts. My observations, analysis and theories about the human condition of togetherness and transformations only exist because of my relationship to the families in Chiapas, the global academic community, my students, my family and friends and just about anyone who I have ever spoken to about parenthood, childbearing and life. I have written a book out of my own words and labour, but the ideas and knowledge are a collective effort.

Since I first travelled to Mexico in 2003, I have met many people who have sheltered me, fed me and welcomed me so that I now struggle to say where I feel most at home. Those people are special and my thanks to them is as it should be, written in their own language below these paragraphs. One person who I do thank in English, Spanish and the unspoken language of intuition is Cris Alonso, a midwife and friend for life who came to be my co-creator of knowledge. Thank you for the freedom and grace to use your words without censorship.

The international world of anthropology has been my dysfunctional family since I first came to study the subject at postgraduate level in 2006. Though I never thought I would think it, I am grateful that my career in social and community work preceded my identity as an anthropologist. I came to anthropology with a distinct critical eye for inequality, social justice and complex human relations thanks to the years spent working in sexual health, substance misuse and families in the UK and Mexico. The combination of these two careers kept me in the belief that research is and should be robust, objective and there to inform but also a form of activism. For support in that belief, I am indebted to Jeanette Edwards, Maya Unnithan and Ciara Kierans. Their mentorship, support and constructive critique of my work has pushed me to produce writing of which I am very truly proud. Jeanette encouraged and guided me throughout my studies and continues to do so to this day. Her detailed written and verbal feedback provided me with focus and the confidence to own my ideas. I am a good academic and researcher today because of the guidance I received at Manchester and the excellent students and staff in the Anthropology Department. Amongst those people I include Gillian Evans, Tony Simpson, Peter Wade and John Gledhill.

I have been lucky enough to travel to Mexico, Brazil, the US and across Europe to share my research on the families of Chiapas. During these trips I have met the scholars who pushed me to be more reflexive and open about the coloniality of knowledge in anthropology and the violent dominance of white privilege in ethnography and international scholarship at large. The political community of scholars I met during the 18th IUAES World Congress, Brazil pushed me to understand better the work I still had to do to centre Mexican thought and perspective in my work. The keynote address given by Mara Viveros Vigoya, 'Entre la extraversión y las epistemologías "nuestramericanas": el lugar de la producción antropológica con enfoque de género', led me to rewrite many chapters from scratch and question my motives for writing in the first place.

I was occasionally lucky enough to get funding for return visits to Chiapas and for this I am grateful to the University of Salford Christopher Hale Memorial Fund, VC Fellowship, the University of Manchester, Humanitarian Conflict Response Institute internal support for researchers.

I greatly appreciate the detailed reviews of the manuscript from peer reviewers who gifted their labour to the publishers. The constructive comments, revisions and suggestions from Robbie Floyd-Davis were invaluable to the final draft. Thank you for your generosity and for having the patience to wade through my punctation shortcomings.

Finally, I would like to thank my family: my parents, my four amazing children and my ex-husband. You all accompanied me throughout this journey whether in utero, person or at a distance. Behind every working anthropologist is an army of support and tolerance.

Y para México

Este proyecto no sería posible sin el apoyo, amor, amistad y consejos de mi familia adoptiva y mis amigos de México.

Primero, quiero expresar mi gratitud a mi familia del alma en Chiapas. A mi hermana Bety y a nuestra madre Felisa, quienes me acogieron en su hogar y su familia hace diecisiete años y me integraron a ella. La relación con ellas me guió para estudiar y escribir sobre la maternidad, alimentación y vida de las familias en Chiapas. Ellas fueron y son mi continua inspiración.

Mi hermana del alma, Bety, ha sido una conciencia crítica para mí con el paso de los años, salvándome durante los meses que sufrí aprendiendo español y guiándome durante las cientas de veces que rompí con las convenciones sociales. Ella nunca tiene miedo de desafiar mis pensamientos y supuestos, por eso siempre le estaré agradecida.

Bety ha estado a mi lado en México durante mi boda, embarazo, vida familiar y las continuas transiciones de la vida. Estoy orgulloso de ser su hermano. Su familia está en mi corazón y su espíritu y guía aparecen a lo largo de este libro; espero que, como su hijo descarriado, se sienta orgullosa de mí.

Me gustaría agradecer a mi buen amigo, el doctor Alejandro Riviera, quien desde su juventud ha trabajado incansablemente para mejorar la vida de las personas con VIH/SIDA y ha promovido campañas a favor de los derechos humanos de la comunidad LGBTQ en Chiapas. Él me ha ensañado sobre la fortaleza, perseverancia y conciencia de las dinámicas sociales y de clase de las poblaciones urbanas en México. Sin él no habría encontrado a mi partera y gran amiga, Cris. Nunca olvidaré el impacto que sus compañeros Gustavo y Arturo – que en paz descansen – tuvieron en mi vida, enseñándome sobre los muchos niveles de amor que existen en las familias mexicanas, ya sea de sangre o adoptivas.

Estoy en deuda con la física y sociología, la doctora Austreberta Nazar, quien me apoyó durante la concepción de mi proyecto y su ejecución cuando intenté entrar a un programa de doctorado en Chiapas, al mismo tiempo que vivía las dificultades mi primer postparto. A través de los años, la doctora Nazar siempre me ha recibido bien cuando regreso a San Cristóbal y me ha apoyado con su experiencia y conocimientos sobre salud materna y comunitaria.

También agradezco a la doctora Georgina Sánchez Ramírez, por su generosidad y trabajo en los centros de nacimiento y partería en

México, y a la comunidad académica del Colegio de la Frontera Sur – ECOSUR – que me ha provisto de aprendizajes y recursos a través de los años y me ha tratado como un académico visitante no oficial.

Finalmente, tengo una enorme deuda de gratitud para las mujeres y familias que compartieron sus vidas e historias conmigo durante largas entrevistas y me dejaron hacerles interminables preguntas para resolver mis dudas. Agradezco – principalmente – a las familias de la Orilla de San Cristóbal, que abrieron sus hogares para mí y mis hijos, me apoyaron en mi embarazo y posparto, cuidaron a mis niños y nos dan la bienvenida cada vez que regresamos a visitarlas. Realmente espero que, en mi investigación, los haya descrito con el respeto y apreciación que merecen.

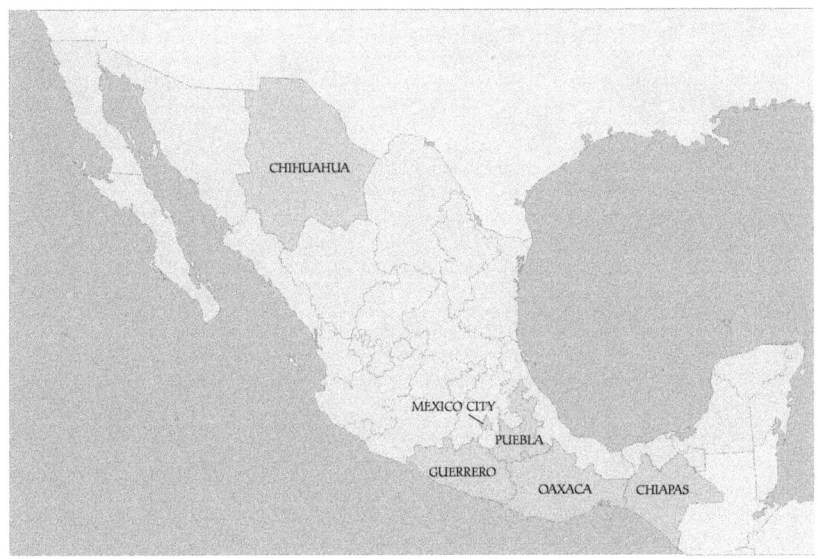

MAP 0.1. Mexico (source: public domain, https://commons.wikimedia.org/w/index.php?curid=4786068)

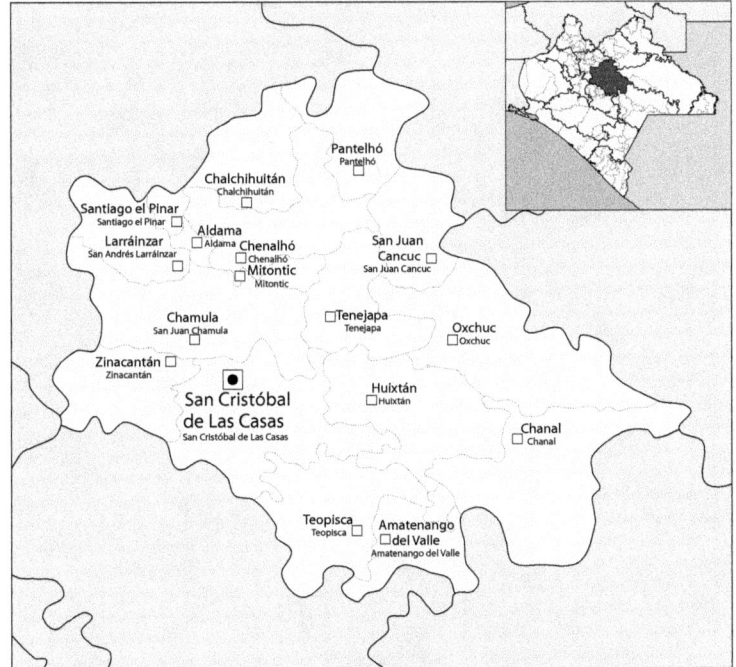

MAP 0.2. Los Altos region, Chiapas, Mexico (source: CC BY-SA 4.0, https://commons.wikimedia.org/w/index.php?curid=88810811)

INTRODUCTION

[T]he space for an alternative feminist discourse on maternity can be cleared only after rigorous interrogation of the cultural representations of motherhood.

—Ewa Ziarek, 'At the Limits of Discourse: Heterogeneity, Alterity, and the Maternal Body in Kristeva's Thought'

I spent most mornings during fieldwork in 2013 travelling back and forth between the small *barrio popular* (working-class neighbourhood) la Orilla and city centre on the *combis*, (converted vans) that move people and packages all over the city from daybreak until the day's end. The *combis* move at an alarming speed, navigating the city's colonial streets that grew gradually bumpier and less defined the further out of town we got. These daily journeys were my lifeline during the first few months, they gave my day structure and enabled me to interact with (and then eventually get to know) women from all over la Orilla who otherwise spent a large proportion of their days in household compounds. Before I got to know my neighbours well the *combi* journeys were essential for the type of 'mother-watching' I wanted to do for fieldwork. This type of public transport was familiar ground for me, having spent the previous years travelling around the city with my eldest child Emilia. On these earlier journeys, women would ask me where and how I had given birth, offer ways to improve my milk supply, check my baby was wrapped up correctly and scold me for not giving her water to drink from a bottle. As a new mother these interactions taught me how to 'perform' motherhood in a way that was acceptable to that environment. On those quick journeys I was offered countless snippets of advice and commentary that I could choose to take or discard the moment I climbed out of the vehicle and merged into the crowds on the street.

When I returned to the city for doctoral fieldwork I was accompanied by Emilia, now five years old and I was seven months pregnant with my third child. We arrived at the beginning of the rainy season. Sunny mornings would give way to the air becoming gradually more oppressive and as the day wore on as the sky would turn black erupting with thunderstorms by early afternoon. One particularly humid morning I was travelling home from the centre having just dropped Emilia off at school. It was just after 8.30am and the *combi* was full of women on their way home from the market. We were squeezed onto the narrow benches lining the sides of the van, colourful shopping bags bursting with vegetables and fresh aromatic bunches of coriander and parsley. Passengers sat with warm sweet breads and tomatoes sweating in plastic bags grasped by the calloused fingers of one hand, whilst another hand gripped onto the bench or dipped into an apron pocket for change to pay the fare. As the *combi* bounced along the dusty road, swerving every few seconds to avoid massive potholes, beep at dogs or narrowly avoid head-on collisions with oncoming lorries, I listened absentmindedly to the conversations as women went about their day. A middle-aged señora was chatting to a younger woman sat opposite who was cradling an infant in one arm and a litre bottle of coke in the other. The señora leaned forward, tickling the baby's legs with her free hand.

'A dónde vas chula?' (where are you going my love?)

'It's my turn to queue for my mum, my sister is with her now, but she has to go to work and my mum has to look after the little ones', she shifted on her seat and opened her blouse slightly so the child could turn its head to feed. 'It's signing on day and she's been there since eight o'clock waiting for her money. Are you going today? I'm told there's a big queue'. She was referring to the periodic signing on process for the pension provision of the conditional cash transfer programme IMSS-BIENESTAR (previously IMSS-PROSPERA).[1]

The señora shook her head, 'no I have too much to do at home, the gas ran out this morning and I have to wait for them to deliver more otherwise there'll be no dinner. I've sent my granddaughter to queue for me'. The *combi* screeched to a halt as another driver jumped out in front to warn ours there was a police check point ahead. The road through la Orilla was the main highway between the highlands and the city, and there were often random police checks for migrants, contraband or arms trafficking. As the van jolted to a halt, a bucket of chayotes spilled out onto the floor, its owner tutted and rolled her eyes at the driver muttering, '*ay joven* we are not cattle in here!' Everybody stretched out with a hand or a foot to rescue one of the spikey vegetables and return it to the bucket which was now lodged firmly between its owner's legs.

The *combi* set off again and the conversation continued. 'Do you have a message for your granddaughter?' the young woman asked. 'Yes', the señora replied, 'tell her I won't be long, I'm just going to do my jobs and I'll be there to sign'. Her voice quietened. 'Do you know who's there [from the municipal government]? The last time they sent me all the way into the centre because I had one digit missing on a paper. If it's the young one I won't have problems but if it's the other, the red head, uuuurrrgghh!' She shrugged her shoulders and pulled a face.

As the *combi* came to an abrupt halt another señora, looking to be in her mid-sixties, plump with two long plaits down to her waist, got on. She was accompanied by two teenage girls who now stood holding onto the handrail as the *combi* continued its way to the entrance to the *barrio*. The smell of warm empanadas wafted from her wicker basket and there was a bucket of *atole* (maize drink) covered with a cloth held steady between her feet. 'Buenos días', she greeted everyone as she shuffled her bottom to make space on the bench. 'Buenos días', echoed various voices in a customary reply.

'Buenos días comadre, what a miracle!' said the first señora to the new passenger. 'Are you off to sign or to sell?'

'Well, a bit of both', she chuckled, 'if I'm going to spend all day waiting in line I may as well make some money whilst I'm there'.

Over time daily life in the *barrio* and around the city taught me that motherwork, intimate relationships and everyday health are never far from engagement with colonial legacy and the global political economy. The lives of people with low incomes are tightly regulated, whether directly or indirectly, by state apparatus, including the unfeasible bureaucracy of identity proof and access to basic health and social services. As such, it is impossible to write about gender and maternal health politics in Mexico without mention of the state and its various apparitions in daily life. Women (as it is predominantly women who partake in this activity and who are the targets of anti-poverty campaigns in Mexico) treat these (dys) functional elements of the state as a *molestia* (an annoyance), a necessary evil that takes time away from crucial economic activity and managing families, but that nevertheless must be done. Yet, at the same time, women collectively invent ways of dealing with the bureaucracy so that their time devoted to the system does not end in vain. In doing so they learn what Auyero (2012) describes as the 'opposite of citizenship', or alternatively what I would define as acquiring an anti-state citizenship characteristic of over-managed populations. Women's positioning (young and old) as mothers, principal caregivers and perceived heads of poor households is what has historically defined their gendered relationship to the Mexican state (as far as the state is concerned). However, what I have come to learn after spending thirty months of fieldwork over a seven-year period (2008–2015), in a region undergoing rapid socio-economic change, is that for most women the state is at the periphery of what gives their maternal identity meaning.

At its heart, this book is a study of Mexican women's experiences of maternal transformation.[2] Yet rather than re-colonizing women as mothers, my aim is to understand this process of becoming as a broader way in which human beings respond to change. This study is a critique of homogenous representations of motherhood and global maternal health logic that exclude the intersection of sexual and reproductive health and that indirectly perpetuate a maternal homogeneity. This book is a project that celebrates ordinary maternal devotion, while castigating the toxic canonization of the mother figure that social systems have historically used to punish and shame women across the globe. I develop my ideas about being a 'good enough' mother in Mexico from the women whose stories shape the chapters in this book, and the hundreds of other conversations I have had with people since I first arrived in Mexico seventeen years ago.

I take theoretical inspiration from María Lugones' writings on decolonial feminism and the coloniality of gender. Lugones' work on the coloniality of gender emphasizes 'the concept of intersectionality and has exposed the historical and the theoretico-practical exclusion of non-white women from liberatory struggles in the name of "Women"' (Lugones 2016). Along with the work of Anibal Quijano (2000) and Mara Viveros Vigoya (2018), Lugones provides my work with the intersectional thinking contextualized in the colonial legacies of Latin America. Her writings strive to make visible the 'instrumentality of the colonial/modern gender system in subjecting – both women and men of color – in all domains of existence' (Lugones 2016). Lugones argued that 'the semantic consequence of the coloniality of gender is that "colonized woman" is an empty category: no women are colonized; no colonized females are women' (2010: 745). Instead, coloniality (rather than post-colonialism) as a process is what lies at the intersection of gender/class/race as central constructs of the capitalist world system of power. The systemic and social oppression of Mexican women in the mother role (and arguably the non-maternal role) is constructed via the coloniality of gender, and this cannot be unstuck from the modernizing efforts of the global health project.

Stereotypical representations of lower income Mexican mothers, as economically tied to the home and dependent upon the state, come about because of the power relations that resonate in transnational feminist critiques of development discourse. Such critiques argue that power relations between state and society maintain homogenous, hierarchal, dichotomous colonial logic (Lugones 2003; Rivera Cuisicanqui 2012; Mohanty 2013). My broader project of challenging the coloniality of motherhood in Mexico does not aim to deny or replace current representations of Mexican women as mothers, but instead seeks to create a dialogue between what exists and what is possible in how we understand the lives of women who are principal caregivers. In doing so I understand my project as a work of creative activism as much as scholarship. With this study I aim to work away from overly ambitious generalizations of what it is to be a mother in Southeast Mexico and instead embrace the instability of the everchanging experience of personhood. The ethnographic material in these chapters highlights how relentlessly emergent contextual variations exist and clash in everyday life, making it impossible to stereotype the archetypical maternal figure in any fixed sense.

It is my aim in this book to take the reader from the ethnographic site of the singular – urban Chiapas – to a deeper critique of the universal by identifying the role that sustainable and healthier development (brought together under the umbrella of the Sustainable Development Goals) plays in shaping aspects of maternity amongst Mexican women. Fertility issues and informal economic activity have long been the focus of poorer women's lives in development and global health discourse, resulting in a homogenous 'frozen' figure of the developing world woman as someone continuously in her reproductive years and striving economically, and in need of regulation. In this way development initiatives exclude other aspects of adult women's social and private lives throughout their life-course. Moreover, understandings of nurture are reduced to a specific period between birth and early motherhood and focus on a distinct care contract between biological mother and child. As the chapters in this book will show, nurture practices are collective, locally constituted and intergenerational.

Though this study adds to the existing body of anthropological literature about families and motherhood in Mexico, a country which straddles the low to middle income economic divide, it does so in an effort to challenge how a narrow positioning of women as reproductive entities recreates a colonial endeavour to keep Mexican women from ever being understood as anything but 'women in developing contexts'. A continuous understanding of motherhood in relation to biosocial reproduction in Mexico remains pertinent. Without such studies untroubled narratives about homogenous female populations without pre- and post-reproductive histories will persist and continue to form the misguided basis of development programmes.

As Indigenous feminist and Zapatista leader la Comandanta Ramona stated firmly often in her speeches, Indigenous women face a triple intersection of oppression: 'Ser Indigena, Ser Mujer y Ser Pobre' (being Indigenous, being a woman and being poor).[3] My thinking is influenced by the feminism of Indigenous women and activists across Latin America. I am preoccupied with how we understand the multiple oppressions together with the writings on intersectionality of Lugones, Quijano and Viveros Vigoya. The collections of Latin American feminist work invite me to ask the following questions: how do we think about the intersecting oppressions of all women of Chiapas across the social strata? And how are women's sexual and reproductive lives affected by the structural violence and misogyny enacted by Mexican men who are also subject to the historical coloniality of violence? With these questions I aim to avoid the destructive and illusionary binaries that wrongly place Indigenous Mexican women on the one hand as other, devoid of class nuance and power, and non-Indigenous Mexican women on the other as one homogenous socio-economic and ethnic group.

The women who appear in the following chapters straddle the public and private divides of the healthcare system; their daily existence focuses on the struggle for economic survival and the pressures of keeping an intergenerational household together. The women in la Orilla do not benefit from the political discourse of the Zapatista movement or transnational NGOs, they represent the households that make up the urban statistics about illiteracy and teenage pregnancy. These women's interests and desires are shaped by sisters, cousins and mothers-in-law, *telenovelas* and the church. Women in la Orilla are ignored by the state until it is time to buy their vote. Most are wives and/or mothers who feed large families on tiny budgets, manage the angers and frustrations of childrearing, they tolerate husbands demands and mother-in-law's interferences. They run businesses from home and account for every centavo that comes into the home and they work the bureaucracy of local government with the skill of a social secretary.

Coloniality of Gender and Critical Global Health

Medical anthropologists have been grappling with what Didier Fassin (2012) terms that 'obscure object of global health' for decades. However, the addition of a 'critical' element is a somewhat newer development brought about by scholars deeply engaged in the intersectional politics of health inequalities and interventions targeted at the Global South (Biehl and Petryna 2013; Adams and Pigg 2005; Biehl and Adams 2016). On the one hand, the turn to critical global health is the renewal of a long-held concern within anthropology: the need for close attention to the broader knowledge field of public health policy and practice. On the other hand, 'critical global health' itself is a construct that emerges specifically through engagement with contemporary biopolitical configurations in which working towards 'something called health' (Pigg 2013: 128) is now shaped, characterized by a 'multiplicity of actors, all vying for resources and influence in the political field of global health' (Biehl and Petryna 2013: 6).

Global health praxis is driven by a data intensive technocratic approach that 'can undermine our ability to think through complex problem solving around evidence that does not lend itself to statistical forms' (Adams et al. 2014: 190). As such, no matter what the intentions are for an all-inclusive agenda in global health, the reliance on measurable outcomes, no matter what area of health is under scrutiny, will always trump alternative ways of targeting what is relevant to any given population at a specific moment in history. Metrics inherent to global health arise from what Lugones described as the 'categorical logic of colonial modernity'. Colonial modernity organizes the world ontologically in terms of atomic homogenous separate categories. Lugones argues that '[t]o see non-white women is to exceed categorical logic' and that involving such categories evades the possibility of intersectional interrogation (Lugones 2010: 742). For meaningful change to occur we must enquire critically into the nature of this thing we call 'global health', examine its historical motives and instigators, and ask why a universal desire for equity in health and wellbeing must come at a cost of devaluing difference between and within populations. What is it about the way in which global health is conceived and constituted that has gone unquestioned? Why do interventions change but the ways in which they come about do not? And what can ethnography of intimate family lives and their relation to institutions tell us about this?

Whilst global health praxis concerns itself with homogenous binary forms of gender, race, poverty and increasingly age, it remains bereft of a contextualized and intersectional analysis, and therefore its politics (gendered or otherwise) are obscured. The colonial roots of this 'bunch of problems'[4] called global health must be examined using a framework that reveals what is hidden from our current understanding of race, gender and sexuality that are themselves a result of colonial and post-colonial modernity. Furthermore, there is a disconnect between the universal ideology of 'equity and justice' and how people live in the ordinariness of the everyday. Many Euro-US ethnographic perspectives continue to overlook variations in the causal processes of inequalities in post-colonial societies. As such, they do not deal with the root causes that are inherently more complex than gender inequalities alone. Whilst contributing to the newer drive for gender equality as a variable in global health, anthropological research has seldom addressed the following questions: how is global health as praxis gendered? In what ways is gender (when reduced to binary categories) prioritized over other inequality indicators and social categories, and to what cost? And whilst global health actors apply universal concepts of gender, wellbeing and health on top of local contexts, does medical anthropology have an appropriate framework that allows us to question these terms from an epistemological perspective?

In this book I confront these questions through two inter-related ethnographic studies: the *barrio popular* la Orilla and a midwifery-led birth centre in the highland city of San Cristóbal de Las Casas, Chiapas. My ethnographic enquiry is about understanding everyday life in the *barrio* through the biosocial process of becoming (m)other with a focus on how young women negotiate the political economy of local health systems and broader societal expectations. The book is organized around three interlocking themes: childbearing, nurture work and globalized health. These themes run centrally throughout the book, including in the third and concluding part which picks up on the issues explored in the ethnographic material and presents a framework for intersectional transnational approaches to global maternal health. Though all the chapters move in and out of the underlying themes they do so at diverse levels. Therefore, they serve as standalone discussions/readings as well an interwoven narrative. I leave my theoretical discussion to the end because I believe it must be foregrounded by knowledge and experience of what it means to become a mother for women of different social classes in the Chiapanecan context.

Notes

1. IMSS-BIENESTAR (known as IMSS-OPORTUNIDADES and then IMSS-PROSPERA at the time of my fieldwork) is a conditional cash transfer programme that has had numerous guises and was started in rural areas in 1997 (titled originally PROGRESA). It was later extended to urban areas. Its aim is to improve education, health, nutrition and living conditions of population groups in extreme poverty, as well as to break the intergenerational cycle of poverty. IMSS-BIENESTAR is the second most extensive programme of its kind in Latin America. Under its implementation as IMSS_OPORTUNIDADES it is also considered to be the most successfully developed example of the region's national public health inspired anti-poverty programmes. It has formed a template for cash transfer programmes in many other low-income countries.
2. The women who appear throughout this book self-identify as Mexican unless stated otherwise. I refrain from using the word *mestiza* as it is not an ethnographic category. *Mestiza* is a problematic term debated mainly in US and some Mexican scholarship. Rather than enter into this debate I choose instead to listen to how the women I meet in Chiapas describe their ethnicity, as noted in the following chapter.
3. Ejercito Zapatista de Liberación Nacional (EZLN), or Zapatistas for short, is a political movement and army founded by the Maya Indigenous peoples of Chiapas with Mexican intellectuals who were in hiding from the Mexican government in the 1980s. They staged a well-documented armed uprising in January 1994 in the Chiapas cities of San Cristóbal de Las Casas and Ocosingo. La Comandanta Ramona (deceased in 2006) was a key military figure in the EZLN and a vocal advocate for Indigenous rights and Indigenous women's rights. This phrase of triple oppression appears numerous times in her recorded speeches and has appeared countless times in publications and news articles discussing the position of Indigenous women across Mexico. As such its actual source is unknown though generally attributed to Ramona.
4. As Arthur Kleinman (1997) describes international health.

Part I

CONTEXTS

Chapter 1

LA ORILLA

COLETAS AND COLONIALITY

Each morning as I set off on the school run with my daughter Emilia, we opened a large metal door and were presented directly with *barrio* life. Our little cabin was situated with four others on a large piece of land surrounded by a high wall. From behind the wall the sounds and smells from the wood fires, kitchens and laundries of my neighbours were a constant reminder that although our house and garden, on one side, looked out onto the surrounding hillsides and quarry in the distance, this was a view far removed from the busy family lives happening beyond the high wall. On the opposite side, beyond the high wall, we were surrounded by dwellings of all shapes and sizes that housed multiple generations of families and that were plotted along the main trade route between the city centre and the highlands. My midwife Cristina first recommended the *barrio* to me. 'You'll be happy there', she told me, 'the rents are cheap, the community is strong and the people are nosey. They're one hundred percent *coleta* [a person originating from San Cristóbal], no foreigners, no bullshit. What's more, if you go into labour I'll be just round the corner!' I was around seven months pregnant at the time and had mistakenly chosen to live in the centre of the city in an overpriced house that also served as a barrier between myself and the local community. I was anxious to settle into fieldwork, find a school for my daughter and settle in a neighbourhood before my final trimester set in. I took a gamble when Cristina gave me the address. Emilia and I jumped in a taxi and travelled to a part of the city I had rarely visited before.

After a month of troubles and false starts in the city centre, arriving in the *barrio* felt like a godsend. I was greeted with the comforting smell of burning *ocote* (pinewood firelighters) and laundry soap, the sound of ranchero music and dogs barking, the heavy chains of the gas truck dragging on the road surface accompanied by the loud tinny jingle that blasted out from the vehicle's sound system. This sensory assortment brought back a reassuring feeling in my body from earlier years living in a similar *barrio* on the west side of the city. I was reminded of when I originally became so attentive to everyday life in the households of San Cristóbal. Though I originally thought that the high wall separated me slightly from my immediate neighbours, I soon learnt that it offered me no privacy at all. My closest neighbours outside the terrain, Doña Frida and Doña Perla, had two-storey houses that looked directly over the wall and onto mine. Within the walled property where my house was, cousins Sara and Ruby's house and garden backed on to mine. At the back of my house was a large concrete and adobe house where a family of ten lived and ran a local business. As much I was aware of my neighbours' movements throughout the day, family mealtimes, preferences in *telenovelas* and music, their arguments and laughter, and the visitors that came and went throughout evenings and weekends, they were aware of mine. My tentative need for privacy, which I was so accustomed to living in England, slowly began to dissipate as I immersed myself into daily life in the *barrio*.

Daytimes in the *barrio* centred round interactions with the women and children who live there. With almost all the men and older boys out working from the early hours to the late afternoon, the *barrio* often felt like a woman's domain during daylight hours. Before I knew it, the daily activities I had originally understood as aside from my fieldwork – the school run, toing and froing on *combis*, fetching water, queuing for tortillas and buying emergency supplies from my neighbours – became the most valuable sources of data and relationship building that would come to shape my research. Through the snippets of conversations I collected during the day I was able to challenge many preconceived notions I had previously held about pregnancy, birth and early motherhood in San Cristóbal. I quickly began to shift my focus on to wider processes and practices of what mothering meant for the women in la Orilla. I became preoccupied with motherhood and nurture praxis as a transitional process with a deeper connection to personhood and colonial relations.

Barrio la Orilla is located to the far east of the city of San Cristóbal de Las Casas and serves as the exit towards the neighbouring municipality of Tenejapa. La Orilla came into existence like many of the outlying neighbourhoods, as an overspill from one of the city's original *barrios*. These outlying neighbourhoods are also described as 'invasion *barrios*' because much of the land was originally squatted with no access to public services. According to local accounts the area of la Orilla was populated towards the end of the nineteenth and twentieth century (CIEPAC 2007; Herrera 2013). Since the 1970s, due to pressure and campaigning from residents, the *barrio* has gradually developed all necessary public services including non-potable water, household waste collection, drainage, electricity and telegraph poles. Unlike in the rest of the city, a local board of representatives run and administer the non-potable water system. Residents also maintain the *barrio*'s drainage system along with much of the rest of the *barrio*'s infrastructure.

Most houses are built from concrete (breeze) blocks, adobe or wooden planks, with concrete or earth floors. Large family groups on the main road have original land plots that have been added to over the years. It is common for there to be three to four generations living under one roof. Families use the outside space to keep chickens, hens, cockerels, goats and pigs for domestic consumption or trade. Houses are either added on to when economic circumstances improve, or they build separate dwellings within the family's plot. Along the main street there are two mechanic and tyre workshops, an electrical repairs shop, a hardware store, a fruit and veg shop, two tortilla shops, a beer station, two small general stores and a hairdresser. *Barrio* women travel to the city centre market to buy wholesale produce to sell from their doorways or door to door. *Barrio* residents must travel to other parts of the city to access health services, public security, secondary and high schools, public offices and for most employment.

The forest area around la Orilla is supposedly a protected ecological reserve. However, without sufficient protection from the municipal government over the years people have taken large sections of forest and built houses or sold land on as their own. Land protection has improved over recent years. Local Indigenous families, conservation NGOs and universities work together to section, guard and manage surrounding forest areas. NGOs also work with resident families on co-tourism projects which gives the families the opportunity to grow crops and preserve native flora and fauna whilst also earning

Figure 1.1 Main Street, la Orilla, Mexico, 2013 © J.M. López

money from tourists. The mixed areas of protected lands, forests and caves are rented by volunteer rescue groups for training exercises, student groups and, increasingly, rock climbers. The upper part of the *barrio* nearer to the forested areas is predominantly inhabited by Indigenous families originating from the neighbouring municipalities of Chamula, Huixtán, Bochil, Teopisca, Chenalhó and Copainalá. Low-income *coleta* households mainly make up the lower half of la Orilla connecting to the two neighbouring *barrios*. As in many of the mixed ethnicity neighbourhoods in San Cristóbal, Indigenous and *coleta* families live side by side yet apart, communicating generally for economic transactions and trade.

In correlation with census data, the households in my study were reliant upon informal economic activity to bolster the precarious salaried work. Most adults and young people have completed primary school and a small proportion go on to complete secondary school. Policy researchers often explain failure to attend secondary school

Figure 1.2 Callejon, la Orilla, Mexico, 2013 © J.M. López

as a lack of desire or aspiration to achieve economic independence, particularly in girls (see Garita Edelen et al. 2016 as an example). When I asked my neighbours why their children did not attend secondary education, they explained how distance was the problem, rather than lack of desire. The nearest secondary school was a thirty-minute *combi* ride away. The distance was both a financial and time expense that families felt they could not afford. Readiness to learn a trade or begin contributing to household or informal labour was perceived as a more pragmatic option in many cases. In terms of gender, men in this *barrio* are principally employed in the construction trade or as vehicle mechanics. Women who work outside of the *barrio* do so as domestic workers in middle-income neighbourhoods. The younger women tend to work in shops or administrative roles in hotels in the city centre, dependent upon their schooling. Most adult women's economic labour takes place within the boundaries of the *barrio* – whether this is informal or formal activity.

When I write of the *barrio*, I refer to what Dalsgaard (2004: 70) describes as a 'loose and primarily experienced unit' as opposed to a cartographic generalization. The actions and interactions of individuals and families define how they understand the *barrio* as a place to belong. On a municipal map the area has well defined boundaries defined by administrative or political divisions. The municipal map does not include the numerous *callejones* and *escalones*[1] on the northwest side of the *barrio* (see figure 1 above). Nor does it consider residents' own interpretations of the *barrio*'s limits or the unregistered dwellings encroaching onto the surrounding forestlands. The families who were my neighbours and interlocuters lived on land plots of varying sizes running along the main street. When I asked about ownership of the different land plots people always explained to me in terms of how many generations the family had lived there. As I gradually learnt the social and political history of the *barrio*, it became clear how earlier generations had acquired land and developed official ownership of it over time. When I first told friends from other parts of the city where I had moved to, I was greeted with mixed reactions. Each person I spoke to would produce a different 'fact' or substantiated rumour about the *barrio*. There were countless comments about the strength and pride of the people in la Orilla, how they were community-minded but not welcoming to outsiders; others said that they were poor, untrustworthy and rebellious. What had first appeared to me as a typical low-income, outer city neighbourhood dominated by a wide and dusty main road leading to the next town suddenly came alive with urban myth and intrigue. In the early weeks I spent a lot of time checking out these tales with older *barrio* residents. I found that, as with most urban myths, there is always a point in history that serves as a root cause to stories that persist over generations. Don Juan and Doña Rosa, the elderly parents of my immediate neighbour Doña Frida, were an excellent source of clarification and myth busting. At seventy-eight years old, Doña Reina, whose family owned a substantial amount of land in the upper part of the *barrio*, was able to help me draw maps of how the shape and nature of the *barrio* had changed over thirty or forty years.

Since my primary research method was participant observation as a resident of la Orilla, I took part in daily *barrio* activities and attended community events such as the patron saint celebrations and residents' meetings. To gain a socio-economic comparison of other birth and caregiving experiences, I conducted participant observation at a local midwifery-led birth centre, attending public courses and talks on maternal health and parenting. I also met other families through my daughter's school and holiday activities. Mothers I met here were kind enough for me to take advantage of play dates and conversations as a way of recording data. In a place where gendered spaces and behaviours are, on the surface, quite clearly defined, my position at that time as a woman, mother and spouse dictated when, where and with whom I was able to spend my time. My positioning as a neighbour and mother was crucial to forging relationships with women in the *barrio*. Carrying out my own motherwork whilst I lived in the *barrio* enabled me to find some, albeit initially superficial, common ground with the women I met in the *barrio*. On doorsteps, at kitchen tables, in the close confines of public transport, and standing chatting on street corners, I gradually became aware of the conversational and social boundaries set by women. I learnt the appropriate ways to ask about and elicit narratives of bodily experience and relationships in ways that, I hope, respected local ways of being and forged relationships of trust, despite our obvious differences.

My understanding of the *barrio* was arguably framed by the mothers, grandmothers, aunts and daughters-in-law I spent my days with. In distinctly gendered spaces it was often the absence and silence of men that helped me to reflect on their role as partners and in childrearing. Younger men were constantly present in the speech of their mothers. Doña Perla who had three sons at home would often cry when she spoke about her eldest Rogelio. He was thirty at that time and still single. Doña Perla was worried he would never find a wife because of his heavy drinking. 'They all go out to work with their father, they work hard for us', she told me one afternoon, 'but I fear for Rogelio. I can't sleep because of the noise when he plays his music. Do you not hear it? He locks himself in his room with his music, later I go in and find him on the floor spark out and I worry one day he will choke. If he had children or a wife like the other two, he would stay sober and be a proper man. When he gets a girlfriend, he calms down. Then he'll cheat on her, she finds out, leaves him and he starts drinking all over again'. These types of comments were commonplace and represent in some form how expectations of masculinity are constructed, and pressures are placed on young men to produce certain ideals. Men's abuse of alcohol, inability to work and lack of marriage prospects were a constant worry amongst my neighbours.

Rigid and defined gendered spaces do not of course equate to gender segregation. I did often speak to men as husbands, fathers and sons of my female interlocutors and through my daily interactions with taxi and *combi* drivers, and water and gas deliverymen. Doña Frida's husband Don Pepe and their four sons accompanied us most evenings as we sat chatting on the doorstep. Don Marco, husband to Doña Carla, often gave Emilia and I a lift to school when the *combi* did not arrive on time. Don Arturo, the eldest son of Doña Reina and husband to Doña Perla, helped me to map out houses and families in the *barrio*. His work in the local building trade and as a part-time handyman to my landlord meant that he was often around fixing and rebuilding the houses. Talking to him reminded me that although I was often tempted by the thought that family organization was a woman's domain, a male head of the household was still the desired social norm. 'It's not the same [since my father died], there's no respect anymore', Don Arturo told me one afternoon when he came to fix my garden steps. As he worked, mixing concrete with a small spade, he explained how he had fallen out with his brother (Don Marco) and they had not spoken for two years. Their argument had been about money and the behaviour of Arturo's eldest son Rogelio, and the heavy drinking that Doña Perla had spoken about. Family members had seen Rogelio on various occasions drinking and fighting in the street. Don Marco had demanded that his brother take control of his son and accused him of bringing shame on the family. An argument followed and each of the brothers refused to back down. Doña Reina intervened and told Don Arturo that she agreed with Marco and that he was at fault for his son's misdemeanours. Don Arturo was hurt by his mother's allegiance to her younger son and felt very strongly that this would not have happened if his father had been alive. 'You need a man at the head of a family', he explained, 'someone to fear otherwise, it all starts to fall apart'.

San Cristóbal de Las Casas: Pueblo Mágico

The colonial city and municipality of San Cristóbal de Las Casas (the city here within referred to as San Cristóbal) is the third largest in Chiapas. During my period of fieldwork (2008–2015) the municipality had a population reaching 209,591 (INEGI 2015). As a municipality San Cristóbal has eighty-three rural communities outside of the city proper (Lazos Álvarez. 2013). San Cristóbal lies at the valley floor of Los Altos surrounded by hills and dense forests on all sides. To give an idea of the mountainous terrain, only 8.75 per cent of ground space across the municipality is urbanized (Ayuntamiento San Cristóbal de Las Casas 2013). San Cristóbal has a relatively young population with 30.6 per cent between the ages of fifteen and twenty-nine and is ethnically diverse with 62,208 inhabitants (in the 2010 census) self-identifying as Indigenous Mexicans (INEGI 2010). The dominant Indigenous languages (out of twenty-five recorded in the whole municipality) are Tzotzil and Tzeltal. The census in 2010 reported that up to 11,540 of the Indigenous population did not speak Spanish (INEGI 2010). According to the 2015 census the city of San Cristóbal has a total population of 158,027 (INEGI 2015). The city itself is made up of 117 *barrios* and *colonias* (neighbourhoods) including a historic city centre zone.

The principal religion in San Cristóbal is Catholicism and each *barrio* has a patron saint and church. Other minority religious groups throughout the municipality are evangelical Christian sects (predominantly Baptist), Mormons, Jehovah's Witnesses and a small community of Sufi and Orthodox Muslims. Although exact population by ethnicity is unknown, the city's population includes Mexicans from other parts of the country and a small transient population of North Americans, Europeans and a small number of Japanese migrants. The most important economic sectors are commerce, services and tourism, which employ almost 67 per cent of the work force mainly centred in and around the city centre (INAFED 2010). The second most important sector is mining, including jade, gravel, stone and metals which are exported to other municipalities in Chiapas and nearby states.

At the turn of the twenty-first century San Cristóbal was designated as a *Pueblo Mágico* (Magical Town), part of a government programme naming specific cities across the country as heritage sites. These cities were given extra funding to promote national and international tourism. In 2010 San Cristóbal was further recognized as 'The most magical of the *Pueblos Mágicos*' by then President Felipe Calderón. Such state decision-making demonstrates the complicated attachment to colonialism inherent in Mexican politics. Chiapas as a region has historically relied upon its diverse Indigenous and colonial heritage for tourism, and as such retains a history that cannot be separated from the asymmetrical power relations between 'colonizer'and 'colonized'. Writing about colourism in Mexico's colonial history, Alejandro Lugo writes ',these incipient inequalities of conquest both evident and embedded in the colouring of individuals, have never been eradicated from the shifting contours of everyday life; in fact, they have left a legacy that only the naive observer can ignore' (2008: 52). Amongst other categories, Mexican society discriminates against individuals based on lightness or darkness of skin colour. Colourism, a historical remnant of the Spanish imposed caste system, intersects with other factors such as class indicators, gender and geographics. There is more nuance in those intersecting factors in relation to how discrimination works than many transnational observers of Mexico have given credit. The contested debates over what makes Indigenous and mestizo identity in Mexico fall short precisely because they create an Indigenous/mestizo binary. This coloniality of identity oversimplifies matters of identity in regions like Chiapas, resulting in a tendency to sweep over the social nuances of gender, class and generations of mixed heritage. For the Indigenous populations alone, it leaves written descriptions of them devoid of the complexities of social evolution and socio-economic status. Homogenous and uncomplex binaries result in homogenous and uncomplex descriptions.

As I mentioned earlier people born in San Cristóbal and with traceable generations to neo-colonial times identify themselves as *coleto/a* (Paris Pombo 2000). This local identifier also has deep roots in the city's colonial past. *Coleto* literally means 'ponytail' and refers to the hairstyle of the original Spanish conquistadors who founded the city (Speed 2008). From around the beginning of the twentieth century the creation of the *coleto* identity was originally a way for men of mixed Indigenous and Spanish/settler (mestizo) heritage to transcend ethnic boundaries and enter the class-based structure of mestizo society based upon birth right as opposed to skin colour and spoken language. Women's *coleta* identity, however, differed from that of men in that they retained the gendered stereotype of a passive Indian woman, which then mixed with the devout and caring Catholic mother figure to create the unique image of the *coleta* woman (Paris Pombo 2000; Speed 2008). When I refer to a person as *coleta/o* in this book, this is because they self-identified as such when I asked them to describe themselves. With the use of this word these people are making it clear they were born and raised in San Cristóbal. For this reason I understood the level of acceptance and *cariño* (affection) held for my daughters when neighbours claimed them as *coletas*, because they were both born in the city.

Despite the outward impression of a multicultural city, the different ethnic groups rarely mix other than for economic transactions and domestic labour.[2] Historical tensions remain and the traditionalist prejudice within the *coleto* population about the violent unpredictability of Indigenous men has, in the twenty-first century, been matched with a mistrust of foreigners. In particular, the *coleto* elite are said to blame the influx of foreigners for a perceived increase in crime and recreational drug use, for threatening local traditions and for manipulating the 'poor ignorant Indians' into rebellion (Speed 2008; Gutiérrez 1999). These social tensions were heightened by the armed Zapatista uprising of 1994 (see note 3 in the Introduction). The city of San Cristóbal was central to the uprising as the municipal building and city centre was the site of a brief yet bloody battle between the Zapatista guerrilla army and the federal army.

The uprising and consequent conflict were instrumental in bringing Chiapas to the world's attention and for urging the recognition of Mexico's Indigenous population on the political agenda. In her analysis of the Indian intellectual after the uprising, Natividad Gutiérrez (1999) argues that whilst capturing the imagination of mainly young, educated middle-class students, the movement has done little to rouse support or empathy amongst poorer Mexican citizens. The lower-income and poorer populations have difficulty relating to or accessing the mainly online writings of (the predominantly male) Zapatista spokespersons and the published communiqués remain the reading matter of the educated left or international supporters.

The significance of the Zapatista movement in the everyday lives of the *coleta* population in San Cristóbal is questionable. Partly due to the effective propaganda machine of the state and the historical barriers between Indigenous and *coleta* worlds, the only daily reminder of the uprising in urban life is the consistent yet subtle military presence and the often muttered 'things haven't been the same since the troubles' whenever there is an outburst in the central marketplace, or the frequent sensationalist reports of revenge killings in local newspapers. In the twenty-first century San Cristóbal remains a very segregated city and *barrio* populations are defined in general by socio-economic status and ethnicity, with the 'diverse population' knowing very little about each other's day-to-day lives and personal relationships. Cristina, my midwife and long-term foreign resident of San Cristóbal described the city as 'very much an unspoken apartheid'.

Although there are significant divides between Indigenous and *coleta* populations, their complex histories mean that many practices and beliefs have shared roots. This appears to be most evident in descriptions of local biologies,[3] cosmologies, uses of plant-based medicine and healing practices. A shared and intersecting history means that in analytical terms these social groupings are not overly discrete ethnic categories. However, in ethnographic terms Mexican, *coleto/a*, Tzotzil, Tzeltal, Cho'l, or Tojolabal identity forms the basis of how a person situates themselves socially and politically. The way in which the people of San Cristóbal declare their *coleta* or outsider identity demonstrates the variability within the local population; that is just as much misunderstood and under-represented in social science and policy literature as the variations that exist within the Indigenous populations.

Chiapas and Coloniality of Motherhood

San Cristóbal and Chiapas may arguably be in a post-Zapatista epoch but the structural violence, ethnic discrimination and inequalities that originally seeded the uprising have not gone away or improved in any significant way. One area where structural violence and inequality is most evidenced is in infant and maternal mortality rates. Chiapas is amongst the country's most marginalized regions, with the highest recorded unemployment levels and lowest educational attainment (completing secondary school) of all thirty-two federal states (OECD 2015). The 2010 census reported that 78 per cent of the state population are economically active in the informal sector (INEGI 2010), and housing and access to public services are below national averages (OECD 2015). Access to public health services is still particularly poor and is associated with wider political economic and social issues. Chiapas has the second highest maternal mortality rate (68.1 per every 100, 000 live births) and the highest infant mortality in Mexico (17.9 per every 1000 children under five years). Over 60 per cent of the population rely on subsidized primary health care (INEGI 2010). When compiling statistics, the various governmental and non-governmental organizations use a combination of employment status, household income and ethnicity results from the 2010 and 2015 census to categorize different sections of the population. In this way levels of poverty and income categorize social groups as opposed to overt identification by social class. Income-based social categories also mirror the language used by people when asked about their social or economic status; people whom I categorize as low-income or working-class will describe themselves as poor or *humilde* (indicating decent, simple folk with little material wealth).

As I mentioned earlier around 27 per cent of the total population of Chiapas self-identify as Indigenous Mexicans (INEGI 2010). Indigenous populations are most concentrated in the highlands, though internal conflict and economic disparities have led to widespread displacement and transmigration over recent decades. The government defines Indigenous identity by language spoken. Following this approach the dominant groups in Chiapas are Tzeltal, Tzotzil, Tojolabal, Cho'l (all Mayan descent) and Zoque (Olmec descent) (INEGI 2010). Changes in migration patterns and the impact of national and global recession have resulted in the rural-urban poverty divide in Chiapas being less distinct. The OECD reports that urban populations in Mexico are no longer significantly better off in access to health services than rural populations. This raises interesting questions for a critical global health analysis. Previously, the emphasis in global health on treating and controlling disease took a 'Magic Bullet' approach – the delivery of specific health technologies to address an issue – which failed to take into account social, economic and political factors, often unleashing unintended consequences (Biehl and Petryna 2013).

This 'magic bullet' strategy to disease control found its way into maternal mortality interventions in rurally defined regions like Chiapas. With increasing pressure to meet the Safe Motherhood Initiative and later Millennium Development Goal (MDG) 5, development discourse promoted increased access to technocratic prenatal care and emergency treatment as the panacea to maternal mortality and morbidity. In Mexico, the requirements were set for a minimum of five prenatal appointments in the public health system. By 2013 this prenatal care goal was achieved across the country. In Chiapas, this happened alongside the building of and improvements to existing maternal health facilities; however, maternal mortality rates remained relatively unaffected and there is little evidence in terms of the quality standards of care provided (OMM 2014). The narrowing of the divide between rural and urban maternal mortality and morbidity in Chiapas – in a negative direction – is one example of the failure to recognize 'how health risks are shaped by law, politics, and practices ranging from industrial and agricultural policies to discrimination, violence, and lack of access to justice' (Biehl and Petryna 2013: 3).

Gender equality as a stand-alone category fares no better than ethnicity or social status via income. Indigenous girls and women are most at risk of mortality and violence in the region for various intersecting reasons (Freyermuth 2010). Chiapas has the highest incidence of forced or underage marriage and adolescent pregnancy (along with its associated health risks). Despite stereotypes to the contrary, underage marriage and premature parenthood are not restricted to Indigenous communities; the most recent Mother's Index study shows the lower-income population of girls and young women in Chiapas as being equally at risk (Garita Edelen et al. 2016). In urban areas reported incidences of gender-based violence, including kidnap, trafficking, rape and murder, have increased gradually and significantly over the last decade, of which low-income *mestiza* women and Indigenous women are represented equally (at least in reported figures, though actual details are unknown due to the complexities of ethnic identity already mentioned). In the case of sexual violence, it appears that gender and social class are factors that trump ethnicity, indicating the dominant force of misogyny existing throughout all levels of Mexican society.

One Sunday Emilia and I walked down to Doña Maria's barbequed chicken stall to buy lunch. This day we had timed it wrong and there was a long queue winding out onto the main road. Not wanting to queue in the afternoon sun Emilia ran around to the doorway from which Doña Maria set up her stall and began to play with three-year old Carolina, Doña Maria's granddaughter. Weekends were always busiest, and Doña Maria had extra help from her three sons and two daughters-in-law. Doña Maria is in her mid-forties and her sons and daughters-in-law aged between seventeen and twenty-two. By the time I was served there were no whole chickens left, just a separate half and quarter and two remaining onions slowly reducing to mouth-watering softness as they soaked up the heat and smoke of the charcoal. As one daughter-in-law Mabel piled our hot food onto a polystyrene tray and wrapped it in tin foil, Doña Maria and I chatted about the recent birth of her second granddaughter who had been born by caesarean section in the local maternity hospital. 'It was an emergency', she explained, 'they said the baby had pooped and they had to get her out'. 'It's different for girls these days, they don't manage [the births] as well, they're too scared, and then they want to carry on afterwards as if everything is the same'. I asked Doña Maria what it was like when she had her sons: 'I was at home with the midwife, everyone did it that way then, it was better'. She pointed to her eldest son Eric: 'I was two days in labour with him, if I'd have been in hospital, they would have had the knives out, as it was, I had the *partera* [midwife] and my mother-in-law and they helped me. I feel sorry for the girls now, it's good they have *Seguro Popular* [basic public health insurance], but it changes things, they don't respect our traditions in the hospital, and they put fear into the girls about giving birth'.

In Mexico national population growth and fertility rates have generally decreased as a combined result of state efforts and rapid socio-economic development (Bringas et al. 2004). The population as a whole has been in a steady decline since the state's efforts to shape the nation's attitudes towards good parenthood, family size and use of contraceptives have not been restricted to policy and welfare interventions. Though the state has traditionally sanctioned and subsidized reproductive health services and campaigns, both federal and state government have used various mediums to influence social attitudes towards family planning. Popular media such as radio and television soap operas, billboards and magazines have long been utilized as a strategy for driving forward the image of the modern Mexican family (Soto Laveaga 2007; Hryciuk 2010).

The targeted use of *telenovelas*, and more recently social media and the cult of celebrity, is a gendered strategy that further implicates women as responsible for shaping national identity. Popular television shows dealing with family, parenting and social issues during my fieldwork in 2013 included *Nueva Vida* (A New Life), *La Rosa de Guadalupe* (The Rose of Guadelupe), *Lo Que Callamos las Mujeres* (What Women Don't Say), and *Mujeres: Casos de la Vida Real* (Women: Stories from Real Life) amongst the numerous seasonal *telenovelas* heavily targeted at female audiences and laden with moral subtexts. Soto Laveaga (2007) found in her analysis of state media strategies that television programmes in particular work to take global concerns, such as population size or reproductive rights, and turn them into 'Mexican projects'. In this way the universal 'rights bearing individual' becomes part of a national identity without the recognition of local cultural constructions (Scheper-Hughes and Sargent 1998: 10).

Due to the success of state sanctioned campaigns, women in urban Mexico are having fewer children and at a later age than earlier generations – with a national average of three to four children per family by 1999 from a previous six to eight children on average during the 1960s–1980s (Bringas et al. 2004; Braff 2009; INEGI 2015; Tuiran et al. 2009). Such national attitudes have been apparent during the years I have worked in San Cristóbal. With women who I spoke to during fieldwork, the consensus amongst old and younger generations was that 'three children is enough work for anyone'. Many of the younger women were happy to stop at two. 'If you get one of each then you have a full set', local hairdresser Angela summed up this attitude concisely. In addition, most women agreed that it was the couple who should decide when and how many children to have. Despite this, none considered that it was a man's responsibility to organize contraception.

In la Orilla, contrary to national trends, the pregnant women and women in early motherhood I met during my fieldwork were generally between the ages of sixteen and twentyfour. This mirrors data recently published by Garita Edelen et al. (2016) in their Save The Children Mexico report on adolescent pregnancy and motherhood. Garita Edelen and colleagues' research found that Chiapas has the highest incidence of adolescent pregnancy and the lowest reported use of contraception amongst young people who are sexually active. To gauge the difference between states that are comparative in economic and population status, 46 per cent of sexually active young women in the state of Guerrero reported having been pregnant at least once between the ages of twelve and nineteen, and in Chiapas this figure rose to 73 per cent. These figures converge with the prevalence of reported contraception use which in the state of Guerrero is 57.6 per cent of sexually active women between the ages of fifteen and nineteen and in Chiapas 35.5 per cent, compared with a national average of 59 per cent (Garita Edelen et al. 2016: 11). These contraceptive use figures are in part linked directly to local economic status, education levels and average mortality rates for the region. Throughout Mexico access to state and private reproductive health services and laws surrounding abortion differ greatly and this contributes to attitudes and behaviours in family planning. In the Mothers Index report authors Garita Edelen et al. (2016) suggested that the high numbers of adolescent parents pointed towards a lack of economic and educational aspiration amongst young women. When I think of the younger mothers I have met over the years in Chiapas, I find this type of declaration problematic. Though many teenage pregnancies are unplanned, a more complex understanding of what it means to be a mother in low-income communities challenges the notion of aspirational deficiency. A lack of qualitative evidence in this type of reporting results in many low-income women from smaller urban neighbourhoods like la Orilla being misrepresented, and as such their experiences and attitudes to reproduction are omitted from global and national reproductive health discourses. Again, a lack of qualitative evidence and listening to the young women results in oversimplistic and sexist assumptions that these individuals hold no aspirations and are trapped in intergenerational cycles of early motherhood.

The Mexican state has used a minority world-view feminist discourse on a woman's bodily integrity and right to a planned parenthood over recent decades as a platform to shape women's overall struggles for equality (Gutmann 2009). Although a continuous drive to reduce the reported 'population bomb', beginning in the late twentieth century, has been successful, lowering fertility rates has not addressed existing gender, ethnic and class inequalities in any significant way. Authors writing on family planning in Mexico argue that the responsibility for family planning and 'good parenthood' is continuously placed upon women only (Gutmann 2009; Palomar 2004; Soto Laveaga 2007; Smith-Oka 2013). Gutmann's (1996, 2007, 2009) extensive and detailed ethnographic studies of male contraceptive use and gender relations in central and southern Mexico have shown that, if anything, men have been actively excluded from participating in family planning. This exclusion from the bodily practices of 'good parenthood' works to reinforce expected gender roles and is at odds with the counter rhetoric of universal gender rights and equality also inherent in the social construction of a modern Mexico.

Gender equality under Sustainable Development Goal 5 (SDG5) has been singled out as an essential element to 'ensure healthy lives and promote wellbeing at all ages' (in relation to Sustainable Development Goal 3) by 2030. Sustainable Development Goal 3 (SDG3) broadens the scope of global health beyond non-communicable diseases (NCDs) and maternal-infant mortality, which should in theory work to address the prior essentializing of women's health as synonymous with maternal and reproductive health. Yet, in most contexts gender equality continues to be a universally feminized concept which is overly concerned with heterosexual women's reproductive and economic lives. In countries like Mexico, where governments were committed and subsequently failed to achieve the lower mortality rates set in 2000 under MDG5, the funnelling of women's health resources into maternal health and mortality related programmes only appears to have increased under the SDGs. Whilst the need for high-quality maternal health care is undeniable, a disproportionate number of women still die in pregnancy and childbirth-related complications across Mexico, more so in Chiapas. Women's access to health as determined by their reproductive capacity continues to miss the mark on what constitutes continuous good health across the life-course. The politics of who gets to live or survive childbirth is very much missing from the dominant global health analysis of why maternal deaths happen. Furthermore, as is highlighted by the numerous anthropological reflections on global maternal health programmes in the twenty-first century, the targeting of mortality rates, to the exclusion of other indicators of good health, plays directly into the hands of neo-colonial biopolitics and does little to improve women's health and mortality outcomes overall (Wendland 2016; Adams et al. 2014; Freyermuth 2015; Alonso and Murray de López 2017; Berry 2010).

Notes

1. *Callejones* are steep winding backstreets, *escalones* are steep alleyways made up of concrete or wooden steps connecting dwellings built on the hillsides to the main roads. They are built and maintained by residents.
2. I note domestic labour separate to economic transaction because there were many instances where I came across Indigenous girls or women who were unpaid as household labour or working in exchange for bed and board only.
3. Here I refer to Margaret Lock's (1993) definition of local biologies as an ongoing dialectic between biology and culture in which both are contingent.

Part II

CHILDBEARING POLITICS

Chapter 2

BETY AND ROSA

> There can be nothing more dangerous to a body than the social agreement that that body is dangerous. We can simplify: it is dangerous to be perceived as dangerous.
>
> —Sara Ahmed, *Living a Feminist Life*

The decentralized public healthcare system in Mexico came out of the structural adjustment conditions of the 1990s. The Mexican government at the height of neoliberalism championed decentralization to give federal states control over their own budgets, therefore targeting the health issues specific to each region. Decades of decentralization have left poorer states with a higher economic burden of insurance contributions for those most in need. During the years of my fieldwork coverage of the government insurance scheme *Seguro Popular* was 82 per cent of the Chiapas population, the largest percentage in the country (INEGI 2015). Existing hospitals and clinics provided services for *Seguro Popular*, with the occasional outsourcing to private facilities. A rapid increase in *Seguro Popular* coverage between 2008 and 2015 led to over-burdened services which were already vastly under-resourced and as a consequence, hospitals and clinics that were unable to provide the equitable services they are responsible for.

The Mexican healthcare system creates a sharp divide between those with employment and those with means-tested insurance. The Instituto Mexicano del Seguro Social (IMSS – Mexican Institute of Social Security) provides workers in the formal economy with contributory health insurance. In Chiapas, the IMSS only serves 12.4 per cent of the population, reflecting the lack of structure and formal employment opportunities throughout the state. Government employees receive help from the Instituto de Seguridad y Servicios Sociales de los Trabajadores del Estado (ISSSTE – Institute for Social Security and Services for State Workers). In 2015 ISSTE social security covered 5.4 per cent of the local population (INEGI 2015). The women whose narratives shape the next three chapters range from being fully or partly IMSS/ISSTE insured to being fully in receipt of *Seguro Popular*. The women in this and the following chapters span the social strata but one thing that unites them is that for maternal health at some point they all divert to paying for private services (professional and lay), therefore indicating that the system is lacking in all or some of its parts. Though the decision to go private over public is a common one, with a broad range of cost and quality options, it still comes at a considerable cost to the individual and their family.

Decentralization allows state governments to target a sizeable percentage of the health budget on sexual, reproductive and maternal health. In Mexico, since 2009 there have been up to thirty-two different policies introduced, at federal and state levels, incorporating maternal health elements. The Mexican government, under the pressure of commitment to MDG5 and, post-2013, the SDGs, has made a clear commitment to improving maternal, child and infant health. The *Plan Nacional del Desarrollo 2013-2018* (National Development Plan 2013-2018), its linked initiative *Programa de Acción Específico para la Atención (PAE) a la Salud Materna y Perinatal (SMP) 2013-2018* (Specific Action Programme for Maternal and Newborn Health 2013-2018), and the *NOM-007-SSA2-2016 Para la atención de la mujer durante el embarazo, parto y puerperio* (National Minimum Standards for Attention during pregnancy, birth and postpartum period 2016) have been designed to target the government's desire to meet SDG3 nationwide and also significantly improve standards of care in the public sector. Detailed in these development plans is the government's aim to reach 100 per cent facility-based birth by 2030.

The obstetric transition (the shift from the home to hospital) has immediate consequences such as normalizing the use of the synthetic oxytocin hormone (Pitocin) to speed up contractions, episiotomy and epidural anaesthetic as common practice. Each obstetric intervention works to further restrict the movement of the woman in favour of being able to monitor the foetus travelling from her womb. The immediate consequences of this shift have resulted in more long-term indirect and unintended consequences to women's childbearing experiences across the globe. The rapid increase in hospital attendance in Mexico has led to disproportionate rates of surgical interventions during and after birth, documented widespread abuse and mistreatment of women, and the almost total eradication of midwifery models of care from all aspects of public health practice and policy (see Murray de López 2015, 2019; Castro and Erviti 2015; Sánchez Ramirez 2015).

According to a National Survey of Health and Nutrition comparative analysis, undertaken in 2000, 2006 and 2012, the number of caesarean sections performed in Mexico increased by 50 per cent over a twelve-year period, an increase of 33 per cent and 66 per cent in the public and private sectors, respectively (ENSANUT 2012). A study of trends in caesarean delivery from 2008 to 2017 in Mexico found the national rate of caesarean delivery in first-time mothers was 48.7 per cent (in 2014), with higher rates in private facilities than non-private facilities, regardless of type of insurance coverage (Uribe-Leitz et al. 2019). Though Chiapas has a much lower percentage of recorded hospital births (54 per cent compared to 94 per cent in central Mexico according to national statistics), increased access to hospitals has changed the birthing landscape in a significant way.

Nazar et al.'s study of public hospitals in the neighbouring cities of Tuxtla Gutiérrez and San Cristóbal de Las Casas found that between 1979 and 2003, the practice of caesarean section had increased almost nine times (870.0 per cent) from 7.8 per cent to 29.7 per cent in the general population and almost four times (394.1 per cent) from 0.0 per cent to 20.3 per cent in the Indigenous population (Nazar et al. 2007). Between 2002 and 2012 the number of registered live births involving caesarean delivery in public facilities across Chiapas had risen from 13 per cent to 32 per cent, representing an increase of almost 120 per cent over this ten-year period (Freyermuth et al. 2017). Both statistical and empirical studies show that one of the largest hurdles for pregnant women in twenty-first-century Mexico is negotiating ones' way through a surgery-free birth. Yet, it is exactly by paying attention to the empirical evidence alongside these disembodied percentages that we can see the long-term impact of unnecessary surgical intervention on women's lives.

To illustrate how good intentions to better poor women's chances of surviving childbirth can turn into a normalized culture of abuse and mistreatment, we must first understand the intersecting and conflicting structures of power at work in everyday health systems. What I am attempting to explain here does not align with the broader theories of power inherent in the Eurocentric social science theory. What I have come to call the 'problem with power', in the reading, thinking and writing about power as a 'thing', is that it becomes unhelpfully abstract and detracted from the first-person experience. Instead, what I am trying to understand here are the social determinants of power relations (of which gender integrates as a category of analysis). I do this in the same way that globalized health tries to get to grips with the social determinants of health for target populations. In brief, my aim is to re-populate understandings of the workings of power with the people who are subject to its varying forces. Childbearing narratives are useful tools for this exercise as the actions and relationships described give rise to questions about the social determinants of successful or harmful health systems. If we begin with the social determinants of power as the basis for designing better health systems, perhaps we could arrive at the point where unintended consequences would be indefensible and much intergenerational trauma avoided. The social determinants of power are tangible, definable and therefore measurable.

This chapter centres specifically on the birth narratives of Bety and Rosa,[1] two distinct women with comparable stories to tell. Although only Bety and Rosa's lives and experiences are examined in detail, their stories are complemented by excerpts from other women who have spoken to me over the years. After a decades' worth of research into facility-based care, I feel it pertinent to include women from across the social strata of the city to reflect the complexities of how birth trauma can unite their bodily experiences as mothers. Though I am committed to an intersectional and eco-systemic framework which will identify the elements of class, ethnicity, age, marital status, nationality, religion, family structure and political allegiance in predicting a woman's likelihood of iatrogenic trauma[2] in childbearing, it is also important to note where the female body and reproductive capacity, as constructed by the medical gaze, also becomes a unifying factor to all pregnant women being at some risk of trauma in the moment of birth and beyond.

The transcript and fieldnote excerpts used in this chapter came from interviews carried out between the years 2008–2013 and refer to several private and public facilities in San Cristóbal. Gathered in the form of life-story interviews, the excerpts narrate women's own interpretations of events. In this sense I do not intend them to be about the nature of events as such, but about the lives of particular people who are deeply embedded in them. Using a language of reflection these women reconstruct events from their lived memories and in the context of their transition to motherhood. The life-story approach I took with these interviews gave women the opportunity to reflect upon how (or whether) the birth experience shaped their initial identity as mothers and how they felt about their child. Split into sub-themes of pregnancy, birth and nurture – in an effort to order the nonlinear order of storytelling – the following excerpts include descriptions of trauma and as such I argue that from a feminist perspective they are not to be tampered with, cleaned up or misrepresented. The women's words are meant to exist in their original (albeit translated) form with the aim that as much as possible they retain the feeling with which they were spoken. Throughout the chapter I interject with discussion and comments on the common themes that arise, but my intention is to foreground the women's words as they were told to me.

Pregnancy

Bety

I met Bety (then twenty-eight years old) in 2013 at the birth centre where she attended the preparation for birth classes. She had come to the birth centre for her third pregnancy where she hoped to have a VBAC2 (vaginal birth after two caesareans) with the support of the professional midwives. She differed from the other women attending the class in that she was a practising Sunni Muslim; she also spoke openly about her faith and life amongst the Catholic community. Bety did not belong to the small community of the Murabitun movement of Muslims which has grown gradually over the last two decades in San Cristóbal. She explained to me how the orthodox (Sunni) and Murabitun did not mix, the latter being critical of the traditional ways of the Sunni. 'They are only interested in converting the Maya folk', she told me when I asked her about the differences between the community. 'They want business with the mestizos and conversion of the Maya. I prefer to integrate. My family here in Chiapas are Catholic and I think segregation is damaging'.

Originally from San Cristóbal, she had studied at the Centro Cultural Islámico de México (CCIM) in Mexico City in her late teens. It was during her days as a student that she met her husband Majd, her Arabic teacher at the time and a first-generation migrant from Syria. 'He was about thirty-five and I was twenty-one ... and well we married but we didn't really have a plan to have children or anything or any long-term life plan, so when I got pregnant it was a bit of a surprise'. After marrying, the couple moved to San Cristóbal so that Bety could be closer to her family. We met on various occasions at the birth centre, and after a few weeks Bety agreed to let me record an in-depth narrative interview with her where she relayed the experience of her first pregnancy and birth, and the period of postpartum depression that followed. Bety had given birth twice before in a low-income private hospital run by nuns (known as charitable hospitals). The births had impacted negatively on her early motherhood experiences and how she felt about her body and her ability to give birth 'as nature intended'.

On the morning I went to record our interview I was met at the door by Majd, a tall man with a mop of brown curls falling down on to his face; he welcomed me into their home and then retired quickly into the background to work at his computer. It was the first time I had seen Bety without her hijab and I was struck by how I was seeing her as Mexican for the first time. Until this point, I had not realized how much I had subconsciously categorized her as 'other', neither Mexican nor foreign, solely based upon her outward appearance. As we sat drinking black tea and chatting about our current pregnancies the conversation steered towards her first pregnancy:

So, when I got pregnant with Adnan I wanted to look for a calm place, where I could trust the people. I remembered that there was a hospital that was run by nuns and they had been part of my childhood, as they were Catholic, they looked after me as a child; they taught me Catholicism. So, I went to see them and my father who is a doctor came with us and we spoke to the director and we explained that we wanted a natural birth, that we wanted something intimate and personal and she said fine, no problem ...

It wasn't private, they call it a charitable hospital but really the charity isn't much because you pay a high price for going there! I remember investigating and all the other hospitals charged so much money. I didn't want to go to a public hospital because I knew that if I went to a public hospital, they would treat me worse than an old rag. So, we didn't have enough money to pay for a private hospital and we went to the place where we thought we knew the people ...

At the beginning the doctor was very friendly and then suddenly she started to behave strangely. It's only now that I realize from the beginning it was a form of obstetric violence[3] because I remember I would ask her something or call and explain – 'It's because I feel [ill]' and she would say, 'No, you need to come now because your baby may be in danger'. Imagine how that felt that you're a first time mother who is in her house in the city and who has to travel an hour or so to arrive at the hospital? If she tells you to hurry because your baby may be dead ... and so really, I felt that I couldn't enjoy the first pregnancy because of so much stress from the doctor. I was always worried and she was always saying, 'let's do an ultrasound because you don't want the baby to have such and such ...' so I was left with this in my head and I started to look everything up on the internet and learn about all these illnesses which made me even more stressed.

Rosa

I had known Rosa, a federal government employee, since 2005 when I was working as a community health worker in the state capital. She later moved to San Cristóbal in 2009 and became pregnant with her first child, when she was thiryt-two years old. Having lost touch over the years we met again by chance in the marketplace one weekend and began to visit each other regularly. Her job in the government legal department meant that she received full health insurance and received medical attention and gave birth in a public health institution for federal employees. I initially interviewed her in 2011 as part of a research project on prenatal care and birth outcomes. At the time of our first interview Rosa was planning to leave the father of her child, and in that first recording, she began to reflect on how her pregnancy and transition to motherhood had made her think differently about her relationship. She had been in a relationship with León (the father) for almost twelve years, but they had never been open to her family. León was separated from his first wife but was not willing to declare his relationship with Rosa because he feared upsetting his estranged wife and daughters. Rosa kept León a secret from her parents because they did not think previously married men were a reliable prospect. The relationship was finally brought out into the open when Rosa fell pregnant, but León still refused to tell his wife and daughters. When I recorded our first interview, I asked her to tell me about her experience during pregnancy and birth. We had had many previous conversations on this subject but, as she later told me, this was the first time Rosa had the opportunity to put all the pieces of the jigsaw together and reflect upon events that happened leading up to her birth:

All the time I was pregnant I tried to be calm and look after myself as you should. I was eating a lot of fruit and vegetables so that my baby would be healthy. Around six months I started to get very itchy all over my body, very, very itchy. I started to think that it might be some kind of animal or bacteria, so we fumigated my room; we cleaned it but I continued to itch. I went to see the doctor and he said that I had a liver infection, but when I had my first ultrasound and blood tests, they said that my liver had been fine. As time went on, I started to feel worse and so I went to see the obstetrician, that was now doing my prenatal checks and they did some tests. They checked loads of different stuff to see whether it was anything to do with my liver and in the end they told me that I had intrahepatic cholestasis[4] and that can seriously threaten the baby's life. I was very scared because it's a very delicate organ. I said, 'But how can this be? They did an ultrasound [before] and said everything was fine. I don't understand'. They explained to me that my liver wasn't happy because something was trying to move into its space and it didn't want to be moved. I was so itchy; I felt like I was having electric shocks all the time and on top of this my morning sickness didn't go away and I was getting very depressed. I knew that I could be doing harm to my baby because I looked this liver illness up on the internet and read that my baby could suffer a lot.

When I was six months pregnant they admitted me to hospital for forty-two days and they did so many tests on me… I was getting so worried that my baby was in danger and every day the doctors arrived and said, 'We're going to check you for cirrhosis, if you have any fat in your liver, if you have liver cancer we're going to take the baby out'. It was always something different. But I thought it can't be anything so bad. I didn't think a pregnancy would make me so ill. And I didn't understand why the doctors kept saying that I or my baby could to die, that my pregnancy was high risk… Thank God that in the end I didn't have fat in my liver, or hepatitis or anything. They just said that I had an infection in my liver but nothing serious, nothing that was going to kill me.

They said I had to get rid of all the toxins that my liver was producing, as there were many. The toxins were poisoning me, it's a very rare illness, poisoning my blood and I needed to get rid of them… In the hospital they said that when I got to seven months, if I still had problems then they would take the baby out so I wasn't putting it at any more risks. They said if I went canary yellow, if my nails went a yellow colour that I should go straight away to the hospital. They also said that if my wee turned the colour of coca-cola that I should go straight away because it meant that the baby had died. Every day I woke up thinking, 'My God has the baby moved?' Sometimes it moved and other days it didn't until around midday and I would touch my belly and try to make it move. I lived in constant fear until I felt the baby move then I would be okay… I lived in torment, desperate to get to eight or nine months.

I just wanted my baby to be born. The doctors had said to me that I couldn't have any more babies after this one, that hopefully they could save this one. They said it would be difficult for me to get pregnant again so every night I was praying that my baby would be born safely...

At seven months I went to a new doctor and he said that it was better to wait to go full term. I felt split because I wanted them to do a caesarean because I thought my baby was suffering. I thought it's better they get him out if he's suffering but also, I was thinking that it was too soon and he needed more time to grow. During the whole pregnancy I was never at peace... Every month they took my blood and did tests and continued to tell me that my pregnancy was high risk. And I would say, 'Yes, I know' and then different doctors would say things like, 'Do you know that you could die?' And I would think, 'Yes, but if die, I die. Only God can decide'.

In both Bety and Rosa's narratives the medical rhetoric of risk guided both medical practice and women's decision-making during pregnancy. When speaking to medical professionals or women I often heard how the use of technology as a way of measuring risk outweighs any existing belief the women may have about their health or that of their growing child. These excerpts show how Rosa and Bety were also preoccupied with a fear of death throughout their first pregnancies. Whilst Rosa's fears were rooted in underlying health problems and pathological symptoms, Bety's fears were evoked by the risk-based approach to medicine her obstetrician employed in responding to her questions. In both cases the use of technology appeared to emphasize rather than obviate negative risk, while in Rosa's case also giving rise to other potential risks. The fear of death and possible damage to their babies negatively affected the pregnancy experience for both Bety and Rosa. Both of their narratives show the gradual path from happiness to anxiety caused by their interactions with medical professionals, searching the internet and navigating their physical changes and individual responses to pregnancy. The impact of this iatrogenic anxiety left the women feeling in conflict with professional advice and doubting their own bodily knowledge.

The treatment that women receive in healthcare services contributes to shaping their experience and more often than not provides the vocabulary with which they begin to talk about childbearing. A woman will describe her pregnancy in the terminology used by the medical professionals she encounters, securely anchoring her reproductive experience in a particular social and historical moment (see Lock 1993). This can be seen in all the women's narratives where there is a distinct shift towards preoccupation with life or death as the women engage more frequently with prenatal care services.

The use and language of technology (which emerges as a way of 'seeing' what the eye cannot) further legitimizes the belief that death can be cheated by avoiding the risk (translated as certainty) of human error. The technocratic model (see Davis-Floyd 2001, 2003a) is clear wherever women recount their experiences of prenatal and birth care in the medicalized environment. The links between technology and relationships of power are revealed where women describe the conflict between their own bodily knowledge and that which is produced via the tools of the medical practitioner. Technology becomes a locus of knowledge which foregrounds the foetus as though it were already separate from the mother. As Claire Wendland so eloquently argues, the mother 'is rendered transparent, invisible; she vanishes from view' (Wendland 2007: 226).

The complex and multiple implications of the technocratic model of birth in low-resource settings are significant in terms of the decision-making that occurs around the pregnant or labouring woman. Public hospitals in San Cristóbal, for instance, often lack the technology (ultrasound, electronic foetal heart monitors, Pitocin and analgesic supplies, emergency obstetric and neonatal equipment) needed to manage pregnancy and birth as defined by the technocratic model. Where equipment is available, it is often found to be out of service or lacking in quantity to meet the needs of the hospital population. As the pregnant woman moves from the stages of gestation to labour the pressure to save the foetus from the hostile environment of the uterus becomes ever more apparent in the actions of those around her.

Birth

In this section the excerpts focus on the event of birth: what was happening to the woman from her own perspective and also memories of what was happening around her. The births described below culminated in emergency caesarean section apart from Rosa who had a vaginal birth. Though these birth stories are personal to the individual, they are also representative of many women I have spoken to and the cases documented by reproductive rights advocates in Mexico.

*Emergency Caesarean Section Outcomes in
Public, Private and Charitable Clinics*

Bety (continued):

I was in labour in the house for around two days but really the contractions weren't very strong; it wasn't anything I couldn't cope with. When I got to the hospital, we arrived in the nighttime, and honestly, I thought the doctor was going to stay with me, I really thought she was going to stay with me during the whole labour. But it wasn't like that. They admitted me and the doctor was there for about an hour and then she said her shift was over and she was going home ... and so the doctor left us and was away the whole night and I don't know if psychologically I was thinking that I couldn't give birth that night because the doctor wasn't there and also the room was very cold, the whole place was very cold, and they treated you very coldly... It's very annoying that [the nurses] just came in and did internal examinations and then left and then came back and did another internal... And you can't just be even in comfortable clothes or you want to get up. It's your instinct to want to stand up but you can't because they've put a drip in you. And you've had a hospital birth as, well haven't you? Can't you remember how they put all these things in you, and you can't move and with each contraction you feel like you want to move? You want to stand up, but you can't. And so, this is how we passed the night time, and my husband was really tired and they put a little camp bed up for him and he stayed there and slept... and it was horrible and really after some point the contractions started to get out of control. They come so fast. You don't really know how much [Pitocin] they're putting into me because the doctor would enter and say, 'Right, give her another injection [of Pitocin]', and then they'd leave and after about 40 minutes they'd come back and inject me again...

In the morning, the doctor came back around 9am... and then she said, 'Oh this is taking a long time. I think we're going to consider a caesarean'. I felt very bad because I really didn't want a caesarean and my husband, I think for his lack of knowledge on this subject he was saying to me, 'Well if the doctor is saying this is what you need there must be a reason' ... It was horrible because it's your body and it's like they're laughing at your body, laughing at your intimacy. It's like this thing that you've dreamed about being beautiful and lovely very quickly turns into suffering... The doctor without even asking my opinion just said, 'We have to break the waters now', and put this thing inside me. It was long and metal that looked like a needle. And so, water started to come out, but it was green. In the moment that she saw the green liquid she said that I must have a caesarean straight away. She said, 'Now it's an emergency caesarean. We can't wait any more time because the baby will start to eat the poo and if it does it...' and so can you imagine how that must feel, a woman in the middle of labour and the doctor tells you that your baby could die, so you say, 'Okay do what you want...'

They did the caesarean and I felt a horrible sensation, very horrible because she said, 'In the moment we take your baby out you're going to feel pain in some of your organs, in the parts that aren't affected by the anaesthetic'... And you know what, it was the worst pain because my husband saw me... I screamed but with desperation. It was a pain that felt like they were touching my internal organs. I don't know if the anaesthetic was done wrong or what... And when they took him out, I screamed because it felt horrible and then after they did that, they gave me a tranquilizer and I remember that I did hear my baby but in between hearing and not hearing him... I was there for three days without seeing him, because of where I was, you couldn't just see your baby when you wanted.

It is evident from Bety's birth narrative how her expectations for a 'natural' (vaginal) birth began to unravel once she entered the clinical environment. Her narrative, together with the others in this section, highlights how quickly women can lose a sense of control over the situation. What is happening around her signals that her body has shifted from something that harbours life to something that endangers it. A common theme in birth stories of long labours resulting in emergency caesarean sections was that women felt they were being prepped for surgery from the moment they entered the hospital. They often spoke of being denied food and liquids, and having their mobility restricted during labour due to either IVs or simply hospital policy. This occurred with women across the social spectrum and so highlights the specificities of the technocratic model of birth across public, private and charitable institutions in San Cristóbal.

Felisa

Felisa, a Tzeltal woman who came to the city to study at high school, was nineteen at the time of her pregnancy. She was part of the cohort of women I interviewed in 2011 as part of a research project on pre-natal care and birth outcomes in Tuxtla and San Cristóbal. She gave birth in the regional maternity hospital where she was accompanied by her elder brother. Felisa had separated from the baby's father at the time she found out she was pregnant but had managed to continue her high school studies and work throughout. She lived with her brother and a younger sister and did not register the pregnancy or attend any prenatal checks. Because of this Felisa was not registered on any assistance programme and her economic status was assessed upon arrival at the hospital. Her birth narrative shows how authoritative medical knowledge and prejudice against young and Indigenous women compromise both agency and bodily integrity:

When I first got my pains, I thought the baby would be born, I didn't know better; it was my first. I went to the clinic and they told me I had a lot longer to go, that I wasn't open yet and I should go and walk around. My waters broke and I couldn't stand the pain, I knew they wouldn't take me at the clinic, so I went to the Regional. I was with my brother. They said that my waters had broken and so the baby had to be born. They said the baby's neck was in the wrong position so it couldn't be born normally. They said I needed a caesarean. I told them I didn't want a caesarean and they said if I didn't have one my baby would die, that I might die. I said I didn't want one, I wouldn't sign the paper. I thought if I die there will be no-one to look after my baby so it would be better if we both died. I wouldn't sign the paper, so they told my brother and he signed it instead and they took me and did the caesarean. They cut me vertically.[5] They said it healed better that way…

It didn't hurt when the baby was born, but afterwards oooh it was painful. The nurses were really nice to me, they knew I was alone, so they helped me with the baby, showed me how to bathe and change his nappy. They were really nice … They didn't charge me a lot because they knew I was alone. They charged sixty-eight pesos, they ask you many questions when you first go in to find out what money and support you have. It wasn't the cost of the caesarean that was hard, it was the medications I needed afterwards. They cost about six hundred pesos. I had my stitches out after a week and went back to work and school ten days later. My sister looked after the baby when I went to classes…

Elbi

I met Elbi when our daughters formed a close friendship at a summer holiday club in 2013. Originally from San Cristóbal, Elbi was a solicitor and her career has taken her across the country. When she became pregnant at thirty-two years old, she decided to move back to her home city to be near her mother. Elbi put her career on hold and settled back home whilst her husband, also a solicitor, continued to work away in Guadalajara. On the day she went into labour she called on her brother to take her to the obstetrician. When I interviewed her, I was struck by where the similarities and differences lay in how she spoke of her experience in a higher-income private clinic to those who had undergone emergency caesarean sections in public clinics. The presumptions made about class and birthing bodies come through clearly in her retelling of her birth:

I had been seeing an obstetrician in Tuxtla, he came highly recommended for normal birth, I woke up with pains one day and we drove there. He said I wasn't in labour and that I should go home, I knew he was wrong; I felt like I was in labour, but then again it was my first baby, and I wasn't sure, so I did as he said. On the way back to San Cristóbal we got stuck in a traffic jam and I started to have very strong contractions. We couldn't turn back to Tuxtla because of the traffic, so we got to San Cristóbal and drove to [a private clinic] which my brother knew. After we arrived, they did an ultrasound and said that the cord was around the baby's neck and that they would have to do an emergency caesarean. I was very nervous as I didn't know any of the doctors or nurses there.

I was really upset because I had dreamed of a natural birth. I said I couldn't decide and would have to call my husband. I wasn't willing to make a decision without him. It was then they started to put pressure on me and say I would have to decide because the baby's life was in danger. All throughout these conversations they were prepping me for surgery. They said if I didn't agree and the baby died then it would be my fault and not theirs. I spoke to my husband on the phone. By this time the contractions were really strong, and I couldn't think straight. He said I should do what the doctors said and not take any risks. He said I should sign the papers. In the end, I agreed as long as they didn't knock me out completely. I wanted to be awake to see and feed the baby. They asked my brother if he wanted to come in with me, but he was too scared, so I went into theatre alone. I remember the staff chatting over me about their lives; I felt invisible. They did the caesarean and the baby was fine... The nurses wanted to know why I hadn't brought a bottle and formula to feed her with. I said I wanted to breastfeed, and they looked at me as if I was mad!... When I think about it, I feel like a failure. For a while I didn't feel like a real mother. I wanted a normal birth so much, but it turned into an emergency and I lost control...

Rosa (Continued)

When Rosa spoke about her birth, she described the constant negotiation a woman enters into with those around her during the second and third stages of labour. Women are unaccompanied in the public labour wards and, as a consequence, are often left vulnerable to pressure and coercion from staff:

At eight months I went to the doctor and they said, 'How far along are you, eight months?'

And I said, 'Yes why? Are you going to take the baby out now?' This doctor said that he needed to check first. It's because the gastroenterologist always said that if the tests came back clear we should wait another month, and then the gynaecologist said, 'I'm going to examine you to see when the baby will be born'. I didn't think it was necessary, but I agreed, and he did the [internal] examination. It was very uncomfortable; they are not as delicate as they should be… I lay back on the bed and he put his hand in my vagina to see if the baby was going to be born. He said, 'Señora, you are dilated one centimetre'. I said, 'That's crazy! How can that be if I'm only eight months?' But I felt something painful that he did when his hand was inside me, I was very uncomfortable afterwards and I was bleeding. I thought that the doctor was bringing on labour because my baby wasn't due to be born yet.

All day I was happy because I wasn't going to make the baby suffer any more. I was finished with the sadness of thinking I was making my baby suffer… I don't think it was normal to start labour this way, but around midday I started to get strong pains. It's quite a coincidence that after going to see the doctor I started to get pains. They lasted all day, small at first but I couldn't sleep, it went on forever. The baby didn't come. I felt like it was going to be born, but it didn't come. I just felt pains and nothing else. My mum said when I started to feel the pains go really strong, I should tell her…

At around four the next morning I woke my mum up and said I thought the baby was coming. I was in so much pain and wanted to go to hospital… We had arrived at 4am and at 8am they gave me a bed and the hours passed – nine, ten, eleven. They said they wouldn't let it go past 2pm. I was in so much pain. I said at one point to the doctor, 'I don't understand, why won't my baby come out?' He said, 'It's because you're not trying hard enough'. So, I started to push a lot and it still didn't come out, and I started to think it was strange that it wouldn't be born. Other women came and went so why not me? So, I asked the doctor again, 'What's wrong, why can't I do it?' He asked, 'Did you drink anything?' And I said, yes, I had drunk some juice earlier. He told me that was a massive error, that I should never have drunk anything. He said that my bladder would be full and would be stopping the baby from coming out… He said I should go to the toilet and empty my bladder. I said I wanted to but couldn't move. Then two student doctors came along, and they told me not to worry that they were going to examine me and see that the baby was born. But that was horrible because they put a hand inside me to make the baby come out, but it didn't, it still didn't come… Another two hours passed and still nothing, so I asked the doctors again what was wrong. They said not to worry, that I should just keep trying. But I was trying as hard as I could, and it wouldn't budge… In the end they said to me, 'Señora your baby is stuck. If anything, else goes wrong then we will have to do a caesarean. If you don't try harder the baby won't be born'.

So, I thought, 'Okay, I'll carry on,' and finally, I thought that it was going to be born.

A doctor came by and said, 'Well, are you ready to have this baby?' He put his hand inside me and said that the baby was stuck behind a membrane. After that the labour pains were a lot worse because he broke the membrane and because he kept his hand inside during contractions, or putting things in me, I had no idea what he was doing. And then he said, 'Right, I think one more big push and your baby will be born. He has a lot of hair, if you were on this side you would notice that you're nearly there'. And then with one last try they took me into theatre and the baby was born, and I was the happiest women alive!

[The doctor] said straight after the birth, after the placenta came out, 'We're going to put an IUD in', and I said no, that I didn't want one. He said that I would die if I got pregnant again and that I should learn from what happened to me. In these moments I don't think you're capable of making a decision... He just said, 'Señora you will die if you have another child'. At this moment I wasn't quite sure what he was telling me. He said they were going to put the IUD in, and I said no, so then he got annoyed, he said 'You are irresponsible, wanting to bring another child into this world, put another child in danger. You are a bad mother because you want to bring another baby into the world to suffer'. I wasn't sure what he was going on about so in the end I just agreed.

The marginalization of the mother in favour of the baby about to be born is present throughout these narratives. The themes of fear, death and culpability continue particularly for the women who faced emergency caesarean sections. Though none of the women questioned the legitimacy of their emergency, they all faced intense pressure to comply with the decision. The meanings that can be associated with a language of emergency and risk are significant. I am not questioning whether the decisions made by the professionals involved in these births were unnecessary or abusive. I am not able to say so and it is not my intention to deny the complications that can occur in childbirth. My argument here is not about the reality of emergencies, but about how emergencies materialize and how they are perceived in an institutional setting. My interest lies in what creates the conditions of emergency, from whose perspective and how language and relationships of power shape the unfolding of events. The construction of what constitutes a medical emergency in childbearing makes for an interesting point of analysis from which we can make direct links to broader reproductive and gender politics. In these narratives power relations are revealed as part of the everyday conditions of emergency in the institutional environment.

The institutional management of pregnancy and birth in urban Chiapas is legitimately preoccupied with high maternal and infant mortality. As previously noted, Chiapas has the second highest maternal mortality ratio (68.1 per every 100,000 live births) and the highest infant mortality (17.9 per every 1000 children under five years). The state has the highest incidences of underage marriage and adolescent pregnancy (along with its associated health risks). The most recent National Mother's Index study names Chiapas as the most challenging place to become a mother regardless of ethnicity (Garita Edelen et al. 2016). Pressure to react to such highly publicized data and meet the aims of international and national development programmes, together with the actual reality of high maternal mortality, means that the level of emergency obstetric cases dealt with in public hospitals will shape societal and clinical attitudes towards the perceived dangers of childbirth overall.

The city of San Cristóbal de Las Casas is an important transfer site for surrounding rural communities and as such has benefited from two new hospitals and maternity clinics built with a view to improving high mortality and morbidity rates. Yet, health inequalities in Chiapas are in large part a result of widespread structural violence, low-intensity armed conflict and ethnic oppression. If we examine this through a lens of intersecting forms of violence, poor and/or Indigenous women of reproductive age are most at risk from social, economic and physical oppression. The sexual, reproductive and maternal health of individuals is significantly affected by intersecting forms of violence and as such plays a significant role in shaping maternal transition for women whether they are directly affected or not. Women arriving in the city from the poverty stricken and isolated communities are vulnerable to complications in labour.

As we see in Felisa's narrative, prejudice from healthcare workers means that rural, Indigenous, young or single mothers are profiled as high risk regardless of any actual complications being present. An emergency medicine culture of 'slice and ask questions later', together with a disproportionate focus on maternal and infant mortality above all else, results in a heightened awareness amongst doctors and nurses of childbirth as a life-threatening phenomenon for all women.

International research arising from the relative failure of MDG5 in many low- to middle-income countries clearly demonstrates that increased access to facility-based emergency care does not improve quality of care or have a significant impact on mortality rates (Berer 2013; Say et al. 2014; van Teijlingen et al. 2014). In Mexico, the national spread of health inequalities further complicates the idea that access to facility-based care is the silver bullet that all women need. Despite having national maternal mortality rates (MMR) on a par with its northern neighbour, the vast inequalities within the Mexican population means that, in practice, the variance in MMR across the country can reveal up to eight times difference in deaths per 100,000 (Freyermuth et al. 2017). This is further complicated by the fact that although the rates of death at the moment of birth may be highlighted as being improved, postpartum death (once isolated from the main MMR data) is rising in Mexico overall (WHO et al. 2015): a possible indication that the increase in emergency intervention at birth is having unforeseen mortality consequences in the days and weeks afterwards.

In the reporting of national statistics, a distinction is made between programmed (elected) and emergency caesarean sections. This distinction poses interesting questions for the circumstances under which the surgery is carried out in public health institutions. In the discourse of global health, state and federal institutions are encouraged to support vaginal birth wherever possible. In terms of technological and financial resource it is cheaper and arguably better for the health and wellbeing of the mother and baby. This means that in practice programmed caesarean sections are reserved for either those with full insurance coverage, women whose pregnancies are deemed high risk for medical reasons or if previous births were by caesarean section. All other caesarean sections are conducted under the definition of emergency. Therefore, in the largest public maternity hospital in San Cristóbal where programmed caesarean sections rarely happen (the women would be referred to an alternative state institution), it is worth asking the following questions: why do emergency caesarean sections make up over half of the birth outcomes? How can women's birth narratives provide a distinct perspective on how permission for surgery is negotiated? And what can this tell us about forms of gender power, resistance, resignation and coercion in clinical environments?

Aside from perceived medical emergencies the expectation of compliance is evident in the narratives in relation to family planning. Reproductive rights discourse in Mexico promotes the universal right for women to control when and how many children they have, regardless of their social situation. Whilst this approach echoes global perspectives on women's bodily autonomy, it also emphasizes the responsibility on women to control their reproductive lives through the use of contraception. Conversely, the Mexican government's continued refusal to legalize abortion at a federal level is a form of limiting women's reproductive options and reproducing the notion of individual responsibility (Gutmann 1996; Lamas 2001). The Mexican public health system provides all methods of contraception for women free of charge. Most commonly women are offered intrauterine devices (IUDs) and tubal ligation, though since the early twenty-first century the contraceptive pill or injection is becoming more available and popular amongst younger women in urban populations. Over the years I have never witnessed a public health programme discussing vasectomies as a contraceptive option for couples. The emphasis in public health (which is also reflected in the local population) is always on how the woman can protect herself from unwanted or future pregnancies via female contraceptive devices.

In his work on sexual health and gender politics in Oaxaca, Gutmann (2009) describes how the introduction of the *Oferta Sistemática* (translated as 'The Standard Plan) around the end of the twentieth century sought to increase the adoption and employment of birth control by women. With the *Oferta Sistemática* every time a woman of child-bearing age came into contact for any reason with a doctor, nurse, or other health care worker, whether in a clinic or in her home, she was offered contraception. Gutmann argues that through this direct targeting of women in the health system a female contraceptive culture emerged and was reinforced by institutions, including through the public health system, so that women were systematically confronted about birth control by health personnel in ways that few men ever experienced (Gutmann 2009).

In the public health institutions in Chiapas the practice is to offer women the IUD or tubal ligation in prenatal appointments. However, this often does not happen for systemic reasons or if the woman has not accessed clinical prenatal appointments before presenting in labour.

'We just don't have time to discuss things properly with the patient', my friend and colleague Dr Ricardo told me, when I asked him about clinical birth management from the physician's perspective:

> I did so much time in control prenatal when I was qualifying and you just have to rush them through, and the other professionals, the social workers, nutritionists, psychologists, we don't communicate. They never come out of their offices, apart from when it is too late. Like for instance ... it is always done when the woman is still giving birth when she is feeling the most pain or just after and they say, 'Do

you want an IUD?' 'Do you want to have children?' 'Here sign this', and the nurse will do it. The nurse has a specific job to do, to check and make sure all is okay for the doctor and so we will say, 'Pass me the paper so she can sign it'. Or if it is in a caesarean section and the women is barely awake, she is between sleeping and awake, we pass the paper and say, 'Sign this'. But if the woman says, 'I won't sign' and she has six children and she is say twenty-four to twenty-six years old we, the doctors and nurses, we won't argue but we go and talk to the social worker, we say, 'Tell the husband or the mother to sign this paper'.

Ricardo's comments give an insight into the priorities of health and medical practitioners and how systemic weaknesses also contribute to creating the conditions of emergency, framed within a language of risk – in this case the need to regulate a woman's uterus and sexual practices. In her paper titled 'Risk as a Forensic Resource', Mary Douglas writes that '[t]he modern risk concept, parsed now as danger, is invoked to protect individuals against encroachments of others' (Douglas 1990: 7). What arises in pregnancy, labour and birth management, in this instance, is a reversal of Douglas' argument where it is the community, an imagined future foetus, the institution and the woman herself who must be protected against the encroachment of the sexually immoral, maternal subject. This idea that a woman who is not averse to risk (of future pregnancies) poses a danger or a threat is evident in Rosa's narrative. When she attempts to resist the pressure to have an IUD inserted or tubal ligation straight after birth, her behaviour is interpreted as irresponsible and the threat of death and suffering is invoked once again to coerce or silence her.

Aside from Bety, the women I have spoken to rarely describe what happens to them directly as obstetric violence or a violation of rights, yet their stories highlight an enforced position of isolation and submission common to definitions of violence against women. In Felisa's case, her wishes were overridden completely when doctors went to her brother for permission for surgery. In all cases the threat of death to the unborn child was asserted in order to obtain compliance. Overt attempts at resistance by the women were met with doctors asserting authority via the use of threats or by turning to the relative or person accompanying them. Acted out in the presence of other doctors and nurses, this type of situation demonstrates that the form of power relations at play requires complicity from others to be legitimate.

Research on mistreatment in hospitals generally concurs that the prevalence of bodily violations and coercive behaviour in hospitals across Latin American countries is congruent with the obstetric transition. Beyond Latin America, the World Health Organisation (WHO) has declared the mistreatment of women during childbirth and associated human rights violations to be a 'global problem' (WHO 2015). The issue was further highlighted in 2015, as UN and regional human rights experts issued a joint statement explicitly calling on states to address 'acts of obstetric and institutional violence' (ACHPR 2015). Despite this, international and regional standards on abuse and mistreatment of women during birth remain in the early stage of development.

Obstetric violence is a product of a multi-factorial framework where institutional and gender violence overlap (GIRE 2015: 14). Obstetric violence is a form of gender-based violence precisely because it is done to women because of who they are (reproductive entities) and what they represent (moral subjects). Obstetric violence violates women's reproductive health rights, and results in physical or psychological harm during pregnancy, birth or puerperium. Perpetrators of obstetric violence can be lead clinicians; they can also be nurses, student doctors and other support staff – regardless of gender. Obstetric violence earned its name because it happens within the space of obstetric logic. Manifestations of obstetric violence can include direct abuse such as scolding, taunts, irony, insults, threats, humiliation, manipulation of information and denial of treatment; pain management during childbirth used as punishment; coercion to obtain 'consent' for invasive procedures; and even acts of deliberate harm to a woman's health (Villanueva-Egan 2010: 148). Systemic manifestations of violence are indicated by high rates of caesarean sections, routine episiotomy, and routine manual examination of the uterine cavity post-birth, all of which are commonplace in the under-funded public institutions in Mexico (Molina et al. 2016; Valdez-Santiago et al. 2013).

In Mexico, there is a disparity in the number of states willing to adopt legislation against obstetric violence and an unwillingness to relate the phenomenon to a broader context of socio-economic, ethnic and gender power relations; this is further complicated by cultural dynamics and attitudes to what constitutes gender-based violence. Over the last decade, there has been an increase in empirical and systematic research on the issue in Mexican public institutions, yet this remains fragmented. Research tends to focus on systemic failure and the attitudes of medical practitioners (Castro and Frías 2019; Castro and Erviti 2015). Above all, beyond activist networks and NGOs, there has been little attempt to understand how women interpret the violations they experience at the hands of health professionals, and how this impacts on their notion of self and being in the world. Identifying and making claims of obstetric violence has become complex because once an issue becomes policy, only certain types of evidence are seen as legitimate. The identifying and defining of what is and what is not violence in a maternal healthcare setting decentres the woman's experience. By listening to women, I have learnt that a more integrated and intergenerational life-course approach to understanding iatrogenic trauma is needed if health systems are ever to evolve. Narrative work tells us that birth trauma arises not from the level of medical complication but how it is dealt with by those charged with supporting the woman through the process.

Elbi's narrative illustrates that acts of coercion can also take place in private clinics which are generally accessed by more affluent women. This suggests that the rhetoric of risk and conditions of emergency are inherent in clinical practice across the board, as opposed to being specifically linked to low socio-economic status or ethnicity. While there are commonalities between clinical practices in private and public institutions, a specific distinction is embodied by the scar left behind after an emergency caesarean section.[6] The women I encountered who had undergone emergency caesarean at the regional maternity hospital, and who therefore were low income or welfare recipients, were clearly marked with a vertical scar stretching from the umbilicus to the pubic region. The scars on women who underwent emergency caesareans in local private clinics were cut horizontally with a transverse incision, described to me by Bety as the 'bikini cut'. The symbolism of the midline or transverse scar vs. a vertical scar has profound analytical consequences in terms of class-based interventions in institutionalized maternal health.

Nurture

In the excerpts below Bety and Rosa describe how their births helped to shape their experiences of the postpartum and early motherhood period.

Bety (continued):

During my recovery I also got a really bad cough, my father said it could be the anaesthetic in my body that I was reacting to. So, I had mastitis, a fever of forty degrees, the cough and without being able to feed my baby because they'd given me antibiotics. It was a terrible time. Even my husband was so tired of seeing me so ill, but he was very patient with me. He didn't lose patience at all. He was always a lot calmer because it was so difficult for me…

Honestly, after having my first son I said I never want to do this again… It was horrible… and like I said the doctor never said that she would visit, come and see how I was after the birth… It was a difficult time, as much for my husband as it was for me. Because I saw him looking really stressed as well but I couldn't help. By this time, I had started to fall into depression…

From the moment I got back home I found it really difficult. It wasn't what I had imagined but I thought maybe after a few days I'll be able to start doing things around the house, but I couldn't. I felt like my body had let me down. I was angry with myself and irritable with the baby… It was very difficult because during this time I started to hear voices. He would cry and I would hear voices saying, 'Don't go to him', 'Kill him; he's bad' and so inside I was very worried because I knew it wasn't right. I thought to myself: How can I do anything to harm my son? He was born from my body, I felt him grow inside me he's made from love; he can't be bad…

I would go to the kitchen and have suicidal thoughts; you see you have no idea how it is to walk around your house and everything you see you think about how you could use it to kill yourself… And so I started to go over to my mother's house for a few days, then back home for a few days and this worked for a while because when I was with my mum I talked a lot. We spoke about everything and, because I was talking, I didn't have the time to think the bad thoughts. In the end I could breastfeed and look after the baby, but it also got to a point when, because of the depression my milk started to dry up. Around 6 months I started to lose my milk and it got to the point where I couldn't even produce a drop…

After the caesarean it took a long time to heal. But they say that the depression has something to do with it, that your body doesn't heal well after the surgery because you feel down. My husband always helped me with curing the wound; he helped me wash and clean it. He said a few times that he noticed pus coming from the wound. That's why I had antibiotics afterwards. But speaking of the wound, the most interesting thing for me is that the wound doesn't stay in your body, the wound is in your heart. Because it's an experience that, although consciously you are saying that you've got over it, but after a long time you realize that you still haven't got over it, when suddenly you get thoughts or reminders that really you haven't got over what happened. It's then you realize that everything that happened is still there. You have it trapped inside and you don't want to let it go. And it carries on hurting you, but you don't want to let it go. When you learn that you can let it go, that nothing will happen, it will go, and you will feel better that's really when the scars begin to heal and begin to disappear…

Rosa (continued):

I wouldn't like to repeat the experience. I wouldn't like so many people to see my body again. It was lovely to have a child, but not the process of having all these people touch you. That was horrible and it wasn't even just one doctor it must have been about seven different people putting their hands inside me… They were all male doctors apart from one and apart from that they were really mean. I heard them say to other women who were screaming out, saying like 'Oh I'm going to die'. They would say, 'Oh yes, and I bet you didn't scream like that when you made the baby'. That's why I didn't cry or anything. I suppressed all my feelings because I didn't want them to shout the same things at me. They were saying to all the women that cried, 'Why are you crying? This is no reason to cry. When you did it you weren't crying were you?' I waited till I got home, when I was alone in my house I thought about the whole situation and I cried…

Being a mother is a beautiful thing and it was worth it, though only once! Two or three times more maybe but I am too scared because of what happened. The situation with my partner isn't ideal either. Today I saw him before I came here, and he was making comments about more children… I don't like having this thing [IUD] inside my body; it has brought about drastic hormonal changes that I don't like. But to be honest I don't want another baby, so for now I won't have it removed… I don't want another baby not because my heart doesn't desire it. I would love to have another child but I'm not in the right situation. We were talking about it only today. My partner said to me, 'Why don't you take that thing out?' But I think he's doing it just because he wants to keep me always for him. He thinks he'll secure me with one more child. You see in Mexico a man won't accept a woman with two children, not even with one.

The culture of blame and individual responsibility inherent in the clinical environment shapes early motherhood in several ways. In the birth narratives I collected, the women repeatedly spoke of coming to terms with a feeling of failure, humiliation and loss of expectations. Women are often left with conflicting emotions and analyse their behaviour during pregnancy and birth, searching for answers of how and where it went wrong. A common theme in the birth narratives presented in the previous section is that although women felt shamed and humiliated by professionals, more than this, they felt let down by their own bodies. The women who underwent unplanned caesarean sections spoke of a sense of failure, which took time to reconcile, and impacted on them as maternal subjects.

Withdrawal from clinical management in the postpartum period resulted in women dealing with many unanswered questions, which they ultimately began to turn inward on themselves. Bety had a challenging time coming to terms with the birth of her first child, and the unwanted caesarean section outcome. Her psychological and physical health were greatly impacted by her pregnancy and birth experience. Though it is impossible to say whether the events leading up to and during the birth were the cause, from Bety's point of view her postpartum suffering was inseparable from what had happened in the hospital. Although her postpartum account (which suggests undiagnosed postpartum psychosis) is more extreme than most, Bety's narrative illustrates how the trauma of birth can profoundly influence early motherhood and maternal subjectivity. In her case an undesired outcome leads to a belief that she is unworthy as a mother, to the point where she wants to do harm to either herself or the baby. Bety describes the conflict between not achieving what 'nature intended' (a vaginal birth), which then develops into 'unnatural' feelings towards her child, and the difficulty coming to terms with what she is supposed to be feeling as a mother. She relates the non-compliance of her body to the perception of being a bad mother, which ultimately affects her personal relationships and ability to heal after a traumatic event.

In her birth narrative Rosa touched upon an aspect of childbearing that is often omitted from maternal discourse: the thoughts and feelings around surrendering the body to the hands of strangers. She provides an example of how women sacrifice bodily integrity for the welfare of the life within their uterus. In the moment of giving birth, the obstetric gaze gives priority to the unborn child and its safe delivery to the outside world. Medical practice dictates that the woman must be compliant for the medical practitioners to achieve this goal. In the hospital women are literally expected to open themselves up, to be examined by multiple pairs of hands, adjusted and cut without presenting any opposition.

Rosa's birth narrative demonstrated how health professionals will often interpret a woman's silence as cooperation and compliance. From Rosa's perspective her silence was a form of resistance, which in turn also served to protect her from receiving a scolding from the doctors and nurses, allowing her to maintain some control over the situation. When she breaks her silence to refuse the offer of an IUD, she is judged for putting herself at risk of getting pregnant again. The Mexican state has promoted the concept of the modern woman in relation to her choices of low-risk behaviour (Smith-Oka 2012). Women who go against medical advice are seen to be increasing their risk of complications and in doing so they are considered bad mothers and a danger to the wellbeing of society. Adhering to medical advice therefore defines women as good mothers because they are demonstrating risk-averse behaviour. Childbearing and childbirth happen in a medical, social and economic context that has the capacity to shape a woman's transition to motherhood beyond the events of the clinical environment. Rosa's strategic use of silence extends to her relationship with her son's father. She tolerates the discomfort of an unwanted IUD to protect herself from becoming trapped in a relationship that may have no future. The compromises to bodily integrity she made during pregnancy and in labour are continued in her roles as good mother and responsible modern woman.

Resistance and Resignation as Everyday Practice

I would like to provide a moment of reflection in this chapter to draw upon Lila Abu-Lughod's work on subtle forms of resistance as a diagnostic of power. Abu-Lughod's assertion that studying less obvious forms of resistance 'will allow us to get to the ways in which intersecting and often conflicting structures of power work together … in communities that are gradually becoming more tied to multiple and nonlocal systems' (Abu-Lughod 1990: 42) ties in well with my attempt to present events from the memories and perspectives of the women who experience a clinical transition to motherhood in Chiapas. I begin with Abu-Lughod's ideas about diagnostics of power as a starting point and extend them to think about forms of resignation, alongside resistance, as a diagnostic of intersecting and contradictory forms of power in institutionalized childbearing. Acts of resistance come about through women's own life experiences and developed coping strategies to the forms of oppression they face. As such, both forms of power and methods of resistance are socially determined.

Through analysis of the childbearing narratives, I have observed two main points about forms of resistance and resignation in relation to space, human action and gendered power relations. These observations encompass both successful and failed attempts at resistance, and how acts of resignation may contribute to producing future acts of resistance. The first observation is that women are afforded greater opportunities for self-conscious resistance in the pregnancy and nurturing periods of maternity. During pregnancy women try their best to identify the support that will allow them to have the birth they desire, and they often withdraw from professionals who threaten their desires and beliefs. These women are not anti-interventionist; their priority ultimately is the safety and wellbeing of their child. Within this notion of wellbeing are collective and individual beliefs about what they deem to be necessary and unnecessary interventions. To carry out this form of resistance, the women must not be dependent on public services and they must have alternative options available to them such as midwives or private obstetricians. This also raises questions about socio-economic status and social networks. In the postpartum period, women will often not return to the place of birth, especially if it holds particularly traumatic memories for them. This is where I identify future acts of resistance that arise from an act of resignation in the moment of childbirth. These women avoid further compromises (acts of resignation) to their own bodily integrity and that of their new baby by staying at home during the postpartum period and failing to turn up for postpartum check-ups. Where women suffered infections postpartum or complications in healing, they reported seeking out alternative care and, where needed, borrowing money to pay for a private doctor rather than return to the hospital where they gave birth. Where they have little choice but to return to the clinical environment, they will arrive with female family members as support.

The second observation is in relation to unsuccessful attempts at resistance in the clinical environment, particularly in the second and third stages of labour. Failed attempts at overt resistance to surgical intervention, intrusive assessment or inhumane treatment remain key factors for understanding forms of power relations at play within the confines of a clinical environment. They show that regardless of women's expectations of, or preparations for birth, or their own feelings on how labour is progressing, once doctors declare an emergency, resistance (to clinical decision-making) is futile. But rather than reading this as a sign of the futility of resistance, it raises important questions about the dynamics of power that hide behind the concept of an 'emergency situation'. It leads us to ask gendered questions about who declares an emergency over a woman's body and how this reflects the coloniality of gender. Declaring a life or death emergency allows doctors (of any gender) to manipulate and coerce women to comply with orders. The use and threats of caesarean section resulting from the evocation of emergency is a strategy employed by the health professional to control the outcome of the birth situation in their favour. The rhetorical question 'do you want your baby to die?' is employed as a coercive strategy that further bolsters the reasoning for ordering an emergency caesarean section, thereby making high caesarean rates, over other forms of surgical intervention, a necessary subject of analysis and possible indicator of other less tangible forms of violence in obstetric settings. The perception of childbearing as high risk and the need to intervene with non-complicit bodies becomes the naturalized rule rather than the exception. The consistent evocation of death and risk of dying present in these women's narratives illustrates the socially constructed danger of childbirth and the insistence in medicine that new lives must be saved at all costs.

The pathological emphasis placed upon childbearing as high risk, and therefore inherently dangerous, portrays the women as needing to be saved from themselves, as though they and their bodies are the root cause of perceived complications or risks. The evocation of risk as danger appears particularly evident in the technocratic environment. Asserting medical authority if a woman is seen to flout best practice does not leave space for considering why she may be doing so – instead, it results in miscommunication, lack of informed consent or perceptions of non-compliance (Smith-Oka 2012). Women's bodies become a site of struggle and where overt resistance occurs professionals misinterpret women's actions, often accusing them of being uncooperative or bad mothers. In the next two chapters I will continue to weave this theme of risk and resistance as I examine the various midwifery models of care available to women outside of the health system. Through exploring birth practices and postpartum care in the community, different ideas about collective agency and what constitutes risk in relation to good mothering will become apparent.

Notes

1. Some ethnographic elements of this chapter are derived from an earlier publication: J. Murray de López, 'When the Scars Begin to Heal: Narratives of Obstetric Violence in Chiapas, Mexico', *International Journal of Health Governance* 23(1) (2018): 60–69.
2. Drawing from an important report by anthropologist Arachu Castro et al. entitled *Iatrogenic Epidemic: How Health Care Professionals Contribute to the High Proportion of Cesarean Sections in Mexico* (2003), I use the term iatrogenic trauma because my exploration is on the impact of mistreatment and individual birth trauma within the broader contexts of women's lives. My aim is to consider how brief yet powerful acts of violence or professional decision-making that result in trauma go on to shape how women feel about themselves, how they view themselves as mothers, how they manage intimate relationships, and moreover, from a health management perspective, how they negotiate interactions with health professionals throughout their lives. Ultimately, this more long-term way of thinking about not only the act, but the consequences of what is commonly termed 'obstetric violence', is an effort to re-centre women in the debate, to try and listen to what women are saying and the things that happen to them at pivotal moments of change.
3. Bety's use of the term 'obstetric violence' is significant and connected her recent contact with the birth centre and therapy she had been receiving there. The discussions among the women, midwives and therapists at the birth centre was often politicized, in that it focused upon raising awareness of reproductive rights and choices. Use of the term is becoming increasingly common amongst specific politicized groups, regardless of social and ethnic category: the common factor linking women who use the term is contact with midwives or obstetricians wanting to break from institutionalized practices. It is not, however, a commonly used term amongst the majority of women I spoke to from the neighbourhood or wider city, whether their maternal practices involved in or out-of-hospital birth.
4. Intrahepatic cholestasis of pregnancy is a liver disorder that can occur in pregnant women. Cholestasis is a condition that impairs the release of digestive fluid from liver cells. As a result, bile builds up in the liver, impairing liver function. All over itching is a core symptom of this condition.
5. The vertical cut to the abdomen known as the classical or midline incision was common practice in this particular hospital which dealt mainly with emergency caesareans. There is no global agreement over the preferred technique in terms of horizontal midline or vertical transverse abdominal incision (see Deka et al. 2010). Medical justification for the horizontal midline incision is for speed of access to the uterus. Although this is undoubtedly an advantage in emergency situations, the disadvan-

tage to the woman is in the scarring left behind, damaged muscle tissue, longer healing time in addition to the risks of caesarean section overall (Gonzalez et al. 2013; Gibbons et al. 2010). If we examine the practice through the intersecting forms of violence paradigm, the question of why the classical incision is carried out in low-resource settings characterized by high levels of structural violence must be addressed.

6. Roberts (2012) also noted the relationship between caesarean scars, class status and ethnicity. In her study it is middle-class women in Ecuador who use the transverse incision scar indicative of private hospitals to remain distinct from the 'governed masses' who need to access social services.

Chapter 3

BRIDGING THE GAP
BARRIO MIDWIVES

Mis nueve hijos, mis hijos hijos y ahora sus hijos todo nacieron en casa con la partera, así es.

[My nine children, their children and now their children all born at home with a midwife, that's just the way it is.]

—Doña Reina, fieldnotes

In la Orilla, many women continue to give birth at home with a local *partera* (midwife) and surrounded by close female kin.[1] As we saw in the previous chapter, with the introduction of conditional cash transfer welfare programmes and commitment to globalized health goals, giving birth at home conflicts with what health systems perceive to be safer motherhood.[2] Whilst I cannot claim that this is a dominant birth model in the city, I came across enough women in la Orilla and other *barrios* across the city hiring the services of a *partera* to make it of ethnographic significance. Part of the problem with documenting homebirth and midwifery-led healthcare is the lack of published statistical records from which to contextualize these. *Parteras* of all types are excluded from public health debate and from contributing to (the right kind of) data to inform policy (Mills 2017). Over the next two chapters I will draw from the lives of *parteras* working in different contexts and women who seek their care. I shift from a prior focus on the state's attempts to eradicate midwifery as a legitimate model of healthcare (see Murray de López 2015, 2019) to understanding midwifery as a gendered category of analysis from which we can ask important questions about the void between what women want from healthcare and what the state provides for them.

This chapter focuses on the continued existence of *barrio parteras* and the tradition of intergenerational homebirth in lower-income families. As part of my broader interest in maternal transition I am interested in how a comparative study of urban midwifery practices can inform my thinking on collective agency and the ways in which 'spaces of contestation' appear through competing notions of risk (Murray de López 2017) and via 'networks of trust' (Mills 2017). In her extensive analysis of Mexican women and maternal health policy, Lisa Mills argues that a functioning health system is a product of, and is reinforced by, mechanisms that increase trust between patient, professional and institution (2017: 11). Such ideas about who or what to trust come about through shared culture and values. Examining how trust networks work outside of an institutionalized environment in turn allows us to think about what happens when that trust is broken – as we saw in Bety and Rosa's stories. Where do women turn when there is little trust between citizens and individuals and what part does risk play in this?

What little is known about the history of *barrio* midwifery in twentieth-century San Cristóbal tells us that 'for reasons of modesty or trust, patients preferred to be attended by women' (Luna et al. 2015). In a paternalistic obstetric environment, a woman's best chance of woman-centred care was (and continues to be) to avoid hospital services all together and opt for the local *partera*. This general feeling that avoiding hospitals altogether is the safer option for women dovetails with the evidence that across the country a higher percentage of women die due to childbirth complications in hospitals than they do in registered homebirths (Mills 2017).[3] In Chiapas, the mortality ratios between registered homebirth and public hospital births are closer, but a lack of clear reporting make it difficult to say for certain (OMM 2014). I found in my own fieldwork that *barrio* women did not seek out abstract statistics when making decisions about birthplace. Instead, they listen to the experience of others and go with intergenerational expectations. When young *coleta* women want a *partera* they turn to mothers, sisters, grandmothers, aunts and mothers-in-law to recommend the right person. The social status and trust afforded to *barrio parteras* places them in a privileged position as facilitators of change. Unfortunately, where this position has been much exploited by the state throughout the history of midwifery and public health in Mexico (and elsewhere), it has rarely been to the benefit of either *partera* or pregnant woman. In other words, the form of trust that the health system expects from women and referring *parteras* is rarely reciprocated.

A persistent dichotomy has evolved in framing Mexican midwifery as traditional/contemporary or lay/professional practice. This unhelpful dichotomy has caused divisions within and between the medical and midwifery community. Moreover, weighing up the pros and cons of this presumed either-or category in public discourse has distracted from the significant role that the *partera* plays in the lives of many families. Over recent years, Mexican anthropologists and sociologists of health have compiled detailed material on the various models of birth available to urban women in Mexico (Nazar et al. 2007; Sánchez Ramírez 2015, 2016; Freyermuth 2018). These works have contributed to a growing counter-narrative to the urban institution verses rural homebirth models touted in policy and maternal health literature. Despite this, these multi-authored works have failed to have any noteworthy influence on current Mexican policy and the works are little cited in English-language publications on women and maternal health in Mexico and Chiapas.[4] Even in the breadth of work conducted in these corners of Mexico, the focus remains on traditional (used in text as synonymous with Indigenous) verses professional midwifery models.

It may be that like the non-registered, non-Indigenous *barrio partera*, descriptions of how low- to middle-income urban households are going about their daily reproduction, on the periphery of state and private health systems, does not fit the universal maternal health narrative that informs policy on national and international levels. In general, maternal health policy targets women who are wholly reliant on the state system and therefore the system is shaped on this form of reliance. Targeting maternal health in this way has indirect consequences for those otherwise healthy women who straddle the public-private divide for their healthcare.

The titles *partera tradicional, partera empírica, partera técnica* and *partera profesional* all pertain to specific paths, background and training in midwifery and appear across literature and policy (in both Spanish and English). These titles denote a long history of the political manipulation of midwifery and the gradual domination of the medical model in childbearing. Because the mixture of women who work under these titles embrace a range of practices and methods of learning, in my own writing, unless otherwise stated, I use the word *partera* in the same way that families I write about do – as a trusted woman they call to attend a homebirth. When I place the *partera* within a socially contextualized narrative such as the *barrio*, her practices and identity are intrinsically connected with the families and their belief systems. Described through these relationships I can understand the role of the *partera* beyond the rigid definitions of traditional and skilled birth attendants that translate from global health governance. It is within the social context that her identity as Indigenous, non-Indigenous, foreign, traditional, professional or *barrio* acquire meaning. I argue that by thinking with this perspective we can also begin to see how damaging and futile the traditional/professional binary is.

The *barrio partera* best fits the definition found in literature of the *partera empírica* (Murray de López 2015; Luna et al. 2015; El Kotni 2019). The *partera empírica* is a person who attends to the mother in childbirth and who initially acquired their knowledge and skills through their own births or by learning alongside others. Whilst not strictly accurate in practice, this definition covers *parteras* who learn through experience and apprenticeship rather than institutional study. The *partera empírica* is the midwifery anomaly. She has recognition and acknowledgment by the state (in a regulative capacity), in that she may register and attend government education initiatives. Like the Indigenous *partera tradicional*, she suffers from institutional exclusion and prejudice from medical professionals. However, unless the *barrio partera* self-identifies or registers with the state as Indigenous, there are barriers to her registering as a *partera tradicional*. This is significant because in Mexico the *partera tradicional* is protected under constitutional rights as a traditional Indigenous practice. The title does afford them certain protections under Mexican Indigenous rights legislation to continue to attend Indigenous women giving birth outside medical facilities. However, this post-colonial attempt to protect Indigenous birth practices restricts the Indigenous *parteras* to the WHO category of Traditional Birth Attendant (TBA). A TBA is excluded from the Skilled Birth Attendant (SBA) definition and therefore a *partera tradicional* cannot be classed as a member of the health workforce either. The *barrio partera* and the women she attends, on the other hand, exist in an unregulated vacuum where she is neither recognized as a TBA nor a SBA. Though this offers her no protection when complications or death occur, existing in this legal lacuna does give the *barrio partera* a level of autonomy to practice without over-regulation of her methods.

When I first moved to San Cristóbal in 2008 I was eight months pregnant, without health insurance and afraid of giving birth in hospital. Whilst searching door to door around the city's *barrios* for a house to rent I also took to asking older women if they knew of a *partera* I could pay to attend a birth at home. My actions at that time did not come from a commitment to humanized birth and a desire to challenge the pathologization of childbearing. This was my first pregnancy, and I knew very little about the world of maternal health in Mexico or anywhere else. I was translating what I knew of my own birth culture in the UK to my adopted environment. If I had been pregnant in the UK, I would have gone to see a midwife (state provided or otherwise) and so for me, it seemed logical to look for one in Chiapas. Up until the latter part the twentieth century, alongside the signs in windows announcing *Aquí se inyecta* (injections offered here), there would have been notices declaring *se atiende partos* (births attended) to advertise a *barrio partera*. Historical documents show that the *barrio parteras* around San Cristóbal tended to be retired nurses or *partera* by life experience.[5]

During my search for a *partera* in 2008, I was met with many unsure or concerned reactions and lamenting responses like 'pues, es que había una señora, pero ya se murió' (well, there was a woman, but she died a while back). As I became more familiar with the city and its residents, and in later years returned to conduct studies in the outlying *barrios* of the city, I began to meet existing *barrio parteras* through the networks of families I met. These families, like those in la Orilla, were low-income and tended to combine state and private services, separating what they felt was a medical need from a social and maternal one. The families were protective over the identity of their *partera* because they valued their services and were fully aware of their precarious existence and broader social attitudes towards homebirth.

Filomena

I first met Filomena on Doña Reina's doorstep after she came to visit her granddaughter Carlita towards the end of her pregnancy. Filomena is a typical *coleta* woman, short and plump, her serious face framed by waist-length black hair, usually tied into a ponytail at the nape of her neck. She spoke in a quiet voice that commanded your attention. Our conversations were often fleeting as she was always on her way to see a family, prepare herbs or source medicines. She was never comfortable with any request for a lengthy interview or recording about her life as a *partera* but was always happy to chat when I bumped into her in the *barrio*. During my first few months in la Orilla, I was in the final trimester of my third pregnancy and upon each meeting she would look down at my bulging *panza*, declare the sex of the baby and estimate how many weeks or days I had left.

Filomena was a regular visitor to Doña Reina's family, and she had attended the births of all her grandchildren and great grandchildren born at home. At forty-nine years old she was relatively young for a *barrio partera*, having devoted twenty-eight years of her life to helping pregnant women bring new life into the world. Originally from the upper part of la Orilla, she has lived in the neighbouring *barrio* since marriage but continues to serve many families in la Orilla as well as in her own *barrio*. Born in 1964, she described how she was brought 'earthside' by her grandmother, also a *partera*. She told me 'in these times there were no doctors or unless my mother didn't know any or have any access to one, life was more difficult'.

Filomena was a well-established *partera* in this part of the city and knew many of the families very well. She was distantly or closely related to a lot of families through blood or marriage ties. Most mature women in the *barrio* make some claim to experientially based knowledge of maternal health, and even the experience of assisting a daughter, a daughter-in-law, a granddaughter, a niece, or a neighbour in giving birth. What sets the *barrio partera* apart from the women who make these claims is the authority she holds within the community, the number of women outside of the family she has attended, and how she charges for her services. Though most local *parteras* (registered or not) have a fixed price of anything between 500 and 1500 pesos for a birth, Filomena was guarded about how much she charged, telling me that it depended upon the family and how well she knew them or their financial situation.

Although Filomena told me she did not differentiate between boy or girl babies, she (and other women) would tell me of *parteras* who charged more depending on the sex of the baby. One of the reasons given to me as to why this was the case was that 'the boy will be the one to go out and work when he is older, he will bring more money to the household because the girl will just stay at home and not earn'. Another woman gave me a more technical reason, that 'to see or attend a birth if it's a boy, it always complicates because the umbilical cord tends to get wrapped around the thing [penis] so that's why they charge more'. Younger women, like my neighbour Rosita, were unsure of why the practice existed or continued. 'There's another *partera* up at the top [of the *barrio*]' she told me, 'and she charges $1000mxn if it's a girl and $1500mxn if it's a boy. I have no idea why or what the difference is, a baby is a baby!'

Like most *barrio parteras*, Filomena's midwifery knowledge has been obtained through generations of women in her family. When I asked her one day about how she first became a *partera*, she explained to me, 'I am a *partera* thanks to my mother and my aunt. When I was twenty my mother started to take me to different births, she showed me how to position and how to catch the baby and that's why now I attend births'. Her description contrasts to other *parteras* I spoke to who often describe their beginnings as a calling or having received a kind of premonition. It is possible that the ways in which many *barrio parteras* find themselves in the role – out of community necessity, prior nursing experience, generational obligation or simply happenchance – result in a more practical reasoning for how they came to be.

Filomena has extensive knowledge of local plants and herbs not only for use in pregnancy, labour and postpartum recuperation, but also for minor ailments and illnesses. Filomena is not registered with the health authority and so she has never accessed any of the training programmes that are sporadically offered to *parteras* around the city. Hence the births she attends are not registered as homebirths but unattended spontaneous births. Her opinion on government interventions such as training programmes is that 'they are a waste of my precious time'. Filomena knows through experience how to recognize potential complications that would need medical help and she is suspicious of 'being told what to do by doctors'.

The relationship between *parteras* and medical professionals is often fraught. This conflict is emphasized by the fact that they generally come into contact when there have been complications during labour or birth. Women will not tell their doctors when they are seeing a *partera* or plan to give birth at home, as this often leads to problems including threats to withdraw treatment in an emergency. In San Cristóbal attitudes varied greatly amongst medical professionals depending on their personal experiences, age and how familiar they are with the city and its populace. Whilst some doctors are accepting of a woman seeing a *partera* for antenatal or non-medical interventions, for example a *sobada*,[6] they feel differently about a *partera* attending an actual birth in a home.

Junior doctors first come into contact with *parteras* when they are completing their training in more rural locations. Attitudes of senior colleagues often impact on shaping younger doctors' ideas about *parteras* and out-of-hospital birth. My friend Ricardo was in rural maternity hospitals when he was a medical student in the early 2000s. He told me once that rural clinic placements were often seen as punishments for student doctors that were not getting good grades. On these placements they had to spend weeks away from city life, work longer than usual shifts and complete large amounts of paperwork connected to conditional cash transfer programmes. In a hierarchical medical education system, the rural clinics were viewed as the back end of medicine rather than the cutting-edge consultancy roles that many students aspired to. Ironically, the clinical and surgical skills required in the rural setting are more varied than those needed for better resourced urban hospitals and experience in a rural setting results in more skilful practitioners. However, students and recent graduates undertaking social service obligations in rural areas often do not have the experience or supervision to deal with the level of emergency care expected of them, and many escape the placement as soon as is possible. Ricardo's views on *parteras* were mixed due to his experiences during rural placements and in his role as director of a sexual and reproductive health rights NGO. In one interview he described in detail the dismissive attitude doctors had towards *parteras*:

> In my experience I only ever saw *parteras* that brought patients in, I saw that *parteras* who believed or considered that something wasn't right [in a labour or birth], they themselves brought the women in… We never let the *partera* in to accompany the woman, nor did we let them explain what had happened. When I think back now, we never asked whether they had given Pitocin or asked how the baby was positioned, or what the complication may be. No, we just left them outside and let the mother or the husband in.

Ricardo's descriptions of his student days demonstrate the non-reciprocal trust relationship between *parteras* and the medical profession. Registered *parteras* are trained by the state on the warning signs of complications in labour or of high-risk pregnancy, and they are 'trusted' to refer and transfer women to 'safety' (i.e., into the hands of a doctor). The *partera* must have faith that a clinic or hospital is the best place for a woman who fits the risk profile or has complications during first-stage labour. Yet, doctors are not educated or conditioned to trust in the skills and experience of the *partera*, nor ask whether she has vital information to share with them, resulting in what Davis-Floyd (2003b) has called 'the trouble with transport'. The gender, ethnic, class and linguistic hierarchies inherent in the workings of the health system create the circumstances for doctors to deny the *parteras* as experts in their practice. When these social factors are reinforced by lack of institutionalized regulation – formal qualification, licensing, adherence to ethical codes – the *barrio partera* is unlikely to ever be legitimized as a member of a recognized health workforce.

The everyday tense relationship between medical professionals and *parteras* cannot be separated from broader health politics. Ricardo explained how sometimes consultants were hesitant to treat a woman transferred by a *partera* at all. 'Many times, I heard [my seniors] advise that if anything happened [to the woman] it wasn't our fault. There was an attitude that no-one wanted to treat that patient because there could be a complication that has actually been caused by the *partera* or the patient themselves'. Pressure on rural clinics to improve MMR and maternal health outcomes can result in a blame game between doctors and *parteras*. With the political power dynamic already skewed in favour of the medical system, the isolated *parteras* will fare worse when it comes to proportioning blame.[7] As doctors move between rural and urban hospitals, their attitude to *parteras* and women who arrive with them do not soften. When I asked Ricardo about how obstetricians in the larger town or city hospitals dealt with *parteras* transferring women, he told me 'I never saw an interaction between the senior consultant, or the obstetrician with the parteras'. This observation echoes the many conversations I have had with both professional and *barrio parteras* about the times they have had to transfer women during labour. Regardless of the ethnicity or nationality of the *partera*, the trust between them and medical professionals is precarious and dependent upon the risk of blame.

In 2011 Chiapas state initiatives to improve working relationships and trust between *parteras* and consultants were re-introduced. This was partly in response to a new rigorous system of reporting MMR in 2004, the initial results of which challenged assumptions that maternal deaths in high MMR regions resulted from giving birth at home with a *partera* (Mills 2017: 160). Instead, the MDG 5 driven data collection revealed that deaths were more prevalent in public health facilities than in those run by social security institutes, or at home with *partera*.[8] As a result, in Chiapas there was political pressure on the public health system to recognize the importance of communication between community *parteras* and frontline obstetric workers. As the obstetric risk assessment focus in maternal health policy shifted to one of emergency obstetric care, the onus was once more placed upon registered *parteras* to assess risk and refer – the idea being that referral should force general practitioners at least to trust and communicate with *parteras*.

Despite this initiative, enduring prejudice among obstetricians continued to threaten any possible autonomy afforded to the local *parteras*. When I asked Ricardo about the new training programmes being introduced in 2011, he was not hopeful. He told me 'I hear consultants, from the obstetrics department, say that they were against the new policies brought in to train the *parteras*. They see the *partera* as someone who was there to trip us up, or who came to judge our work as doctors'. During a conversation in 2013 about effective regulation and professionalization of midwifery, Ricardo confided how the state secretariat had limits to its trust of midwifery models of care, adding that 'the support is there only when the *parteras* serve as health promoters, the attention [at birth] should be provided by the institutions, they will never consider professionalization'. It is little wonder that the unregistered *barrio parteras* prefer to maintain their autonomy from the state.

The tensions between medical professionals and *parteras* affect childbearing women directly. In interviews women described how they are careful not to mention to medical professionals that they may be seeing or plan to see a *partera* for all or part of their care. Doctors can accuse women of irresponsibility or ignorance and threaten them with the refusal of services or vital documents. The institutional paperwork, so lamented by Ricardo and his colleagues, is a necessity for women, not only if they are to make claims for conditional cash transfer programmes but also for registering the birth and obtaining a birth certificate and social security number for the child. The exclusion and lack of legal recognition of *barrio parteras* mean that families must find strategies to work the system to obtain the legal documents required for their children to participate in society as full citizens. Though this is arguably more difficult for Indigenous families in cities, *coleta* families also require strong local networks and resilience to make this happen for new generations.

The fact that numerous families in low-income *barrios* like la Orilla do continue to give birth at home with unregistered *parteras* despite their dwindling numbers serves to highlight that the everyday significance of childbirth continues to outweigh the hierarchical logic of the medical system for such families. This observation is nothing new to anthropologists of maternal health, midwifery advocates and scholars or families themselves. And so, we must ask why do policy decision-makers remain resistant to thinking about how to incorporate homebirth options in the public health system? In terms of understanding maternal transition within the life course, it is also pertinent to ask that with so much structural power working against them, why do younger generations of women continue to seek out the services of a *barrio partera* and what does this have to do with the kind of mother they wish to become? The consensus of women who continue to give birth at home, and who encourage their own daughters and daughters-in-law to do the same, is that hospitals are not safe places to give birth. For most *barrio* women birth is not something that should be experienced alone without the presence of close female kin. When I spoke to women about why they did not want to use public hospitals they always remarked on the likelihood of ending up with a caesarean section or being subjected to poor treatment. Women form their opinions through prior experience or through other women they know. They do not view pregnancy as an illness to be treated, as such women make up their own minds about the kind of birth care they wish to receive, and they seek out the support they trust. Women in la Orilla were aware that caesarean section is a common outcome in public and private facilities. By hiring a *partera* they are consciously taking action to avoid it. Both mothers and *parteras* consider homebirth as the only viable alternative to a caesarean section and suffering indignity in childbirth.

I noticed early on in my conversations with women in the *barrio* that they did not prioritize the pain of childbirth in their birth narratives. This is in a stark contrast to the women describing or preparing for births in a hospital where fear of pain appeared to take precedence over any other aspect. For women who give birth at home, there is an emphasis placed on the body as naturally capable of carrying and giving birth to a child. The idea of birthing at home with family and a *partera* as being 'proper' is used synonymously with 'nature's way' or 'how things should be'. For the women who hire *barrio parteras*, childbirth itself is not understood as high risk, but as a natural, everyday event. Within this perspective, women do not equate beliefs about birth as a natural event with a negation of interventions when needed – whether they be herbal, spiritual or tactile. Mirroring the woman-centric approach to transnational midwifery models of care, women do not speak about the labour pains as negative, but as a necessary part of the transitional process. Homebirth women explain that having the support of close female relatives and the *partera* was a way of coping with the pain or 'uncomfortableness' of the stages of labour. Even when I was able

Figures 3.1 and 3.2. Examples of walk-in clinics, Mexico, 2013
© J.M. López

to ask new mothers about pain within days of them giving birth, their responses were along the lines of: 'Well yes I suppose it hurt but I don't really remember it now'. It is impossible to generalize as to whether women experience pain differently in the home as opposed to hospital, particularly as the pain-as-suffering narrative was omitted from most homebirth descriptions. However, it is the way in which descriptions of pain are omitted in one type of birth narrative, and dominant in another, that suggests that although pain is experienced by all in some way, it is perceived differently depending on the environmental context.

There are three key stages of the reproductive life course where women seek out the services of *parteras* like Filomena. These stages are during pregnancy, childbirth and the postpartum period (lasting traditionally up to forty days). Aside from childbearing women also access *parteras* for fertility problems and abortion care. The antenatal period is the time that younger women in San Cristóbal use a combination of *partera* and gyno-obstetric services. The commodification of and easy access to technologies such as ultrasound has also undoubtedly increased antenatal attention and increased pregnancy intervention for current generations. There is no doubt that the technocratic model of birth translates into a profitable business for the private health economy, though whether it has any overall increased benefit for women is debatable. A woman can find clusters of walk-in gyno-obstetric practices, laboratories, and ultrasound clinics on almost any street in the city centre. On the advice or insistence of doctors in public hospitals where these resources are not available, women with sparse economic resources will pay for numerous ultrasounds and lab tests (bloods, urine, amniocentesis, etc.) throughout their pregnancies. Mills' (2017) research found that even where these resources are available some public hospitals in Chiapas continue to charge patients unnecessarily.

The public and private antenatal services available to women are plugging a gap not prioritized by previous generations accustomed to hiring the local *partera*. Prior to the influence of goal-oriented globalized health, women did not give antenatal care, in its medicalized sense, the same importance as the care provided at birth. In la Orilla I observed strict rules pertaining to what a pregnant woman may or may not do, but in a way that differed from the pathologized management of childbearing (weight, blood pressure, urine checks, gestational diseases and conditions). Once pregnancy is confirmed (by home test kit or lab test), many women will not call upon a *partera* until they reach the second trimester when the woman begins to show (around five to six months). This first contact is usually to check on the progress of the pregnancy and to have the *partera* estimate the actual gestation. Many third- or fourth-time mothers will not call upon a *barrio partera* until they are in labour. In this local midwifery model of care, the woman and her female relatives, not the *partera*, are the active decision-making subjects. Increased universal primary health coverage is providing wider access to antenatal services, which in turn is changing attitudes towards this aspect of childbearing.

Protection from external forces such as spirits or other people's emotions or actions remain at the forefront of young women's care throughout pregnancy. Rather than replace or reject old notions of risk for new ones, women incorporate biomedical and global health messages into local systems and local biologies. The young women in la Orilla use their close family networks and access to credit to navigate intersecting knowledge systems and meet the needs of their pregnancies. Like elsewhere in the world, women becoming mothers in twenty-first-century Mexico are 'tied to multiple and non-local systems' (Abu-Lughod 1990: 42) and they demonstrate this through their decision-making. They are accustomed to using a variety of private practitioners (among which I include *parteras* and *curanderas* [healers]) as a strategy to avoid the undesired or dysfunctional aspects of the public health system. The way in which younger women spoke to me about care during pregnancy suggests that any active resistance to medicalization is arguably a 'secondary, unintended outcome' (Unnithan-Kumar 2001). Instead, their use of a mixed economy of care is a way of incorporating local biologies and beliefs about bodies, maternity, family and social values with competing notions of risk.

Lupita

Lupita and her parents were the only family in la Orilla whom I knew before my fieldwork there in 2013. I first interviewed her towards the end of her pregnancy in 2011 when she was just turning twenty-eight years old, and then subsequently in 2013 and 2015. When we recorded our first interview, she had been married for two years to Diego, her partner since high school, and they were looking forward to the arrival of their first child. Lupita commuted to work in the state capital on nearly a day-by-day basis. On the days that she could not face travelling back to San Cristóbal she stayed in Tuxtla Gutierrez with her siblings who were studying there. The travelling between cities not only involved an hour or so by minibus but also a significant change in altitude between the two locations. It meant that she was constantly torn between life at home with her parents and new husband and her commitment to her Government administrative job and social networks in Tuxtla. When Lupita became pregnant, her dual location also involved navigating healthcare in the two cities. She had health insurance provided by ISSTE (Institute for Social Security and Services for State Workers) and as such she had to attend appointments at their facilities in Tuxtla. Despite this Lupita was determined to give birth at home in San Cristóbal where she could be close to family and rest in the postpartum period. As she explained to me, this did not stop her from seeking out a combination of public and private services:

> In Tuxtla I have to go to the ISSSTE because of my insurance. I like it better here in San Cristóbal because I can see *parteras* or *curanderas*, to me they are more human. I also have an obstetrician in San Cris who is fantastic, I pay to see her. The other doctor who saw me at the ISSŞTE, she was very against me going to see *parteras*. I didn't like her because she told me I had to take medicine, whether I like it or not. They were iron tablets and they made me feel awful. When I found my doctor here in San Cristóbal, she said, 'If they make you ill, stop taking them, eat lots of green vegetables instead' ... The other one in Tuxtla she was very narrow minded, my appointments never lasted more than five minutes. She would be like, 'Anything wrong?' Pues no, nothing, 'How are you?' Pues Ok, 'Did you bring your test results?' And just like that, 'See you in two months then!' ...
>
> The doctor in Tuxtla also said I couldn't travel and for me this was a problem because my family are here in San Cris and my work is in Tuxtla. I didn't want to stay in Tuxtla, but she told me I was at risk if I travelled. The nice doctor here said it was fine, as long as I felt healthy and took care of the changes in altitude, and so now at eight months I'm still travelling to and fro without any problems.

Lupita's story also tells us about the varied attitudes of doctors, depending upon their environment and flexibility within which they work. Lupita's private obstetrician in San Cristóbal ran her own practice and attended women at the local public hospital when they went into labour. In the private antenatal appointments, there was less pressure on time and space to explore Lupita's desires and expectations. Many women go to see a private obstetrician to look for someone who can confirm their attitudes towards giving birth. Lupita hoped to give birth vaginally either at home or in hospital and she wanted to have this choice. She chose a doctor who was familiar with local family practices and who therefore respected her wishes to see the *partera* from time to time. This doctor also gave her the reassurance that she could have a vaginal birth when the time came. However, the ISSSTE doctor in Tuxtla fits the description of an institutionalized practitioner. When Lupita attends appointments in Tuxtla the power dynamic between doctor and patient is apparent. This doctor will see high numbers of women in a day and will be under pressure to process women through pregnancy and labour, keeping them alive for the benefit of mortality statistics. Notions of risk and danger appear not only when doctors scold Lupita for using a *partera*, but also when it came to her desire for a 'normal' (vaginal) birth. When I asked her about the ISSSTE doctors' attitude towards vaginal birth she told me, 'When I started to see the doctor in Tuxtla, she always talked about how hard it was to have a baby and when I said I wanted a normal birth she would say "Do you think it's that easy? Do you think it will happen so easy? Giving birth is hard you won't be able to do it normally"'.

The normalization of caesarean sections is one way in which institutionalized maternal health expresses ethnic and class-based discrimination. Doctors' attitudes towards Indigenous and non-Indigenous women's bodies are denigrating on different levels and are dependent on context. For example, I observed on occasions medical and health professionals in Tuxtla (mainly in public hospitals) describe Indigenous women's bodies as 'made for birth', as though it were an unquestionable evolutionary fact. Doctors in the capital city often explained to middle-class women that their bodies are not built to withstand pain in the same way as Indigenous or poor women, or that they may want to preserve their vagina by having a caesarean (to be sexually available to prevent their husband straying). In contrast, in San Cristóbal the population is more diverse in class and ethnicity, and attitudes are more flexible around women's abilities to give birth. Instead, doctors use descriptions of Indigenous bodies as a comparison to show how women of all shapes and sizes can give birth and breastfeed without complication or intervention. It is worth noting that caesarean sections and resources are less available in San Cristóbal public hospitals, and this will change the motives of obstetricians and their interpretations.

In both Tuxtla and San Cristóbal the ways in which women's bodies are racialized, hypersexualized or desexualized brings colonial praxis to the forefront in twenty-first-century Mexican maternity. The study of the doctor-*partera*-woman nexus points directly to how gendered bodies and racialized power are reproduced by what sociologist Sylvia Rivera Cusicanqui describes as 'day by day via micro-oppressions and silences, despite successive attempts at the radical transformation' (2018: 25) of institutions and society. *Barrio parteras* are unregulated and misunderstood. The middle classes tend to see *barrio parteras* as part of an underdeveloped past of Chiapas that the state and upper classes have worked hard to distance themselves from since the intense neoliberalism of the 1990s.

Lupita is an example of a generation of women who negotiate within and among local and globalized health practices. Her decisions on where to seek support depend upon her own perceived medical need, obligations to fulfil health insurance requirements, her personal feelings towards services, family networks and cultural and religious beliefs. When I asked her why she decided to look for a *partera*, she told me that there were 'things that you can feel but that the doctors can't see'. She sought out the services of her local *partera* on the advice of her mother and aunts. Lupita was always open with doctors about seeking the services of the *partera* and found their attitudes differed according to whether they interpreted the proposed treatment as threatening to medical practice (such as labour intervention, external positioning of the foetus). Like most women I spoke to on this matter, Lupita valued the expert knowledge of the *partera* and her ability to ease physical discomfort with a relatively hands-off approach. She also deemed the *partera* necessary for dealing with the symptoms of *mal de ojo* (evil eye), *susto* (fright), and other forms of emotional unease:

> I had been very uncomfortable with my back and one Saturday my mum sent me to see the *partera*. I was about six months pregnant. At first, she didn't even touch me. She took me out into the garden and asked me to walk around and she just stood watching me. Then she asked me to go and get her some water for the bathroom and to carry the bucket with my right hand. I did so and when I had finished, I carried the full bucket to her outhouse. I thought she just needed help carrying heavy things. Then we went inside her house, and she gave me a *sobada*, though only for a minute and an herbal tea. I'm not really sure what she did but my backache never came back! ...

The next time I went was when I had a false alarm. I thought I had gone into labour about eight days before I was due, my hips hurt a lot and my mum called for the *partera*. They put me in a bath, and they poured very hot water over my hips and back, and they gave me a tea made from *mishto*[9]... They told me if you're ready to give birth this will quicken everything up and if not, it will help to calm the pains and that's what happened. The pains calmed down.

In her chapter on 'Authoritative Touch in Childbirth: A Cross-Cultural Approach', midwife and anthropologist Sheila Kitzinger wrote how '[t]ouch given or withheld by those present during labour and delivery may be a central theme to the social analysis of the culture of birth' (Kitzinger 1997: 209). The *barrio parteras* in my studies do not do a vaginal examination before or during birth. All knowledge is gained through external touch and observation of the woman, what she is saying and sensitivity to her environment as well as the *parteras*' intuition. As Rosa and Bety's birth stories in the previous chapter demonstrated, unwanted touch and vaginal examinations during the first stages of labour, by strangers, impacted significantly on how the women felt about their bodies and their births. Something the institutionalized model of birth does not recognize is the link between emotion and touch. Touch ignites sensations and triggers emotions during labour. The sensory apparatus of touch (and withdrawing touch) combined with intuition are key tools within midwifery models of care. Paying attention to the bodily form of others also includes attending to one's own body in relation to others and the environment.

When I write of intuition in this context, I refer to a physical manifestation of the *parteras*' sensitivity to the environment and the pregnant body they are attending to. Intuition as 'sense' is neither arbitrary nor biologically determined but culturally constituted. This use of 'intuition' in practice results in an action or non-action on the part of the *partera* – whether this is to suggest the labouring woman move position, change something about the environment or sit back and observe further. Though observation plays a significant role in deciding when to give or withdraw touch for example, *parteras* will often speak of using their intuition when it comes to decision-making. The limited verbal communication (from the mother to those around her) often associated with second and third stages of labour requires the *partera* to attend with her own body in to support the labouring woman – both instinctively and physically she must feel the best action to take in that given situation.

'Cobra Poco y Atiende Mucho'

Aside from the social value of giving birth at home there is a significant moral economy at play concerning the hiring of *parteras*. Cost is often one of the first things mentioned when discussing the merits of the local *partera*. The importance of how much money families are prepared to pay a *partera* for her services indicates not only her worth as a practitioner but also the value of her gendered labour. Historically, the *barrio* or community *partera* did not charge for her services as the role she played was one of pure vocation, though compensated through high social standing. Instead, families would provide all the materials she needed and sustenance throughout the duration of the birth and postpartum period. The *partera* would stay with the new mother for as long as was needed following the birth at no extra cost. The need to negotiate a fair and affordable price for the services of a *barrio partera* demonstrates how trust in her runs deeper than monetary value. Families measure trust and weigh up forms of risk through experience. They question the skills of a *partera* who charges too much. The price families are willing to pay is also linked to the popularity of a *partera*, as was indicated by Rosita when she first advertised the services of her mother to me – 'cobra poco y atiende mucho' (she charges little and attends a lot of births).

One afternoon I had popped over to visit Doña Reina and while I waited for her to answer the door her younger son Felipe arrived home from work. We said hello and he asked me how my pregnancy was going. I was getting towards the end of my pregnancy and starting to think about a plan for when I went into labour. Felipe asked me whether I was planning to go to hospital. I began to tell him that I had a *partera* nearby and would give birth at home or in in the birth centre she ran. He nodded in agreement. 'It's proper to have your babies at home. My three were born here with Doña Filomena. She's good a lot cheaper than the others and has loads of experience'. I asked him how much she generally charged. Up until now she had been guarded whenever I asked her myself, so I saw this as a good opportunity to get an idea about her prices. 'Well, it differs', he told me. 'She didn't really charge us for attending the birth, but I paid for the herbs and bits and pieces. I've probably spent about 1000 pesos on each child. She doesn't charge much; wages are very low around here you can't earn a great deal'. I wanted to know a bit more about the 'bits and pieces' so I asked whether she saw his wife during pregnancy or just when she was ready to give birth. He thought about it for a moment and said 'she came three times, once or twice to position the baby and then for the birth. She comes afterwards to cure the bellybutton and stuff. I can put you in touch with her if you want. How much does your *partera* charge?' At this point it was my turn to feel guarded about giving away my *partera*'s price as I knew he would think it ridiculous. 'I think it's about 8000 pesos now', I told him, apprehensive as to how he would react. He raised his eyebrows and smiled: 'That's a lot, I can find you a cheaper one if you want'.

The concern with how much it is proper to pay a local *partera* is juxtaposed with the expense that families expect to pay for the services of private obstetricians, ultrasound clinics and paediatricians. The families in la Orilla are of varying low incomes and most are entitled to primary health care under *Seguro Popular* or the conditional cash transfer programme, though as mentioned many use a mixed economy of health services depending upon perceived need. Antenatal care in the clinical sense had not traditionally been a priority for women in the *barrio* and many are happy to attend appointments at the public facilities to be registered there for emergency treatment. They attend the conditional *control prenatal* appointments and pay extra for private scans and tests as requested by the doctors. At the same time, they hire a *partera* because they describe her as meeting 'different needs'. Despite the opinion that one should not pay over the odds for the services of a *barrio* (or any type of) *partera*, the women and their families are very clear about what value the *partera* holds in the moral economy of reproductive and maternal health care.

Notes

1. The word *partera* translates to mean 'traditional midwife' in policy and maternal health literature. The contents of this chapter will demonstrate how questions of class, ethnicity, economics and generation are ways of denoting the type of *partera* a person is referring to and what their practices may entail, as the practices of *parteras profesionales*, despite many overlaps, in general differ considerably from those of *parteras tradicionales*.
2. Here I refer specifically to the Mexican governments' commitment to the Safe Motherhood Initiative (SMI) (during the 1990s and early 2000s) which was most active and successful in Latin America. Combined with an

already fervent human rights culture, the SMI (later Safer Motherhood) was particularly active in Chiapas and made many failed attempts to better incorporate *parteras tradicionales* into local health systems. Such failures can be attributed to existing patterns of structural violence and desire to control Indigenous populations. Attempts to recognize *parteras tradicionales* as part of legitimate birth options were further doomed by the WHO excluding traditional birth attendants from its definition of Skilled Birth Attendant when the MDGs were launched.
3. I must highlight however the difficulty in evidencing this statement as so few homebirths with *barrio parteras* are registered for reasons explained throughout this chapter.
4. In writing this book I have taken the conscious decision to foreground local social scientists who have over two decades worth of published research on maternal health in Chiapas. I have learnt a lot about localized models of care from these authors' works and their generosity in meeting with me during fieldwork trips to share their findings and provide critical feedback on my own work. I would argue that the lack of recognition for Mexican social scientists in US and European texts is a form of citation bias practised amongst those authors in maintaining a coloniality of knowledge on Mexico. I do recognize the canon of English publication anthropology on maternal health in Mexico (and beyond). These works formed the basis of my postgraduate education and shaped my earlier thinking on the subject. However, in the commitment to de-canonize and de-colonize ethnography my practice is to foreground the influence that Mexican and South American scholars have had on my understanding.
5. As noted by Luna et al. (2015) in their chronology of institutionalizing midwifery in San Cristóbal de Las Casas from 1940 to 1970.
6. A massage to help pain in the lower back or help position the baby in the final trimester.
7. Similarly, Nicole Berry's (2010) ethnography of the Safe Motherhood Initiative in Guatemala highlighted the practice of blame-making by doctors who have the power to document how and where a maternal mortality occurred. The pressure to show how facilities lower the MMR led to a focus on where a death occurs, rather than the nature of the death and the social context within which it may be prevented.
8. I remain hesitant to make too strong a connection with the data system as there are still no mechanisms for recording homebirths with unregistered *parteras*, and, as found in Berry's work in Guatemala, when under political pressure doctors can be found to manipulate data for more favourable outcomes.
9. *Mishto* is the Tzotzil word for myrtle: a species of plant that plays a vital role in the treatment of a variety of folk illness throughout Mexico and Central America, especially *susto*, also widely used for gyno-obstetric related conditions.

FIGURE 4.1 The lilac façade of the birth centre, Mexico, 2015 © J.M. López

Chapter 4

CRIS, SOFI AND ESME
THE BIRTH CENTRE

> The birth centre is more integrated, more westernized. That's why the traditional *partera* is not for me. Here I felt the possibility of feeling heard and understood as someone who was between two cultures ...
>
> —Sofi, 2017

Luna Maya birth centre is situated two *barrios* away from la Orilla on a quiet street about a fifteen-minute walk from the city centre. Though most people in the city cannot tell you its location, once you are aware of it, the brightly painted lilac house becomes instantly recognizable (figure 4.0 above). It is a place, like those who work and birth within it, that generally goes unnoticed by the broader population of the city. Whereas I could give the name of most public and private maternity clinics in the city to a taxi driver and they will know where to go, with Luna Maya I have always had to give the street name and house number. The centre's subtlety is strategic, in part due to the precarious positioning of professional midwifery and out-of-hospital birth practices[1] and in part because the idea is that women and families feel the centre is a home away from home. Like their *barrio* counterparts, the birth centre *parteras* gain a reputation by word of mouth more than anything else. Ironically, under Mexican law the birth centre cannot advertise as a place to give birth and the *parteras* working there cannot legally offer their services as a skilled birth attendant.[2] Women generally find the birth centre at a time in their lives when they most need it, either through social media or recommendation from existing clients. However, unlike the almost complete invisibility of the *barrio parteras*, birth centre practitioners are more overtly politically active in terms of sexual and reproductive health promotion and education.

The birth centre *parteras* work actively to promote their services locally and online within the confines of legislation, seek out alliances with sympathetic obstetricians, paediatricians and gynaecologists, and engage with medical schools and health secretariat where possible. There are numerous reasons that privilege their ability to interact on this level with considerably fewer negative consequences than their Indigenous or *barrio* counterparts. Instead of the more common title *partera profesional*, I have chosen to discuss the birth practitioners in this chapter using Hanna Laako's term *partera autonoma* (autonomous *partera*). According to Laako, 'The concept of autonomy is fundamental in the collective action of these midwives as their profession lacks autonomy in Mexico. However, the concept of autonomy also emphasizes the anti-systemic character of these midwives [and] their critique of the biomedical system' (Laako 2016 171). I find the title *partera profesional* increasingly problematic in terms of how it results in a hierarchy that suggests traditional or empirical *parteras* are somehow lesser as opposed to different, which is not the case in practice, nor is it the opinion amongst the broader community of *parteras*.

The birth centre clientele are women without any previous medical conditions that impact on a healthy pregnancy, women profiled as low-risk and who intend to go into labour without medical intervention. Across Mexico there are approximately eleven birth centres all operating under their own distinct model, registered either as private clinics or as Asociación Civil (third sector organization) (Sánchez Ramirez 2016). During my period of fieldwork (up until 2016) Luna Maya was the only state registered birth centre which is also an Asociación Civil in the country.[3] Both regions are characterized by significant structural inequalities, ethnic diversity, political upheaval and high infant and maternal mortality. In comparison to northern and central Mexico, Chiapas and Oaxaca have historically had higher rates of recorded out-of-hospital birth amongst Indigenous and rural populations due to demographics and structural underdevelopment. However, in recent years there has been a shift and out-of-hospital birth amongst upper- to middle-class Mexicans has become increasingly popular.

With the lack of regulation, underground nature and lack of official records, there is no evidence base to measure the exact increase in popularity and so to speculate one must work ethnographically and qualitatively. For a while between 2010 and 2017 another birth centre did open and function in San Cristóbal, run by a Mexican doctor who self-trained in midwifery models of care. The existence of this other birth centre does indicate a consistent if not increasing demand for more out-of-hospital birth options during the years I did fieldwork in the city. Other alternative birthing spaces in urban Chiapas have come and gone over the years, either because they were eventually shut down by the authorities or the *parteras*/birth attendants have moved on elsewhere.

The image of the autonomous *partera* as cosmopolitan and 'not Indigenous' helps the middle-class couples who face a great deal of resistance or pressure from their families committed to the perceived safety of medicalized birth. Comparable to other types of *partera*, critique of the autonomous birth centre *parteras* is not limited to medical professionals or behind closed doors of the health secretariat. Autonomous *parteras* and the birth centres they run have faced critique from within the out-of-hospital birth community in recent years. Non-governmental organizations working with Indigenous *parteras* and the broader eclectic maternal health community throughout Mexico[4] have accused this new generation of autonomous *parteras* of, amongst other things, appropriating Indigenous practices and commodifying them for a middle-class audience, and promoting health tourism whilst excluding those most in need (see Vega 2018). It is interesting to note that these accusations of appropriation are spoken about on behalf of the Indigenous midwifery community rather than directly from Indigenous *parteras* themselves. This oversimplified critique tends to distract from the more important question of why women from across the social spectrum seek out alternative spaces in which to give birth in the first place.

Spanish-American CPM[5] and public health consultant Cris Alonso founded The Luna Maya Centro de Partos[6] in 2004. Initially, Cris came to Chiapas to work with a state programme to lower MMR in Chiapas (Maternidades Sin Riesgos). Dissatisfied with the paternalistic approach of the state programme, she decided to set up a midwifery-led birth centre in response to what she felt was a crucial absence of midwife-led midwifery training in the approach to improving maternal mortality. In the interview extract below Cris explains how previous approaches to improving mortality failed to recognize the importance of local traditional and empirical *parteras* in communities. Her approach in using the woman-centred midwifery model of care values the active role of the *partera*, rather than just seeing her as a point of reference to the hospital:

> [At the time] they were publishing all that stuff about emergency obstetrical care and the basic understanding at that time with maternal mortality was that out-of-hospital birth is attended by people who don't have the competencies to identify obstetrical emergencies. So, if you can set up systems for identification, transport and rapid attendance in hospitals then maternal mortality rates will descend. What was missing in that structural programme was an understanding that midwives actually have better outcomes.

Aside from the misdirection of policy interventions, Cris also saw that there was a need to address the sexual and reproductive healthcare of women in the region. Her goal from the outset was to provide sexual, reproductive and maternal health services that were respectful and empowering to local women. The concept of a birth (or maternity) centre is not new to San Cristóbal or other cities in the southeast region. Throughout the 1970s the ISSSTE, for example, subcontracted services for lab analysis, surgeries and birth attention. ISSSTE subcontracted out maternity services to established *parteras empíricas* who had set up an early style of birth centre known as the *sanitorio maternidad* (maternity clinics). Luna et al. (2015) documents one of San Cristóbal's most established *partera empíricas* Doña Amelia Quiroz Gutierrez in an interview with her daughter-in-law. Doña Amelia was a single mother, which in part explains the relative freedom and motive she had at the time, in the 1950s, to pursue a career in midwifery and open her own *sanitorio maternidad*. During the 1970s ISSSTE paid Doña Amelia for each woman that they referred to her. She had a local doctor on call in case of any complications (Luna et al. 2015). And so, much like Luna Maya today it appears that birth centres and certain types of *parteras* in San Cristóbal have historically been tolerated and even supported by public health services. Despite this, the formal regulation and professionalization of *parteras* has never occurred and autonomous *parteras* fall out of favour depending upon the politics of the time.

As well as taking inspiration from local midwifery models of care, Luna Maya is informed by a transnational approach and inspired by the Bumi Sehat foundation of Indonesia and the higher-turnover midwife-led birth centres in Jamaica. Luna Maya's approach combines education with public health based on addressing the psychosocial and physical needs of its clients. Since its beginnings, the birth centre has served women from all sections of local society.

It was a key step for Cris, who first set up on her own, to attend women regardless of their economic means as not only a personal philosophy but also to gain a trusted reputation. As I noted in the previous chapter, *barrio parteras* come recommended by the number of births they have attended and the low cost of their services – anything from between the cost of basic medicines to 1500 pesos. One hurdle that Cris had to overcome was the value families placed upon the number of births attended and the low cost provided by existing *parteras*. From the outset she attended a mixture of poor women with no social support, foreign residents and more affluent Mexican couples. Although the additional services that the birth centre grew to provide – prenatal group, yoga, parenting skills, counselling, natural gynaecology and alternative therapies – are marketed at a clientele able to pay competitive prices, Luna Maya's beginnings as a social action and education provider means that as a civil association it maintains a responsibility to the population at large and has a history of adapting their services charges appropriately and when necessary.

Cris' vision for Luna Maya was not to reinvent or appropriate the local and traditional models but to develop a curriculum based upon the needs of local *parteras* and families. The birth centre came to fruition in 2004 when she received international funding for a project to work with traditional *parteras*, community health promoters and doctors in the nearby town of Tenejapa. She took this opportunity to develop a midwifery-led approach to community health that began with creating relationships rather than interventions. 'What we did was we went up there and we started scouting them out', she told me when I first interviewed her on record about the project's beginnings. Through previous experience with the *Maternidades Sin Reisgos* programme she knew that building trust *partera* to *partera* was the best way to approach the Indigenous *parteras* in Tenejapa. She explained: 'We would say you know, "I'm a midwife, I'm not here to tell you what to do. I told them we wanted to build a circle of midwives so that we can all improve our competencies together'. The *partera* to *partera* approach had some success and initially broke some barriers within the group. 'They wanted to talk about stuff that all midwives talk about, stuff that frustrated them that the medical community would say to them like – "Just don't do breech!"'. By building relations with the traditional *parteras* the project was able to figure out a peer-informed training programme that simultaneously suited *parteras* and spoke to funders' concerns. 'We did a five-year training thing where we taught them competences previously denied to them when the interventions were run by medics. The first year we had to do the emergency transfer stuff to keep the funders happy and focus on maternal mortality'.

Through taking this peer approach Cris and her colleagues were able to find out how the traditional *parteras* felt about the numerous interventions they had been subjected to over the years. 'It was interesting', she told me, 'At the first circle of midwives they said very clearly that maternal mortality has to do with violence. Women who die in labour are women who are isolated from the community: that aren't attended by midwives but by their husbands or whichever inexperienced person may be at hand'. What the *parteras* in this first circle talked about mirrored the arguments about violence that local maternal health researchers had been arguing for some time, and that was still being ignored by policy-makers.[7] Cris went on to describe how the *parteras* in the circle were clear that 'if [these women] didn't die in childbirth, they would die of violence. They would die of malnutrition or they would die of whatever because they were women who lived in horrific violent situations'. Through having these peer-led training circles it became clear to Cris that the dominant narrative for funders in educating traditional *parteras* about early transfer or referral of women conflicted with what was needed. 'It felt totally pointless to do this kind of training', she said, 'Because they knew they were not the problem, and for the last twenty years or so they'd been drilled with emergency stuff. So, we focused on a theme for each year that the *parteras* in the circle defined, combining actual and perceived needs from the point of view of the circle and based on global evidence'.

The Femifocal Model and the 'Right Kind' of Evidence[8]

The basic premise behind Luna Maya was that it would become a centre for improving the lives of local women and provide an integrated midwifery training programme that would incorporate the best of regional and international midwifery models of care. As the number of *barrio parteras* decreased across the city Cris saw an opportunity to develop a locally specific midwifery model as a middle ground for those wanting to avoid the potential violence of a hospital birth but influenced by years of over-medicalization of pregnancy and birth.

Alongside the day-to-day running of the birth centre and education programmes, the political mission of the organization and communication with midwives and researchers from across in the world, Luna Maya as a collective set in motion a conceptual lens for a universal midwifery model of care. Taking a holistic and life-course view of sexual and reproductive health, the practitioners in Luna Maya wanted to respect the characteristics of the matrifocal and culturally mother-centric society that Mexico is. At the same time they worked to challenge the exclusion of women who fall beyond the parameters of motherhood, for whatever reason. Ultimately, the aim of the organization was to work towards a less maternal-centric shift and to acknowledge motherhood as one option among the many that can be presented to women. From this approach Cris and colleagues devised a femifocal model of care. Femifocal can be understood as a mindset, which can then be used as a model to inform policy and behaviour change (Alonso et al. 2018).

On the one hand, the femifocal model recognizes that a woman is at the centre of her own social, political and cultural ecology. On the other hand, it recognizes that an individual is inseparable from and is informed by her environment, including her family and community. Therefore, this model works with local belief systems of intergenerational connectivity and community, and also works conceptually to antagonize a set belief that goes against individual experience. By replacing the matri(focal) with the femi(focal) Luna Maya extends midwifery care to include women and girls who are mothers, have been mothers, those who have never been mothers, those who aspire to become mothers and those who intend never to become mothers. The femifocal approach honours the original meaning of the name 'midwife' in English, describing a woman who is 'with-women'. In addition, influenced by the *parteras* who have served women for generations in Mexican communities, the femifocal model captures the notion that any individual woman encompasses many spheres of experience and existence, rather than solely being viewed as a biological machine that needs medical attention (Murray de López and Alonso 2018).

Femifocal care understands that humans are nested within larger contexts that can be positive and negative, often comprised of loved ones, family, friends, community, culture, political structures, built environment and natural geography. The femifocal care model works with a woman, taking these multiple contexts into account. Femifocal care supports a woman across and throughout her life course, in recognition of the fact that she is accumulating experiences and history as she grows and develops. The model recognizes the woman as expert in herself and with agency to define her own health needs. The ability to understand the woman throughout her life-course transitions is enabled by the fact that, ideally, she is seen by the same practitioner the whole time, that there is consistency in her care. All femifocal care is rooted in a woman's desire to participate (with informed consent) in her treatment and care, as well as in her elucidation of what her unique health goals are. This latter element forms part of the activist and educational element of the model as few women who approach Luna Maya have ever been asked to consider their own health needs. An additional challenge, yet a necessary one, is to promote the idea of informed consent within a society characterized by elevated levels of gender-based violence, human rights infringements and institutionalized violence.

Luna Maya's transnational and international connections and the autonomous *parteras'* commitment to social change mean that they understand the importance of creating a solid evidence base. In terms of gaining the ear of the health secretariat and global health bodies, Cris understood early on that numbers matter. Since 2007, Luna Maya *parteras* and the organization's apprentices have collected antenatal and birth outcome date using the MANA Stats data base. MANA Stats is a web-based data collection tool designed for out-of-hospital midwives by the Midwives Alliance of North America (MANA) Division of Research.[9] In 2017, Cris and I began to work with this decades' worth of data to provide further evidence for the case of midwife-led birth centres as a viable option for low-risk women in Mexico (Alonso and Murray de López 2017). MANA Stats collects baseline information on midwife education and licensure, as well as demographic, clinical history, pregnancy, labour, birth, postpartum and neonatal information. In total Luna Maya *parteras* collected and translated into Spanish 182 pre- and postpartum cases for the birth centre data system. The total Luna Maya dataset included records from 587 women receiving prenatal care at the first time of registering with the birth centre. Our focus was the analysis of birth characteristics (shoulder dystocia, meconium presence, blood loss, preeclampsia) and birth outcome (transfer rates, vaginal or caesarean delivery, mortality rates). As such we removed from the dataset women who transferred care to another provider prior to the onset of labour and all neonatal deaths (including stillbirths, miscarriages and abortions) from the analysed data set. Thus, the final sample for analysis was 410 women who reached full-term and went into labour under the care of the birth centre *parteras*.[10]

Under Luna Maya's organizational policy, previous caesarean sections, twins and breech presentations are not deemed high-risk profiles on their own. The *parteras* work with women using an informed consent model, and the women with previous caesarean births, breech positions or twins chose midwife-led care for their birth. It is important to note that there are occasions when women opt to birth out-of-hospital despite being high-risk due to fear of obstetric violence or non-consensual care. Following the informed consent model, the role of the autonomous *partera* in these cases is to inform and support the woman as best she can in her decision-making. This is one aspect where birth centre women differ from those who give birth with a *barrio partera* and where the risk taken by the autonomous *partera* is most heightened due to her precarious position.

In comparison with the medicalized model of risk, maternal age, education and socio-economic status are taken into consideration by birth centre *parteras* but not used in themselves for exclusion from medium- or low-risk status.[11] The reason risk criteria remain so flexible is that often women seek care from Luna Maya because they have been automatically scheduled for a caesarean delivery in the public or private sector, which they are seeking to avoid. Currently in Mexico women under eighteen years or over thirty-five years of age, or women with previous caesarean sections, are automatically labelled as high-risk and scheduled for caesarean delivery despite an ample clinical evidence-base to the contrary. In terms of the mode of birth of the 410 women in the sample, 86.3 per cent completed an out-of-hospital birth (either at home or in the birth centre). The spontaneous vaginal birth rate for the sample was 90.2 per cent, including vaginal births after transfer to hospital. In the total sample, forty-nine women had a vaginal birth after one, two, or three previous caesarean sections (VBAC, VBAC2, VBAC3). The total VBAC success rate for women over the complete sample (n=410) was 85.2 per cent. The total intrapartum transfer rate, over the ten-year period, was 13.7 per cent (n=72) of all planned out-of-hospital births. Six out-of-hospital births were breech presentation. Of the seventy-two intrapartum transfers, thirteen were urgent transfers, forty-nine resulted in a caesarean section, giving an overall caesarean section rate for Luna Maya mothers of 9.8 per cent. The most common reason for urgent transfer was maternal exhaustion (n=13, 57 per cent of intrapartum transfers) and, very closely behind it, failure to progress (n=12, 52 per cent of intrapartum transfers). Other reasons included desire for pain relief, hypertensive disorder, and malposition sans meconium. There were five postpartum transfers from the whole sample (three urgent) and seven neonatal transports (five urgent). All women are recorded as being out of the *parteras'* care as soon as transfer takes place and *parteras* are unable to accompany the women into hospitals. As such, Luna Maya transfer data is most important in terms of what is missing. The void in communication between autonomous *parteras* and hospital staff leaves a gap in any measurable data that can only be accounted for qualitatively if the woman chooses to return to the birth centre during the postpartum period and/or agrees to follow-up visits from the *parteras*. The MANA Stats systems at present lacks the cultural translation to consider what happens in the 'lost hours' between transfer and postpartum. This aspect is unlikely to change unless there is a significant shift in governmental attitudes towards wanting evidence collected by birth centres and autonomous *parteras* in regard to quality of care and out-of-hospital-birth outcomes.

In the total sample of 410, over the period of 2007-2010 there were five perinatal deaths and zero maternal mortalities. The benefit of working with a small dataset is the ability to cross-reference mortalities with the *parteras'* written records and living memory of events. Of the five perinatal deaths, four cases are distinct and can teach us about women's agency and determination to subvert a hospital system that structurally oppresses them. The first perinatal mortality happened within forty-eight hours from an undiagnosed condition leading to rapid deterioration and ultimately death. The baby was born at home without complications and with a healthy Apgar score. Three of the four cases suffered complications during labour and the women refused transfer to hospital. All three women had previous experience of obstetric violence with previous births. The first woman was full-term (forty-four weeks) and refused induction and transfer through fear of abuse. The second woman had a previous caesarean birth; she also had untreated hypothyroidism and a breech presentation. She refused transportation through fear of a second caesarean and abusive treatment in hospital. The third woman had suffered a previous neonatal death due to congenital malformation. She refused transportation through fear of mistreatment and having her baby removed from her if it had malformations. The fourth woman had a foetus diagnosed with malformations incompatible with quality of life. The woman and her partner knew the baby would not survive long after birth and that hospital practice would be to remove it without giving them time to grieve. The parents refused transfer through fear of birth trauma, forced caesarean and lack of respect for the condition of the foetus. In this last case the parents sought support from the birth centre prior to labour stating that if they could not have support from a *partera* the woman would give birth unassisted.

These four perinatal mortality cases highlight the strengths of the femifocal and informed consent models available to women and also the ethical challenges that autonomous *parteras* must face. Above all, these cases demonstrate the effect of iatrogenic trauma on women and the intergenerational impact of obstetric violence over the life course. Unlike the medical model of birth that emphasizes the separateness of the foetus to the mother and paternalism, the midwifery model treats the mother-infant unit as one, prioritizing the bodily autonomy of the mother and taking the burden of shared responsibility for the outcome.

Though the number of Luna Maya's clients cannot be compared to those in nearby hospitals and clinics, the MANA Stats dataset is the only detailed record of out-of-hospital birth outcomes in the country. As such, whatever the sample size it is significant in providing a case for further action on understanding the fragmented populations of women who have autonomous *partera*-led continuity of care. Furthermore, the data challenges clinical risk models regarding breech positioning, multiple births and previous caesarean sections. Luna Maya's data provide the evidence that with sufficient training and resources, out-of-hospital and community midwifery practice can deal with complex situations in low-resource settings, and, moreover, with less reported birth trauma for the woman and newborn baby. With a caesarean section rate of 9.8 per cent for low- to middle-risk women, the birth centre outcomes fall well within global expectations of what is acceptable in any country and far outshines the national average which in 2016 reached 41 per cent of all births in public hospitals (with an estimated 96 per cent in the private sector). Furthermore, with the global health concern with MMR, the birth centre average of zero maternal mortality is worth focusing on.

Despite such excellent outcomes, lack of progression as a recognized profession has resulted in years of frustration for autonomous *parteras* like Cristina who continue to attend births and make vast improvements in women's overall health. Along with their traditional and *barrio* counterparts, these *parteras* are unable to have their presence and contribution to improving maternal and infant mortality legitimately recognized and unable to obtain recognition as a profession. For the time being, the issue of what kind of data and health professionals matter intersects with a historical prejudice against *parteras* and out-of-hospital birth. Though the quantitative data is limited, it does combine with strong qualitative case examples to support the birth centre model in a region in need of maternal health system strengthening.

Over the years, alongside *parteras*, I have spoken to researchers (local, national and international), medical professionals, NGOs and people working within the health secretariat who repeatedly pose the question: why are people not looking at the evidence on qualified *parteras* and birth centre outcomes? While on a personal level doctors, politicians and heads of departments appear genuinely interested in midwifery-led models of care, the consensus among decision-makers within private meetings remains that midwifery will never become a recognized and respected profession in Mexico. Ultimately, the commodification of every aspect of obstetrics in both public and private facilities and in the political economy of public health means that there is simply too much to lose for medical practitioners, providers of surgery equipment and the pharmaceutical industry. Effective public health programmes in Chiapas (urban and rural) rely on collaboration at every level of community and health services, in addition to the mutual respect among all active practitioners. Furthermore, the health secretariat and medical professional would need to meaningfully recognize the notion of informed choice and autonomy for all women. This latter element provides the largest barrier, as Cris explains:

> The problem is that there's no legal hole for [birth centres] you know. There's no place to place us, as a place that does out-of-hospital birth ... When there has to be a medical intervention we transport to a medical centre. But it has to do with the same thing that with no professional midwifery, then where do you put birth centres? ... And we have done [work] at a federal level with a group of midwives. We've done a couple of processes where we worked on a competencies document for educating midwives at a federal level. But I never see that any of these initiatives make it past the offices where we work on them. I've had people saying, 'Yeah we need to regulate birth centres'. 'Yeah I totally agree we need to regulate midwives etcetera', but nobody wants to be the person to do it.

How Equitable are Birth Centres and Autonomous *Parteras'* Work in Practice?

So, why do women choose an autonomous *partera* and a birth centre? Despite the structural, systemic and social barriers to women choosing out-of-hospital birth and autonomous *parteras*, Luna Maya continues to thrive. The endurance and extension of Luna Maya's work arises from the organization's commitment to community engagement and the collective agency of their clients who feel strongly enough about the type of healthcare they wish to have. The public face of Luna Maya – the birth centre – may reinforce the idea that this is a contemporary and imported culture of humanized birth available to middle-class Mexicans and foreigners; yet the commitment to the community midwifery model speaks equally to urban Indigenous and poorer *coleto* communities.

San Cristóbal's migrant Indigenous subpopulations have increased tenfold since the early 1990s due to a combination of conflict-related forced displacement and labour flow. Many of the cities outlying *barrios* (la Orilla included) are populated by Tzotzil, Tzeltal, Chol and Zoque individuals and families fleeing religious or political persecution in the rural highlands. Increased opportunities for girls from Indigenous and rural communities to study at secondary and high schools in the city have also led to a new type of subpopulation living without the protection of community elders and vulnerable to exploitation. Whereas the *coleto* families have well-established links with the *barrio parteras* still in existence, the transient migrant neighbourhoods lack the traditional *partera* families would usually turn to.

Two neighbourhoods in particular stand out in their relationship with Luna Maya's early community development: Ranchería Limón and La Mancha.[12] Both these neighbourhoods are extremely poor; homes are made of plywood, plastic sheeting and lack indoor plumbing. Most homes have dug out latrines and do connect to a neighbourhood electric grid. Women marry young, often before eighteen years old and have an average of three or four children in their lifetime. Women who birth in La Mancha seek out *parteras* late in their pregnancy (if at all) and are mostly concerned with the baby's position. They do not attend childbirth education classes and inherently believe that birth is a natural event that should occur at home with other women. They are afraid of the local hospital and believe that all women who birth there end up being mistreated and forced to give birth by caesarean. Luna Maya began working with La Mancha when one woman who was at a birth that had lasted two nights decided to call one of the *parteras* to ask for assistance. The traditional *partera* attending the birth was asleep and could not provide more support or diagnosis. The baby was in an asynclitic position, meaning the head was sideways, and posterior presenting (the baby's back was lying towards the mother's back). Using the *rebozo* (Mexican shawl) to help better position the baby, the Luna Maya *partera* supported the mother to have a successful birth and avoid transport to the local hospital. From that moment, women from La Mancha chose to birth with Luna Maya or call their *parteras* when births were not going well to ask for assistance.

The first birth attended by a Luna Maya *partera* in Ranchería Limón was a breech. It was the woman's second pregnancy and she was told by doctors at the hospital it would have to be a programmed caesarean. She began asking around for support for a vaginal breech birth and eventually found Luna Maya who offered to attend the birth. The birth went very well, and since then the women from Ranchería Limón have gone to Luna Maya for maternal, paediatric and family health care. This community has no traditional midwives or healers and suffers from mass structural inequalities. Families in Ranchería Limón eat on average one plate of beans a day. Alcoholism is rampant among males in the community and therefore violent acts against women in the home or street are commonplace. The city's expanding overspill *barrios* become zones of economic and social abandonment[13] encompassing all the conditions likely to cause premature mortality and exclusion from public health services.

For six years Luna Maya also worked with a local *Hogar Comunitario* (Women's Hostel). Founded in 1994 the Women's Hostel provides sanctuary for women fleeing violence either in rural communities or the city. Indigenous women and girls are often forced to flee their communities if they become pregnant outside of marriage. Safe abortion is not legal or easily accessible in Chiapas and before 2016 medical abortion was not legal in cases of rape without a judge's order. The Women's Hostel therefore offered a safe space for pregnant women to live during the end of their pregnancy and for a period afterwards. Before Luna Maya, all pregnant women were referred to the local maternity hospital. Luna Maya worked with the Women's Hostel from 2005 to 2010, attending births in-house and training the nurses who worked there in midwifery skills. The nurses eventually became skilled enough to provide the care themselves and Luna Maya remained in a consulting role for the staff.

Luna Maya's commitment to providing safe and respectful healthcare to all women and training other healthcare professionals in the same skills is one of the less documented activities of the organization. The organization's economic model of charging higher rates to families who can pay to subsidize individuals who cannot remains a core philosophy of the birth centre in San Cristóbal today. The *parteras*' work with poorer and more vulnerable women tends to go unnoticed to the broader society and is often unknown to the more affluent clientele seeking full-spectrum care and services from the birth centre.

As I previously mentioned, the birth centre's majority middle-class clientele hail from nearby Tuxtla Gutierrez and San Cristóbal; they pay full price for services at the birth centre and tend to use a mixture of sexual, reproductive and family health services before, during and beyond their pregnancy. The average age of women seeking antenatal and birth care at Luna Maya is twenty-eight years old and they tend to be very proactive in their own health education and decision-making. As with most Mexican women, they are hyper aware of the high caesarean section rates in public and private hospitals and they are generally open to alternative ways of thinking about birth. Through listening to women who attend classes, events and appointments at Luna Maya, it is clear that they distinguish between the Indigenous or barrio *parteras*, and the autonomous professional *parteras*, though they discuss this topic in terms of their individual needs rather than hierarchical preference.

The women who attended the birth preparation courses during my fieldwork seemed less concerned with the comparison between traditional and transnational practices of *parteras* and more focused upon negotiating a safe physical and emotional transition to motherhood. The naturalizing of all aspects of pregnancy and birth is emphasized as soon as one steps into the birth centre environment. From the artwork on the walls, the cloth nappies, sanitary towels and baby carriers for sale in the reception, to tinctures and oils, and birthing manuals available to borrow from the small library shelves, the spaces that make up the birth centre are the antithesis of a stark clinical environment. The small entrance leads through a wooden framed glass double door into the reception, shop and small waiting area. Off to the left are a couple of steps leading to the old house kitchen. The old kitchen is used for preparing herbal remedies and the far side of the area is used as office space. There are desks with computers, phones, storage boxes and a large white board detailing the shifts of tasks for centre staff and volunteers. Towards the back of the original building, there is another waiting area, toilet and two examination/treatment rooms with an adjoining bathroom.

At the back of the building is a large walled garden where families are free to congregate and for labouring women to use during their brief stay. Along the garden wall are two outbuildings built especially for the birth centre, providing a yoga and workshop space, and a family room. One outbuilding is occupied as a birthing suite complete with a single bed and a large bath for waterbirths and postpartum treatments. The birthing suite contains all equipment necessary to deal with emergencies complications in labour, though a visitor would never know as everything is stored in cabinets so as to maintain the non-clinical feel of the space.

The home from home environment works with the overall ethos of the community midwifery model of care: that pregnancy and childbearing is a profound experience, which carries significant meaning to the woman, her family and the community, and in addition that midwifery care takes place in partnership with women, recognizing their right to self-determination, and is respectful, personalized, continuous and non-authoritarian.[14] This approach extends to the language used in the birth centre with individual women and in groups. In the hours I spent listening to women in the antenatal support classes there was a noticeable transformative process of 'letting the body take over the mind' in the weeks that women spent preparing for their birth.

The language used by the Luna Maya *parteras*, and consequently their clients, connects cosmologies of mother earth and female bodies that foreground the woman's transformative role in the process. The language is highly feminized (and heteronormative) and speaks of hidden powers and reconnecting a woman to her previous (matriarchal) lineage and nature. The language is also politicized in challenging the pathologizing of childbearing, as we saw with Bety in Chapter two. The discussions in the antenatal groups introduce women to the terminology associated with the human rights framework to health and it impacts positively on their worldview. I have heard many women describe how they have been transformed by contact with the birth centre, informing how they understand themselves and their relationships beyond motherhood. The birth centre environment and lexicon represent a polar opposite to the medical model, yet in a way that also becomes a hyper-naturalization of childbearing. The *parteras* and therapists provide reassurance value via this language precisely because many women (and their partners) desire a counternarrative to the hyper-medicalized processes of childbearing they are offered elsewhere. Despite its own limitations in terms of adopting a meshwork of world spiritualities and cosmologies, this politicized natural birth discourse works to reassure women that they do have a role to play in defining their birth and family-making, regardless of whether they choose the obstetrician or *partera* for their care. Rather than provide a problematic extreme opposite to the hyper-medicalized model, the various options and pathways open to families means that the birth centre provides a more fluid, plural approach to healthcare.

Sofi

Sofi came to a focus group in Luna Maya where we had recruited participants specifically to gather information on women's perceptions of security and decision-making. Originally from Italy, Sofi came to Luna Maya during both her pregnancies and chose to give birth with the midwives for the second child. At twenty-nine years old she fits into the average demographic of the birth centre – middle-class, university educated and navigating a mixed economy of healthcare. Like the other women who come to the ante- and postnatal groups she has been proactive in her own health education and decision-making about motherhood. Sofi was one of three women to turn up to this focus group[15] and throughout the first hour of recording she dominated the conversation, barely pausing for breath as she jumped around her maternal chronology describing her experience and process of transformation. She sat talking while holding her youngest child in her arms, a boy born a few months earlier at the birth centre. Whilst nursing him intermittently she spoke with ease for a good forty-five-minutes or so about how underlying fears had shaped her maternal health-seeking behaviour and trust-building with health professionals. Throughout the whole interview Sofi was very animated, her storytelling reflecting the conflict between medical advice, personal experience, and what she described as the rational and irrational emotions affecting her decision making:

> Well, I was grateful to have a space in San Cristóbal like Luna Maya, because I knew that being supported was integral, and I had it super clear, that here [LM] was a type of support, and in the hospital, it was another. At the time of the first pregnancy, I was coming to Luna Maya but also, I was still very connected with the deep-rooted belief that the hospital was safer, I still am in many ways. I have a personal family history of several diseases, some very serious, that have been solved in the hospital, so it is clear to me that you need them. I felt that if something could have happened, then the best solution, would

have been the hospital. But at the same time, because all talk of a home birth, well, it caught my attention too, for a more humanized birth, because I knew there was another story, right? A different approach. For example, when I had a urinary infection, on the one hand the doctor is saying 'antibiotics' and here they tell you 'plants', and you are there in the middle thinking 'what do I do?', no? But it was the beauty of the journey I was on, the one that I chose, which reflects my insecurities and where I go, right? Because suddenly, of course, my heart says 'plants', but in my head there are fears that bring about doubts. So, it was nice, for example, it was nice to stop and say 'Orale, I'll try the plants and if that doesn't work, then the antibiotics', and so it was. And of the two infections, for example, the first one was plants, and in the end the second one was antibiotics because it just wouldn't clear.

For this generation of women, who attend and pay for various classes and services at the birth centre, it is clear they feel they have a role to play in deciding how to get the best out of birth and parenting. There are always family and societal pressures, more so for Luna Maya's *coleta* clients, but women like Sofi are demonstrating a proactive need to be listened to. As Sofi describes above, what women appear to be looking for when they come to Luna Maya is a middle ground that speaks to their desire to have as natural a birth as possible, while also having the reassurance that *parteras* have a level of clinical or nursing training to deal with potential complications. The underlying fear that there is always something that can go wrong tends to weave its way into all elements of decision-making for those accustomed to medical models of care. What resonates in Sofi's and other women's narratives is needing to know there is a choice when it comes to managing fear and weighing up risks. Luna Maya clients find they go there when the time is right. They may attend antenatal or parenting courses and appointments with a first or second pregnancy and then decide to give birth in hospital. They then return with more confidence in themselves and their *parteras* to try a homebirth with the second or third child. Where this kind of back-and-forth decision-making is discouraged in the medical environment, the Luna Maya *parteras* understand this as part of the woman's ongoing process of empowerment. Unlike many doctors, the *partera* will not reprimand or scold or a woman for going to hospital and then returning to the birth centre for her postpartum care.

Sofi began to attend the groups and workshops at the birth centre during her first pregnancy, while still undecided about where she wanted to give birth. Always wanting to research every option, she joked that at one point her peer group assumed she had got a scholarship to attend so many classes. However, as she explained, no amount of therapy and group conversations could take away her inner fears and doubts about something going wrong at the birth. She began to think about what she would be risking if she needed a transfer mid-labour and whether she could cope with the guilt if anything happened to the baby:

> If something was going to happen in the transfer between Luna Maya to the hospital, I knew I would be to blame! And I still have the memory clear, in spite of all your messages, your history of public hospitals, about how shit they are, I had it clear: my birth is going to be blocked, I said: 'I'm going to get scared during the birth process' because I couldn't get rid of that fear of transfer. So, with Diego it was 'Do you know what? I feel calmer in a hospital', despite everything I was super clear about that decision.

It has always been interesting to listen to women reflect about different birth experiences and choices because through these reflections come ideas about how birth experiences bring about personal transformations. When women talk about what they learn from each experience they piece together their own steps in learning and track how their own perceptions change over time. Sofi spoke candidly in this interview about how her fears of something going wrong during labour or the consequences of having to transfer did not subside over the five years to her next pregnancy. However, her attitude and way of coping with the fears had changed and this contributed to her decision to have her second child with the *parteras* at Luna Maya. In her narrative she kept returning to the point that the space provided at the birth centre and the opportunities to talk openly with other women about all aspects of mother and womanhood guided her through decision-making. She repeated on several occasions the importance of continuity of care and getting to know her care provider, of building trust so that she could listen to frank and honest information, as she described 'all the doubts, the complaints, everything, because it is from these points that we grow'.

The need to reflect upon their own personal histories and fears is part of the psychological preparation for birth and transformation that is built into the femifocal model of care. The *parteras* at Luna Maya do not teach women that their fears are irrational. Instead, they offer to explore them along with the women and to identify coping mechanisms. Often when I would discuss with Cris the topic of transfers and the likely reasons as to why a woman would end up requesting an ambulance mid-labour, she would comment how their heart was not really in a home or birth centre birth from the outset. 'When the whole *partera* and birth centre thing comes from the partner rather than the woman', Cris explained, 'it is obvious from the start she will ask for a transfer, she never really wanted to be here in the first place'. Having a choice in where, when and how she wants to have her baby impacts greatly on a woman's confidence postpartum, and ergo her self-transformation in early motherhood. As Sofi's narrative shows, this is not always about choosing the midwifery model of care, but more about feeling she has a role in how decisions are made:

> There is clearly a need for women to have a more rational explanation, clearly, of how everything will work, the emergency and all that. But also, for the emotional support, of the fears you have, you need support from elsewhere, so the woman must decide how to find support for these fears. My fear was transformed after the first birth, because I chose to go to the hospital, it was on my terms. The nice thing for me is that I don't have to compare the two births in this aspect. Because my son sometimes asks me 'But why was Flavio born in water?', Right? And in these moments, it's nice to also talk to him, right? How I was at that time and I appreciate that. And I even appreciate the bloody episiotomy because I had to go through that at that time, period. I had to give birth that way in that moment because I had all those fears. I didn't feel safe in the birth centre and the second time I felt differently. It's good in the birth preparation courses when fears come out and you see how different we are as women. What scares me is not scary for you, and vice versa. And then everyone is their personal history. It's about where you feel safe.

Esme: 'la historia de no tener un parto feliz o un parto deseable'[16]

Amongst all the positive stories of Luna Maya women, there are of course many births that do not meet with women's high expectations. When births do not go according to plan, forms of physical and psychological trauma occur. Births rarely go to plan in the exact sense that someone following a natural birth plan cannot predict when and where they will begin labour, nor how long the three stages of labour will last. When complications occur and unexpected birth events remain unresolved, women spend months, often years, picking apart the details and trying to find answers that help to settle feelings of guilt or distress. The midwives at the birth centre maintain an open dialogue with women who want to come and discuss their experience. The femifocal model in practice enables both care provider and client to explore unresolved issues and creates a learning opportunity 'to learn from the pain and anguish of [unplanned] events' (Sánchez Ramirez 2016). It challenges all those concerned to identify the part they played in the process and how it played out. It can take many years before a woman is prepared to examine a traumatic experience in detail and it can often cause further disillusionment if she is unable to get the resolution she imagined. The benefit of being able to revisit birth narratives over time and with support is that women can eventually feel a level of ownership of a situation within which they originally felt helpless and out of control. Though this may not find them the exact healing they hoped for, women at the centre have described a sense of acceptance that would never arise from trying to seek answers from physicians.

Esme is a *coleta* woman who came to the birth centre when she was pregnant with her first child in 2015. Her story, as described in her own words, was not 'one of a happy or desirable birth'. After enduring a long labour at home and attention from the centre's lead *partera* and student midwives, Esme's first experience of childbirth resulted in a traumatic double transfer to private and public hospitals and an emergency caesarean section. Two years later she was invited to attend the same focus group as Sofi. On the day of the group's interview, she arrived late, about an hour into the conversation just as the women were debating whether or not it was beneficial to know the things that can go wrong in a homebirth. Esme entered the room where the focus group was taking place, took her seat and spoke immediately about her situation. Her voice was shaking when she spoke and for the first few minutes there was an urgency to her tone. The words escaped quickly from her mouth, a mixture of events and questions in no particular order. 'When I got the call to come here today', she began, 'I nearly didn't come. But then I thought, I need closure'. She explained how she needed to complete her own process of healing, that she still felt so angry when she thought about her birth and had many unanswered questions. It was Esme's hope that by attending the focus group some good would come out of her pain, and that by helping others learn from her experience it would in some way be given a purpose.

Esme's pregnancy had passed without complication, everything about her records suggested she was a normal low-risk case, an ideal candidate for a home birth. Throughout the pregnancy she attended courses and groups at the birth centre and was confident in her preparation for the birth. On the day she began in the slow first stages of labour her waters broke and she began to lose fluid. Her voice became focused as she explained her first three days of labour in a methodical tone.

> I was told that the membrane had ruptured a little and that I shouldn't worry. I'd heard stories, other things that people would say. I was told, if you listen to the allopathic version that if there's meconium that you go straight to surgery. I wanted to trust the *partera* and so when she told me to look for anything green coming out and to keep an eye on it. It was like that for three days, the *partera* checked me, she knew there was meconium, but she didn't seem worried. The first time I called her she came and she said to me 'calm down, you have two centimetres dilated and this will take a long time, you have to stay calm'. But you never touched me, so how could you know I had two centimetres. I understand that you said it could be a pathway to infection, so how could you now how much I was dilated to two? And you left me that night, with my waters broken and with meconium. I felt like I could have given birth that night, but you just left me. I mean, in all the courses there's this talk of humanized birth but with me there was no [cervical] contact. How can there be a humanized birth without human contact?

The relative risk of foetal distress associated with the presence of meconium, clinically referred to as meconium-stained liquor (MSL), has long been a contentious topic in global maternal health. Like most potential birth complications, the presence of MSL as a response to hypoxic stress is dependent upon other factors. Unfortunately, a lack of clarity on the topic leads to a medical assumption (and accusation) that all MSL is life threatening, requiring emergency intervention. However, MSL may be a sign that a foetus has reached maturation but is not an indication alone that the foetus is in distress. Following foetal maturation theory the presence of MSL in late gestation reflects normal foetal physiology (Wong et al. 2002). At the later stages of gestation foetal heart rate rather than meconium is an indicator of distress. Other factors are determined by the colour and consistency of the MSL.

According to the Royal College of Obstetrics and Gynaecology (cited in Addisu et al. 2018), meconium-stained amniotic fluid is classified as either significant MSL and non-significant MSL. Non-significant is described as having a thin yellow or greenish tinge and significant MSL dark green or black. The Luna Maya protocol lists thick meconium (significant) under the conditions that require transport to hospital during labour. The written *partera*'s records from this case show that transfer happened once there was clear evidence of thick meconium and there had been a failure for the labour to progress after forty-eight hours, but that the foetal heartrate did not show signs of distress. What is not clear from Esme's recounting of her labour is whether her thoughts about neglect relating to meconium has arisen from months of trying to identify a point of blame for her birth trauma and in the negative treatment she received from doctors at the hospitals she was transferred to.

> I had been waiting three days for this natural delivery, all throughout the pregnancy I had given myself the illusion of how it would be. Then suddenly, like out of nowhere, everything goes from perfect to pfum! Panic, transfer, caesarean section! I really didn't want to get to crisis point. You transferred me to the hospital, and well, that's another thing I wanted to ask about. When you told us you had doctors that you worked with for complications, we understood that it was a proper partnership. But that didn't ring true. When we got to the first hospital you put us in their hands and then you have no part in it. I still wanted you to be with me, I asked for you to come with me when I was admitted but you didn't, you just left.

What Esme is describing here echoes Cris's comments earlier on and is typical of the exclusion of all midwives regardless of ethnicity or type from the institutional environment. Despite years of campaigning, preferences of global health policy and promised intentions at state level, midwives are consistently refused any kind of hand-over between health professionals or entry into treatment areas. As we saw in Chapter three, the presence of midwives often instigates forms of punishment towards women from obstetricians and nurses leading to acts of obstetric violence. One could be forgiving of midwives who did choose to leave the transfer scene as a form of self-protection, though this is not the practice of Luna Maya staff. At the point in Esme's monologue where she accused the *partera* of abandoning her at the hospital, the *partera* interjected, saying quietly but firmly 'I was there'. Esme listened to this and paused for a second. The interruption had clearly brought her out of her memory into the present, but she was eager to get back to her thoughts to complete her retelling of the birth:

> Well, ok yes you were there, but for the doctors it was like you were invisible. I understand that it was an emergency but really, there was no collaboration at all. I don't understand this after we were told that these were doctors that you worked with. But once we were there you had no part in it. Then there's the other thing I don't get. At the

first hospital they couldn't even help me because they didn't have the right equipment for the baby. We had to transfer again to the public hospital, all that time me thinking that my baby was going to die. You had said in the courses that if there was a complication we would go to the private hospital where you had a good relationship with the doctors, and that if there was an emergency we would go straight to the public hospital. Was this not an emergency? Three days with meconium and an affected heartrate! If you had taken me there in the first place, then what happened wouldn't have happened.

When we got to the second hospital it was so late, they told me that my baby was going to die. The doctor, whilst they were cleaning me up after the caesarean section and checking the baby, he said that she was stillborn and that in the best-case scenario, in that hospital only forty percent of babies ever survive. Imagine, I'm lay there, after hours of trauma, I can't move, and he starts telling me off for going with a *partera*! It was like they were punishing me. Even afterwards, when I was recuperating in the bed, the other doctor she said to me, 'all you can do is pray for your little princess'. I don't know if you understand the degree of shock and trauma that I've suffered.

At this point Esme broke down and sobbed quietly. There was silence in the group and Sofi handed her some tissues. Cris gots up to make her some herbal tea and everyone waited for the air to settle. No-one tried to lighten the mood or fill the silence and Esme was given this moment to grieve. When she was ready, she continued to ask about the decision to transfer and why it was not treated as the emergency it was. She wanted to know why the *partera* had allowed her to feel safe, to not react to the presence of meconium and to suddenly change tack after three days. It was a point that she fixated on and clearly something that she identified as a turning point. When I look at my fieldnotes from this day and when I came to translate the transcript some months after, I counted over ten reframed versions of this question in Esme's contribution to the focus group. It was clearly a traumatic experience and a memory that had haunted her over the previous months, and something to which she had failed to gain resolution.

Esme mentioned repeatedly over the course of her story how she had spent the last two years trying to figure out who was to blame, though rather than using the exact term *culpar* (to blame), she talked about professional responsibility and negligence. In this aspect process and paperwork served as a tool for indicating there may be someone to blame for the unwanted events. 'I remember reading the paperwork', she said referring to the client contract with

Luna Maya, 'The part where you declare you [the midwives] are exempt from responsibility in the case of transfer, and I remember my husband asking you, "and if there's negligence?", because there can be negligence on your part too! But it looks like there's no place for you to take responsibility, how do you explain that?'

There is potentially a lot to unpick here in terms of the commodification of healthcare and the sense of culpability and measured risk embroiled in the bureaucracy of contracted relationships between patient and provider. The contract that a woman enters into with a birth centre *partera* is symbolic of the way in which families hire a *partera* in the *barrios*. It is a relationship based largely on trust, hence why so many women are content to sign a contract agreeing that the *partera* is devoid of responsibility for what happens post-transfer. At this stage, most women trust in the birth centre model enough to convince themselves that a transfer will not apply to them. Yet at the same time they trust that the *partera* will transfer should a complication occur that puts the woman or baby at risk. The women have high expectations which work to counteract the fear of ending up at hospital in the hands of an unknown physician. For the *partera*, this section of the contract is important because it documents the limits on her power. It is an acknowledgement on all sides that she has no influence whatsoever in an institutional environment and that she is not legally classified as a healthcare provider. The statement of exemption serves simultaneously no purpose and every purpose. The statement comes into symbolic significance when things do not go according to plan. The introduction of paperwork into a traditionally non-bureaucratic form of healthcare is a reminder of how quickly trust in the midwifery model of care can be eroded. The necessary introduction of the contract between the birth centre/*partera* and pregnant woman provides us with an example of 'interpersonal trust' (Mills 2017), an integration of both the reliability of the provider and her moral obligation to honour the trust bestowed upon her. It is an effort at self-regulation which is ultimately futile for all because there is no state regulation or legitimate recognition of midwives or their profession.

At the point in the conversation where Esme becomes distressed, Cris opens up the discussion to the other women in the group and asks how they interpret the need for a contract between health provider and client. She asks the women what it signifies to them to sign a waiver, whether from *parteras* or medics, which confirms that they as patients accept the responsibility for what will be done to them. Addressing the group, she asks 'I want to know what that means to each of you. What does responsibility mean, and who does the responsibility belong to?'

Esme is the first to respond and continues to relate her ideas about responsibility directly to the healthcare providers: 'I don't know, well on the one hand responsibility means that the person has enough experience to know what to do in cases of emergency and will act on that. They'd know the protocols that are used in hospitals and they'll know what doctors will do when there's a transfer. You know, just have general knowledge'. Nayelli, a Spanish postgraduate student, reflected on the idea of shared responsibility: 'Because I trusted in my body and my ability to give birth from the outset, I was sure nothing bad was going to happen, so I didn't feel the need to sign anything'.

The women's different responses to this question are inseparable from their initial expectation, memory and outcome of their births. Nayelli gave birth as she expected, in the birth centre with no complications and supported by the *parteras*. She felt no need to consider responsibility within a framework of blame because nothing had gone against her expectations. Esme, however, had lived through traumatic circumstances with her birth and was looking for resolution involving blame. Esme's contact with medical professionals prior to becoming a mother, during pregnancy, birth and postpartum was shaped by risk and surrendering bodily autonomy to the authoritative knowledge of health professionals. The signing of a waiver serves for doctors working under oath and protected by a legal system against claims of negligence. Outside of the hospital and in the more equitable space of midwifery and birth centres, the waiver and contract serve to critique *parteras* as irresponsible or powerless to help in an emergency. Bureaucracy of this kind therefore is a tool of hierarchy, meant to sustain unequal power relationships. It arguably has no place in an equitable femifocal model of care.

Some Final Notes on the Social Construction of Natural Childbearing

I would like to conclude this chapter and section of the book by reflecting on what these women's stories tell us about the social construction of natural childbearing. I will also return briefly to how the femifocal model of care grapples with this increasingly contentious and commodified issue. Women across the social strata seek out *parteras* because they desire a 'normal' birth, by which they mean to give birth vaginally. Other women who give birth in hospitals with obstetricians generally hope to do the same. Just about every conversation involving a newborn begins with the question: 'fue normal o cesarea?' The distinction is made between how the baby came out of its mother and whether the method was natural per se. There is no agreed global definition of what natural childbearing entails, as it is no less a culturally constructed notion than the idea of 'non-natural childbirth'. If natural childbirth involves working with the body, then how one conceives of the body will determine its scope. The most useful biosocial definition in the literature on this topic is provided by Cosans (2004) who suggests the use of 'naturalistic practices' rather than the problematic and constructed term 'natural'. By this she means placing emphasis on working with the physiological processes of the labouring body as opposed to against it. Cosan's definition is useful for thinking about natural childbearing in the context of San Cristóbal because for most women, use of epidural or other forms of pain relief, episiotomy or forceps delivery do not take away from whether or not a woman had a natural birth. This raises important ethnographic questions surrounding what women and *parteras* understand natural childbearing to mean.

Terminology such as 'normal' or 'natural' in relation to birth contributes to the cultural construction of childbearing as a biologically determined and natural event. The natural (and in Mexico humanized) birth movement places emphasis on the power of women's bodies and their unique ability to manage the natural process of reproduction as a way to counteract the pathological and highly technocratic models of birth that dominate the public health system. However, the idiom of nature sets limits which, from either perspective, result in reproducing the notion that women are natural caregivers whose bodies are pre-programmed for childbearing and rearing. Although this is meant to empower women who more often than not are at the mercy of obstetric violence and submission in the medical environment, the promotion of natural childbearing draws upon traditional ideologies and fetishization of motherhood that the state has historically used to oppress its female citizens.

So how can the femifocal model serve to resolve these biologically worded rationales explained in reference to ancient ways? The femifocal mindset that places the woman at the centre of her social, political and cultural ecology provides an in-between space to explore the intersection of nature and desired intervention. This intercultural model of midwifery practised in Luna Maya enables middle-class women, conscious of feminist politics and their rights as women, to also negotiate the desire to embrace the cultural ideology of becoming a mother and being 'maternal' in the Mexican sense, all without feeling like they are compromising their agency as twenty-first-century women. Choosing to embrace motherhood with the femifocal mindset becomes a conscious, political action for middle-class women, something arguably not afforded to poorer *coleto* women – and this is possibly where the good intentions of the autonomous *parteras* and the intercultural model of midwifery will always reach their limits in creating social change.

Notes

1. In this chapter I tweak the term 'out-of-hospital birth' to incorporate the community midwifery model in San Cristóbal that offers both homebirth and a non-clinical birth centre as options for women. This shift centres the environments in which the *partera* practices and allows for discussion outside of policy and legislation that restrict midwifery attended birth to the woman's home.
2. Birth centres cannot legally advertise their services as a place to give birth under Mexican law. The *Norma Oficial Mexicana NOM-007-SSA2-2016* sets out the rules that a planned birth must happen in a hospital delivery room with a delivery bed or table and emergency obstetric and paediatric equipment, as well as in the presence of a registered skilled birth attendant (*parteras* of any type are not considered as such because they are categorized as a traditional practice not a profession). This means they are constantly at the whim of the authorities who tend to turn a blind eye to their existence unless a client complains about treatment, there is a situation that attracts attention (an infant mortality or clash upon transfer) or simply a change in directorship in the local health secretariat to someone opposed to out-of-hospital birth models.
3. Luna Maya opened a second birth centre in Mexico City in 2013 serving predominantly middle-class urban families. Since 2016 at least three other birth centres have registered with the state and serve small populations in Guadalajara, Michoacán and Yucatan.
4. Within this eclectic community I include activists and academics.
5. Certified Professional Midwife (CPM) refers to the US government-recognized technical qualification that Cris Alonso and a few other autonomous/professional midwives in Mexico hold. In this work I will use the term *partera* when discussing all birth centre midwives as we remain in the Mexican context, and all have taken a varied path to their practices.

6. Although known locally as the *casa de partos*, Luna Maya has the official title of Centro de Partos (Birth Centre) because of the complex legal implications regarding registration and places where birth can be planned to occur.
7. For example, see the work of Mexican anthropologists and sociologists Graciela Freyermuth, Austreberta Nazar and Georgina Sanchez who all have an established history of research in the region.
8. A version of this section on the femifocal model and the following description of Luna Maya's history appear in Alonso et al. 2018.
9. See Cheyney et al. 2014 for the excellent statistical outcomes of nearly 17,000 CPM-attended births.
10. It should be noted that this sample included data from a second Luna Maya birth centre which opened in Mexico City (LM-CDMX) in 2013. As the purpose of this analysis is to examine the impact of midwifery practice, which is comparable between the two centres, it would not be worth separating the births from LM-CDMX from the sample under discussion.
11. High-risk profiles include chronic diseases such as diabetes and cardiac problems. Women are referred to institutional care for pregnancy complications such as preeclampsia and gestational diabetes.
12. These place names are pseudonyms.
13. Here I refer to Joao Biehl's (2013) concept of 'zones of social abandonment' as he describes the increasing urban phenomenon of spaces where marginalized societies are left to find ways to fend for themselves. The lack of any infrastructure and the desperate self-sufficiency of these communities creates a convenient state of ignorance on the part of state interventions or responsibilities. This concept lends itself well to the overspill *barrios* around Chiapanecan cities that arise from the migration and displacement of Mayan Indigenous peoples.
14. International Confederation of Midwives (2014) Philosophy and Model of Midwifery Care Core Document, https://www.internationalmidwives.org/assets/files/definitions-files/2018/06/eng-philosophy-and-model-of-midwifery-care.pdf.
15. Focus groups are rarely well attended for many different reasons. Much like in the *barrio*, birth centre families preferred the more relaxed arrangement of happenchance notetaking and occasional recording at group meetings or over coffee. The request to attend a focus group with a specific aim tended to repel rather than attract women who were otherwise often happy to discuss their experiences. It was also less likely that Mexican women would attend a recorded focus group and more likely that European or American clients would volunteer.
16. The story of not having a happy or desirable birth.

Part III

Nurture Work

Chapter 5

LUPITA AND CARLITA

It wasn't easy, it's never easy, being a person who produces milk.

—Valeria Luiselli, *Faces in the Crowd*

The first time I encountered the postpartum *cuarenta días* (the forty days) in San Cristóbal was in 2008 shortly after my first child had been born. Although I was very used to seeing babies, toddlers and children in every kind of public space in San Cristóbal, it wasn't until this point that I noticed I could not recall having ever seen any babies outside of the house who were less than around two months old. A neighbour's daughter Sandra had recently come to stay in her natal home after giving birth in a local clinic. While I had been alone at home dealing with the first emotional and practical throes of being a first-time mother, Sandra was convalescing surrounded by the comfort of hot food, warm blankets and female relatives. I can still clearly remember the first time I was invited over to visit, the impact of going into a warm, darkened room at the back of the house has stayed with me ever since. The windows let in no natural light as they were covered over with bed sheets. The only light was a lamp giving off a warm glow from the corner of the room where under a mountain of fleecy blankets, on a large wooden bed, lay Sandra feeding a barely visible baby shape wrapped up under yet more fleece blankets. Sandra and her baby would not leave that cocooned environment for around a month. At the time I thought it reminiscent of a womb, a serene warm space that protected the senses from the harshness of daylight and the realities of the world outside. I remember the smell of warm *atole* and sweet bread wafting in from the kitchen mixed together with the scent of baby talc and laundry soap, the muffled sound of the *telenovela* in the adjacent sitting room, and all throughout the visit fighting back an overwhelming desire to crawl under those blankets with my own baby and have the women take care of me for a few days.

Being new to motherhood in 2008, I had no knowledge of the type of forty-day postpartum quarantine that many Catholic families abide by in San Cristóbal, nor what the physical and emotional implications were for both mother and baby, but my visit to Sandra did raise specific questions that still help me think about this practice today. What is happening here? Who are the experts in this space? Is the new mother still a novice during this period, whilst older female relatives take care of all but feeding the baby? And how does this forty-day period begin to shape the type of mother she will become? What type of bodily transformations are taking place? Where was her husband? Where were the men? How is the marital relationship affected by the temporary return to the maternal home? How does the need for a forty-day bed rest conflict with work duties, other children and how does this work for lone mothers?

The *cuarenta días* is certainly not unique to San Cristóbal; it is practised in homes throughout the country and versions of it are prevalent in both Indigenous and predominantly Catholic families of low to middle socio-economic status. Variations of forty-day quarantine practices appear historically across cultures from medieval England (Kitzinger 1997) to modern-day China, Jordan, Lebanon, Egypt and Palestine (Kim-Godwin 2003). It is a tradition in Maya communities that women convalesce for twenty days or less and anthropologists suggest that the extension of the rest period to forty days probably derives from Spanish colonial influence (Jordan 1993; Katz 1996). The literature on the Mexican postpartum quarantine (anthropological and non-anthropological) is sparse and mainly restricted to reports on immigrant practices in the US (Martinez-Schallmoser et al. 2005; Niska 1999; Waugh 2011) or Indigenous postpartum practices in the Highlands of Chiapas or Mixtec Highlands of Oaxaca (Katz 1996; Groark 1997; Jordan 1993; Resau 2002). I have yet to read a detailed description of postpartum practices in homes in urban Mexico. As such there remains a disparity of analysis in motherhood studies in Mexico (and elsewhere) that identifies conception, pregnancy, birth and nurturing practices as an interconnected process within a broader socio-political and economic context.

This chapter centres on the postpartum narratives and nurture practices of my friend Lupita and my neighbour's daughter Carlita. Over the next few pages, I pay particular attention to the way in which the *cuarenta días* occurs in la Orilla. In 2013 both Lupita and Carlita were first-time mothers and although their situations were different, their confinements were typical of new mothers in the *barrio*. These women's narratives demonstrate the struggle for recognition as a 'mother' in the family hierarchy and highlight the need for *primerizas* (first-time mothers) to be mothered by those with more experience. Though there is a significant age difference between them (around fourteen years), both Lupita and Carlita are members of a generation that straddles the divide between *barrio* and family tradition on one side, and contemporary motherhood influenced by social media, television, films, the 'borderless, fast-pace dissemination of commodities and styles' (Freeman 2001: 1010), and rapid advancement in reproductive health technologies on the other.

Carlita and Lupita's narratives reveal how the *cuarentena días* is located and embodied within a wider entanglement of competing cultural metaphors and ways of measuring risk – akin to the management of birth discussed in the previous chapters. I define postpartum cultural practices in the sense of a 'moral community in which members share a similar perspective about what constitutes moral outcome' (Rouse 2004: 517) and who share a common cosmology and language. I limit this moral community to the families in la Orilla, where discourses and dispositions are shared amongst neighbouring families and framed by predominantly local ideas about what constitutes a good mother. In the context of this chapter, I limit the postpartum period to the first two of three continuous phases described by Romano et al. (2010): the acute period, the first six to twelve hours after birth; the subacute period lasting two to six weeks; and a final delayed period lasting up to six months. The first two phases orient us toward postpartum practices within a comparative biomedical framework that recognizes both bodily transition and the healing that takes place within a specific timeframe. The acute and subacute phases are, in essence and in a temporal sense, comparable to the concept of the forty-day confinement commonly practised in low-income Catholic homes in Mexico. It is during the *cuarenta días* confinement that new mothers have the opportunity to heal, establish feeding and milk supply, and also when they are most likely to remain in contact with medical professionals in regard to either maternal or infant health.

Carlita[1]

I knew that Carlita was coming close to her due date when I bumped into her walking with her mother (Doña Carla) one early evening in July. The afternoon rains had begun to ease off and the cool breeze coming down from the mountains made perfect conditions for walking. I recognized the wide gait of a woman reaching the end of her pregnancy, the slow, heavy and methodical steps up and down the uneven concrete pavement as she held onto Doña Carla's arm. Her large *panza* had now dropped to her hips and was protruding out between her sweatpants and knitted poncho, one hand placed under the bump as though gravity itself wasn't enough to hold it up. Everything about her movement said heaviness. I stopped to say hello. 'We're on our way to the temple steps', Doña Carla explained as they stopped to greet me. The local church sat at the top of a hill looking over the town and with over one hundred steps to climb to reach the top it presented a challenge to anyone carrying extra weight on their body. 'We're on our way to the church steps', Doña Carla nodded in the direction of the church. 'Is it time to give the baby a nudge?' I asked. Doña Carla smiled and shrugged her shoulders: 'Something like that', she answered.

There are many different ways to help bring labour on with full-term women and it is common to try everything in order to avoid a visit to the clinic, particularly when women plan to birth at home. Although women do not declare this intention openly, the activity surrounding the pregnant women as she nears her due dates, such as walking, extra visits from the *partera* for massages, baths and herbal teas, suggests an attempt to help things along without medical intervention. Walking up and down steep steps is the least intrusive method and one that does not require calling the *partera* out unnecessarily, thus avoiding a small charge. It was a common sight to see accompanied, heavily pregnant women quietly huffing and puffing their way up and down the steep temple steps in the early evenings. When reaching the top it is also common for women to attend mass or say a prayer for a safe passage into the outer world for both mother and baby.

It is generally the female head of household who decides what action to take when a woman's pregnancy is reaching full-term. In households like those of my neighbours in la Orilla where women give birth at home, it is more likely that these practices will occur, and if over-due a visit to a maternity clinic will be the last resort. It is also in these circumstances that there is evidence of the absence of men in the decision-making. The way that male family members are consulted (or not) is similar to the strategy used with health professionals: a method of hoodwinking in order to maintain the peace and a façade of compliance with medical opinion. In the week or so leading up to Carlita's due date I noticed a conflict between the plans for birth depending on who I spoke to. The women of the household and immediate neighbours were calm about the progress of the pregnancy, making the necessary preparations for when they would need to call the *partera*. As the family *partera* Filomena in this instance was also Carlita's *suegra* (mother-in-law), she benefitted from extra visits almost daily towards the end of her pregnancy and there was no suggestion that the outcome would be anything other than a home birth. When I spoke to Don Marco (Carlita's father) he told me that a caesarean section was programmed for the following week upon the advice of the obstetrician they had been seeing for check-ups and ultrasounds. Whenever I bumped into Don Marco in the street or when he gave me a lift on the school run, he appeared unaware of the women's intentions to make sure the clinic's deadline was never met.

I visited Carlita around one week after her baby had been born. The baby girl Alison had been born at home attended by Filomena, Doña Carla and Doña Reina. There had been no complications and the labour had been relatively quick for a first-time mother, around twelve hours in total. Carlita's boyfriend Raul briefly visited each day though was not permitted to stay for a long period – 'mejor que se duermen en paz' (it's better they're left to sleep in peace), Doña Reina responded when I asked why his visits were so quick. Carlita and baby Alison had left the house just once since the birth to go to the maternity hospital to register the birth and obtain vaccinations. As Filomena is not a registered *partera* the family had to register the birth as a spontaneous unassisted birth at home and obtain a signature from a doctor at the maternity clinic to legitimate the birth of the Alison. Without this signature the family would not be able to obtain the birth certificate or social security number and Alison would not exist in the system. The exchange involved having the newborn physical exam and first round of vaccinations before they can leave the clinic with the paperwork.

At sixteen years old Carlita was still very much a girl in the eyes of her family and particular care was being taken to ease her into the role of mother. Carlita had originally planned to move back in with her *suegra* after her *cuarenta días* which is common practice with young couples. She had been living there since she found out she was pregnant but moved back home when she was nearer to her due date. 'She's always on her own because of her *suegra*'s midwifery duties', Doña Carla told me, 'She needs to be here where we can look after her'. During her final weeks of pregnancy, Raul visited on a daily basis but he was not permitted to stay overnight. On the morning that I visited Carlita she was being looked after by her maternal grandmother, mother and sister-in-law Dulce. A room had been set aside for her *cuarenta días* that was normally the marital bedroom of Carlita's brother Marco Jr, Dulce and their two-year old son. The family members had cleared the room apart from a double bed and a child's single bed on opposite sides of the square room, a large, dark wooden wardrobe with a television positioned on top opposite the double bed, and neat piles of baby clothes in white, pink and yellow placed on a small dressing table. Next to the clothes were packets of baby wipes, sweet smelling creams and nappies. A curtain made from bed sheets hung across the width of the room as a barrier to the door, ensuring that any cold air or light from outside would be kept out of the room and away from mother and baby. There were no other windows in the room and a bare light bulb hanging from the ceiling provided the only light. There was also a warm, orangey glare from the daytime show 'Hoy!' which beamed out from the television on the top of the wardrobe.

From underneath the blankets, I could just about see the top of Carlita's head as she smiled and nodded to say hello. She remained quiet whilst Doña Carla directed the conversation. 'Look at hers', she said, chuckling and nodding in my direction as I sat feeding my own daughter. 'Not like our little ones', she said, referring to my exposed breast, 'You could feed all the babies around here with those! Do you have lots of milk?' She turned to her own mother who was sat to my left, 'See mamá, they feed their babies like we do'. The older woman turned to me and smiled; she reached over and adjusted my *rebozo* to cover both breast and baby.

I answered Doña Carla, 'Yes, I'm lucky I've always had good milk'. I looked across to Carlita who was watching us with amusement. 'Has your milk come in yet?' 'I think so', she said quietly, 'she's feeding quite a lot, so I suppose so'. 'Yes, it's coming', interrupted Doña Carla. 'The midwife gives her fennel tea and she also drinks plenty of oat milk that helps it come in. What do you use for your milk?' she asked me. I hesitated a moment and then answered,

'Dark beer'. Doña Carla's eyes widened. 'Doesn't that damage the baby?' she said, not quite sure whether to believe me. 'Well, I don't drink it every day, just one or two to help get things going. It's what women do where I come from'. I shrugged as I spoke, though in my head I was already regretting making the comment about drinking beer. I was worried about judgement from the older women who I had never seen drinking alcohol, not even at fiestas.

After a short while Doña Carla and her mother left the room and the tone of the conversation changed. Carlita and Dulce were very intrigued about the idea of drinking beer to help the milk supply – 'though we just couldn't', Dulce said, 'we should only drink oat milk'. Before I left, I asked Carlita about the birth and how she was feeling in her body. 'No, I just feel sore but also I have my *faja*, are you still wearing yours?' Carlita lifted her jumper to show me a shop bought girdle; looking at her tightly bound torso made me suddenly very aware of my own soft, fleshy midriff still recovering from its third gestational stretch, I felt open and loose. I started to regret all the neighbours' offers to *fajarme* (bind me up) after the birth and wondered if it was too late. 'I didn't use one, is it comfortable?' Carlita shrugged: 'It's okay I'll wear it for a month. How are you so slim? Where did your *panza* go? What about your womb it can fall?' 'I don't know I feel alright, maybe I'll try one next time', I said thinking that maybe I should.

Within two weeks, Carlita's *cuarenta días* was interrupted by the sudden illness and hospitalization of Alison. One afternoon she had begun with a fever succeeded by her coughing up what looked like a bloody mucus; in a panic the family called an ambulance and Carlita and Alison went, accompanied by her parents, to the public hospital. During the time that they were in hospital, Alison's illness went without a clear diagnosis, and after four days in hospital, following the administration of antibiotics, she was discharged. Carlita and her mother had permission to stay with Alison in the hospital during this time, but Carlita was not allowed to breastfeed or express her milk. Doña Carla later told me that two days after returning home Alison had begun with a fever again and this time the family took her to a private hospital in the city, still concerned that they had no clear diagnosis. This time Alison and Carlita stayed for twenty-four hours under observation and were then sent home. During both times in hospital, Carlita and her family were given various non-specific explanations from the emergency doctors and a paediatric consultant.

Shortly after the second hospitalization, I sat with Doña Carla outside her house, and she told me the following: '[The doctor] says the baby has a stomach infection that went up to her head. We had only left the house with her once', she explained, 'to get her checked and registered at the clinica'. Many midwives working in the city *barrios* have not attended government training, are not registered with the state, and are unable to provide families with a birth registration certificate. To obtain a birth certificate under these circumstances, a family will take the newborn to a local clinic in the first few days following the birth, to ask a doctor to register it as a spontaneous homebirth. Doctors, in general, will accept the explanation, although they often use the opportunity to scold the family for being irresponsible and delaying coming to the hospital. The family will obtain the birth registration certificate upon completion of a newborn examination and first round of vaccines.

Over the course of several days, I learned more about the circumstances and explanations for Alison's mysterious decline in health. These details began to paint a picture of risk, or more specifically, of efforts to transform women like Carlita into a source of risk. The first doctors to assess baby Alison, when she was transferred by ambulance, claimed the illness was brought on by the infant not receiving all her vaccines at birth. I wanted further clarity on this, so I asked if she remembered which shots they gave her in those first few days after birth. Doña Carla thought for a moment and replied, 'I don't know, all of them. I think. [The doctors] said it was our fault because we must have missed one that goes in the leg'. As she said this, she pointed to her thigh. 'Do you remember what it is called?' 'No, it's just the shot that goes in the leg. I don't know what any of them are called', she said.

When the infant was first admitted, the emergency doctors were told that Alison had been born at home, and they took this opportunity to deliver a diatribe of blame, telling Doña Carla that her family should be ashamed for having taken this risk. This assessment was displaced later, when Alison was admitted the second time. In the private hospital, the paediatrician told the family that the infection had not resulted from missing vaccines, but rather that it was passed to Alison through Carlita's milk. 'She has colitis', Doña Carla told me, '[Carlita] suffered with it a lot as a teenager, and he said it will have made her milk infected'. This time, blame was directed away from the family birth practices and towards Carlita's individual body, with the suggestion that her milk was 'infected' with her colitis. This doctor told Carlita to stop breastfeeding straight away and substitute with formula that he would prescribe. He explained that if she continued to breastfeed, then Alison was at risk of further illness. The notion that colitis can be passed from mother's milk to infant has absolutely no epidemiological basis; at most, infection can be passed via a contaminated nipple, not the milk itself.

The interesting thing is that the doctor's admonishment of Carlita regarding her posing a risk to her infant by way of her own supposed history of colitis is not uncommon. The way in which colitis is used by doctors in Mexico to explain all varieties of bowel-, stomach- or colon-related conditions makes it impossible to say whether Carlita's past diagnosis was a contagious form of the disease or not, let alone whether there was the near impossible risk of her contaminating her nipples with the disease and infecting the infant. Nevertheless, the perception on the part of the doctors who cared for Alison was that Carlita herself was a source of danger to her infant. As others have noted, medical professionals can regulate and control maternal bodies by 'creating risk' in a variety of ways (MacKenzie and van Teijlingen 2010). This approach to 'risk equating to danger' results in a complex series of decisions made by biomedical caregivers who feel the need to protect babies from the traditional behaviours of mothers like Carlita. That these equations of risk and danger are widespread and normative means that doctors will tend to err on the side of caution; and thus, a rare possibility becomes factual explanation and guide for medical advice and diagnosis.

Carlita and Alison completed their *cuarenta días* without further complications and Carlita continued to breastfeed without having to substitute with formula. This is not the first instance I have been told about mother's milk or the mother's body itself making a baby ill. Such explanations generally come from the women themselves based on family knowledge or interpretations of medical advice. Local postpartum advice often included how a woman should wash her breasts before feeding her baby as dirt on the mother's body could cause stomach infections in the baby. On occasions when babies were taken ill with stomach upsets older women would comment on how the mother must not have sterilized her breasts properly. The practice of washing breasts resembles very closely the public health advice given to women around bottle feeding and home hygiene. Doctors and nurses validate this belief often in the prenatal *platicas* (conversations) at public clinics and reinforce the moral notion of the mother's body as a source of contamination for the baby. Women also spoke of personality traits in mothers and emotional outbursts that could cause a mother's milk to turn bad, making the baby ill or interrupting milk flow and feeding. The sources of such understanding were various: from personal experience, public health messages, often dramatized in *telenovelas*, local ethno-methodologies and religious beliefs about purity and women's bodies.

Lupita

Like many young couples in the *barrio* Lupita and Diego's families knew each other very well and were closely linked through social roles and community. They both came from fairly middle-income Catholic families and they were relatively well educated compared to other families in the *barrio*. The three eldest children in Lupita's family had all studied at the university in nearby state capital Tuxtla Gutierrez; this is quite rare in the *barrio* and so it resulted in the family being well known throughout the *barrio*. Lupita's parents ran a busy general store on the high street and were a good source of knowledge about most goings on in the *barrio*. Although resident in the *barrio* at weekends Lupita worked in Tuxtla and spent the week there, travelling home on Fridays. Lupita had always worked in Tuxtla since studying at university there. The couple had a large loan they were paying off for their house and the secure job she had as a State government administrator was vital to keep up with the payments. Wages differ as much as by 50 percent between Tuxtla and San Cristóbal, and job security is rare in either city.

Her workload had not lightened during the pregnancy and she often worked from seven in the morning to ten at night Monday to Friday, and sometimes weekends, which prohibited her from getting home. Most free weekends were spent fixing up the new marital home, a small breeze block house on a plot close to her parents and in-laws in the lower part of la Orilla. Diego worked during the week in a paint shop and had a second job at weekends. The couple were accustomed to making the most of any time they had together, though Lupita admitted this did place a strain on the relationship. They began to argue a lot because Diego spent his wages going out drinking with friends whilst Lupita put all her spare cash back into the house. During their arguments he often told her 'You are away what am I supposed to do stay at home alone crying and waiting for you?' The couple had married against their parents' wishes and Lupita's mother also expressed concern over the pregnancy, arguing that the couple were not ready for the responsibility of a child.

Lupita, the second of four children, had fought with her mother for independence and often stated that she was overprotective and controlling. When I first recorded an interview with her when she was eight months pregnant, she spoke at length about her joy of becoming a mother:

> I've cried a lot because I've been alone [in Tuxtla], so it's very difficult, for example the first time I felt the baby move it was beautiful, but I was alone ... Now I worry about eating well. If I get stretch marks or not that's okay; it's nothing serious, they go away and if not so what ... Maybe it's a crazy idea I have but I feel like the baby is looking after me from the inside, or I don't know, as if he came to cure me of everything, all the anguish I had. Because of the colitis, I was nervous. I was hysterical all the time. Now I'm calm. Because I am pregnant, and I have him inside I'm very calm and I've always said that this baby came to make me better from the inside out ... [the pregnancy] has been wonderful, very beautiful.
>
> I told you how this baby came to help me prepare for many things. For example, sometimes I wake up in the night, but it's okay I still get up for work and I do everything I need to. I just go to bed earlier these days, I think I'm going to be run off my feet, but anyway I'll get on with it alone ... the love for your child, everything you have to do, for him to be okay and you also, I have to make sure I'm okay so that I can be there for him.

Lupita wanted to give birth in her maternal home to be close to family. She originally planned to give birth at her aunt's house using a local *partera* known to her mother and godmother. Although her mother and godmother knew the *partera*, Lupita did not meet her beforehand and received no prenatal attention from this *partera* in particular. The day that Lupita went into labour her godmother was out celebrating her *barrio*'s patron saint day and could not be found to track down the *partera* to attend the birth. Her private gyno-obstetrician, who she had seen for prenatal check-ups, would have attended her in the local public clinic, but she had recently moved cities and was not available. Lupita managed to arrange a new obstetrician just three days before she went into labour. She took the decision to go to a private clinic so that her mother could accompany her during the birth. 'I couldn't bear going to the regional', she later explained, 'I felt really vulnerable and I needed to have someone with me. I knew if I turned up to the regional I would have been alone because they don't let anyone in with you'.

After six hours of labour Lupita had an emergency caesarean section at a cost of 30,000 pesos plus extra treatment for the baby. Lupita stayed in the private clinic for three days after the birth and then went to her aunt's house in order to begin her *cuarenta días*. Faced with a large medical bill to pay, Diego took on some overtime at work. He visited Lupita most evenings before either returning home alone or staying at his mother's house. Due to her employment, Lupita was entitled to twelve weeks' maternity leave which enabled her to complete her *cuarenta días* in San Cristóbal.

In 2013, almost two years after the birth of her son Mateo, I interviewed Lupita about her postpartum experience. Her life had changed significantly since our first recorded interview. Around one year after Mateo was born, Lupita and Diego separated. Problems, in part caused by balancing her job in Tuxtla and married life in San Cristóbal, and Diego's reluctance to curb his drinking and partying, had led to him eventually returning home to his mother. Lupita continued to manage her job and lone motherhood in Tuxtla during the week, returning at weekends to the couple's house in la Orilla. She hired a girl to help with childcare, domestic work and ultimately companionship and was going through an on and off battle with solicitors to obtain regular child maintenance from Diego. During the interview she reflected on how the postpartum period could have affected her marriage:

> So, as I said [after the clinic] I went to my aunt's house. It was uncomfortable very uncomfortable. If I have any more children, I'm going to go back alone to my own house! I would wash the [section] wound. When I bathed, I would wash it and my aunt helped me to dry because I didn't have bandages or anything but they did bind me. First, they buy a venda (wide strip of cotton), very tight, a normal one, one of these about 30cms wide and then they put a body sock and then the *faja* (girdle). It was cotton the one I had because there are others that are made from polyester but they make you itch. So, I had one made from cotton. And well, I could only drink *atoles*, eat chicken and nothing else, *atoles* and chicken. Because of the *faja*, it was so tight I could hardly breath and I couldn't eat, my food would get stuck in my throat ... I said to my mum 'Please take it off!'... I didn't have any milk at first.
>
> For the first eight days, [the nurse] said I couldn't feed because of the medication after the caesarean section. They had given me antibiotics. My milk hadn't dropped so [my aunt and my mother] gave me an herb bath. There were a lot of herbs *juncia, medallon, eucalypto, arnica,*

la azucena de chamula and I don't remember what else. It was very funny because I remember that Mateo was lying down nearby and they started to pour the hot water over my back, they put you in a bath with the herbs and they pour the water over you. It's very hot, it burns it's so hot, but it was funny because suddenly drip, drip it started then drip, drip, drip quickly. So, they said, 'Bring the baby' and they took Mateo's clothes off and put him in the bath with me and he started to feed and from then on it was fine ... Also, because they didn't let me do anything with the baby, for example when I wanted to bath the baby alone I had to lock the door, because they would arrive and be like 'Leave it, leave it I will see to the baby'... I couldn't change him, bathe him. For example, there were times in the early morning or the middle of the night when he cried and suddenly my aunt was in the room 'What happened, what's wrong with him' 'I don't know, he's crying I think he's hungry' 'No, give him to me' and whoosh, she'd disappear with him! There was my aunt, my mum, my suegra and anyone else who wanted to come, there were too many women...

[Diego] stayed with me sometimes but sometimes he went out or he would say he was very tired, and he'd go and sleep at the house. I was twenty days in my aunt's house, I couldn't cook or do anything I was very uncomfortable because Diego would arrive after work and wanted to eat but sometimes my aunt hadn't made the food and I couldn't move a lot. It's not that I couldn't move it's that they wouldn't let me. They would say, 'No hija', but I felt fine because I would walk up and down stairs without problem, but my aunt would be like 'No, no leave it to me, I'll do it' and so Diego would say 'You know what, I'm going to eat with my mum' and he would leave me with the baby.

After these twenty days I went to my mum's house and it was the same. My mum would make Diego's food, but it was complicated because she made what she could and when he wanted it, whilst I was with the baby. Like I said they didn't let me see to the baby much and it got to a point where I'd had enough because they wouldn't let me do anything, I couldn't see to him. If I went to clean his belly button, they would say 'no, you're doing it wrong'... After the cuarenta dias was up I went straight home to my house. By that time Diego had said to me 'okay that's enough we need to go home'. We went home and it was much better, I felt a lot better because I could see to the baby and do things in my own house. I felt much better, free. I felt more sure of myself because all the time they would tell me what to do and how to do it and in my house it was just me and the baby.

Embodying Transformations

> Upon becoming a mother, one returns to, remembers, and relives one's early intense experiences of being with one's mother ... This is because the mother's relation to a new baby is immediately corporeal, sensuous, tactile, and non-verbal ... The sensory experiences unique to this relation ... arouse in the mother varying levels of memory of her preverbal bodily past. (Stone 2012b: 135)

Both Carlita and Lupita's narratives shed light on the significance of home postpartum care in reproducing and producing maternal practices that are socially constituted and individually experienced. These narratives also reveal how techno-scientific models of risk that first appear during pregnancy and birth continue throughout the postpartum period to shape women's lives as modern citizens and good mothers. If we pay attention to the way in which new mothers feed, comfort and cradle their babies in the postpartum environment, it reveals shared dispositions and examples of bodily learning that help to explore how women develop as mothers based upon a notion of instinct. Conceptually, I understand the *cuarenta días* environment to be an intersubjective milieu of developing embodied knowledge and a meshwork of human interaction consisting of 'entangled lines of life, growth and movement' (Ingold 2011: 63). In this way analysis of the *cuarenta días* focuses on forms of power and agency that interrelate in an environment with specific and temporal boundaries in relation to bodily practices. Within these temporal boundaries, growth in the form of transformation of self takes place, 'in part moulded through the superimposition of readymade structures' (Ingold 1998: 26). '[R]eal humans, however, grow in an environment furnished by the presence and activities of others' (Ingold 1998: 27). The type of bodily and social transformation of self that takes place during the postpartum period is wholly reliant upon who is providing the care and where it is taking place. In this sense embodiment is one and the same as the development of the body as-organism in its environment – socially constituted and individually experienced.

The *cuarenta días* is a particularly good subject for exploring how maternal knowledge is learnt and internalized through intersubjective and 'intersensory states for which we have no common language' (Sacks 2005: 33). Anthropological theories of embodiment and sensory ethnography have helped me to think about Mexican postpartum environment and practices.[2] Carlita and Lupita's postpartum experiences provide a way to consider ideas about embodiment as having multiple potentials, as opposed to a binary split between fleshy, environmentally incorporated processes and more abstract notions of inscription and being-in-the world. The physical and conceptual boundaries created through the practice of the *cuarenta dias* provide a temporal environment in which competing cultural metaphors of the body intersect with interpretations of risk and constructions of maternal identity. New mothers find themselves in an inbetween space where interpretation of risk is dependent upon the importance of being a good mother in the eyes of the state and clinical practitioners or adhering to intercultural norms of mothering. In the narratives struggles over the meanings of maternal bodies and practices are present which bring about questions concerning the role of embodiment in orchestrating objective social outcomes.

Throughout the *cuarenta días* transformations take place that begin to shape women's understandings of their bodies during recovery. Two transformations arise in both Carlita and Lupita's stories. The first is the importance of binding the abdomen (*fajarse*) and its significance in terms of embodying local biologies and gendered expectations. The second transformation is when the maternal body, no longer occupied by an infant in utero, becomes a site of conflict and a threat to the health of the newborn. The vulnerability of mother and child to illness and death caused by *aire frio* (cold air), *mal de ojo* (evil eye) or other type of contamination are taken very seriously. Thermal dynamics are deeply rooted in Mexican illness belief systems and can be found both transnationally and locally (Palazuelos and Capps 2013). The hot-cold dichotomy inherent in local thinking represents a complex system of understanding and interacting with the world that has been influenced by history and is reinforced through important social relations. Definitions depend upon who you are speaking to but in general it is a belief system based on the principle that health is maintained when the body is both internally balanced and externally harmonized with the natural world and society (Palazuelos and Capps 2013).

Aire frio provides the largest threat to postpartum mother and newborn and all preventative practices are focused upon creating and maintaining bodily and environmental warmth. Within this belief system from birth babies are understood as cold and are deemed not to be able to retain enough heat to survive on their own. 'Its lungs are simply not ready to defend against the air', Doña Reina explained to me. As the baby develops during the initial *cuarenta días* it will become stronger and develop a better ability to retain heat. For women, the postpartum body is left cold, open and susceptible to physical and spiritual illness. The concept and embodiment of thermal dynamics plays an intrinsic role in how the senses shape and inform action in local postpartum practices. The theme of vulnerability and openness intersects with notions of increased susceptibility to negative vibrations (caused by *mal de ojo* or the negative emotions emitted by others) which in turn can cause illness or mental distress to mother or infant. Awareness of these thermal dynamic beliefs brings a cosmological interpretation to the women's actions and demonstrates how local biologies contrast and converge with universal obstetric knowledge about postpartum healing phases. The context of thermal dynamics in local belief systems demonstrates the ways in which people understand transformation as inseparable from their physical environment.

I have identified three main elements of postpartum practices in the *barrio* homes in San Cristóbal: 1) the importance of hot and cold; 2) the necessity of confinement during a specific period of time after giving birth; and 3) the vulnerability of mother and baby in this period. These three elements converge with the beliefs around thermal dynamics which are also deeply rooted in local Mayan cosmology. The close proximity and shared social spaces between Mexicans (many of whom in Chiapas share mixed heritage over generations) means that it comes as no surprise that cosmological and environmental understandings appear across ethnic groups. The Tzotzil people traditionally believe that everything in the universe is thought to contain a different quantity of heat or dynamic power (Classen 2005: 149). Steam baths or *temazcal* (sweat lodges), along with the use of medicinal herbs, are used to restore heat to the woman's body after birth, to promote lactation and to restore and maintain the reproductive organs following birth (Groark 1997). The warmth of the steam bath, for the Tzotzil women, is considered essential to the physical and spiritual wellbeing of both mother and child. In the period immediately following birth the Indigenous *partera* will enter the *temazcal* with the mother to help facilitate postpartum recovery and the baby will be brought to the mother to benefit from the heat (Groark 1997; Katz 1996). Though it is rare for houses in la Orilla to have a *temazcal* built in the patio, herbal steam baths are carried out in postpartum bedrooms using tin baths and hot water boiled on the kitchen stove (as we saw with Lupita). Marking the transition from *dando luz a la vida* (to give birth, translated literally as giving light to life) to actual motherhood involves binding the abdomen tightly in order to close the body.

After bathing, the mother's abdomen will be tightly bound with a wide strip of cotton (*venda*) and then with a shop bought girdle called the *faja*. She will continue to wear the *faja* for the duration of the *cuarenta días*, only taking it off to wash.

In Chiapas (and across Mexico) families understand the postpartum body as being open and vulnerable to external forces such as *aire frio* and infection. These beliefs manifest physiologically in the openness of the uterus and cervix after birth, whether from vaginal birth and/or the open wound of both uterus and abdomen after a caesarean section. The notion of the body being open and vulnerable lasted for the *cuarenta días* period, usually also around the time that vaginal bleeding stopped. However, binding often continued for up to six months post-birth. According to the women I have spoken to in Chiapas, binding the abdomen has a variety of purposes including closing up the uterus, healing incision wounds and returning a body to its pre-pregnant state. The practice of binding signifies a return to the mundane and domestic life of a woman and is an embodiment of expected gender roles. Binding allowed women to return to duties around the home within or soon after the forty-day period. With everything held tightly in place they could pick up other children, shopping or heavy loads of washing without causing a hernia. Women's explanations about why it was necessary to bind straight after birth revealed much about local biologies and understandings about the internal workings of women's reproductive organs. Experienced mothers and grandmothers explained to me that binding was essential due to the 'looseness of the womb' and the 'floating organs' that were at risk of falling out if they were not bound into place. Women also saw binding as essential to healing caesarean section wounds, even when, as Lupita experienced, it caused a lot of pain and discomfort.

Younger mothers (generally those under thirty) spoke of binding as essential to flattening the stomach and pressing it back into shape. Many young women were concerned with physical appearance soon after birth. Pressure from the constant media coverage of national and international celebrities who appeared to get pregnant, give birth and reappear in an instant as their former selves contributed to younger women's attitudes to postpartum binding for cosmetic rather than physiological reasons. Like the assumptions made about the pregnant body, the postpartum body is a source of conflict in terms of how it can at once protect and endanger the newborn. This conflict is prevalent in both medical and social discourse where ideas about risk are not mutually exclusive but continuously intersecting.

Emotion, temperature, diet, illness (stomach upset, colds, pains) are all factors in the mother that can put the baby at risk during its first forty days of life outside the womb. Ethnotheories and beliefs about the continuing physical connection between mother and baby serve to validate how women were feeling. Medical professionals and families all use this local knowledge and these beliefs to intervene in and regulate postpartum bodies. The opportunity for external intervention inbetween mother and baby is very much present in the success and failure narratives of breastfeeding. The passing of milk from one body to another provides medical professionals with tangible evidence of the intimate connection between mother and baby that has the potential to be harmful.

There are stark differences between how difficulties with breastfeeding are dealt with at home and by medical professionals. For the women who observe it, the *cuarenta días* provides a vital period for new mothers to establish a milk supply and much care is taken straight after birth to ensure success in breastfeeding newborns. The beliefs and concerns about the risks and consequences of mothers' milk 'gone bad' were manifest in both lay and local biomedical knowledge practices, though the approaches to managing this and retaining the corporeal and emotional connection between mother and infant were in stark contrast. It is through the contradictory and indeterminate nature of medical discourse that competing cultural metaphors of the maternal body and mothers' milk exist and are negotiated. Rouse (2004) writes, in the context of competing bodily metaphors in the case of a dying child in the US, how universal discourses are often contradictory and indeterminate in practice. She contends that these contradictions open up a space for social contestation and, in her fieldwork, semiotic transition through the manipulation of social work and medical practice values. Rouse describes how marginalized individuals can employ a 'currency of ethics' in order to change the perceptions and practices of those who hold power in a situation. In the case of Carlita, though the doctors and the *partera* do not communicate, it is Doña Carla, mindful of the social significance of breastfeeding, who negotiates and interprets Alison's diagnosis in a way that incorporates the recognition and need to treat illness with the long-term necessity to breastfeed.

Local practices and maternal thinking consider mothers' milk and breastfeeding to serve a purpose that goes beyond nutrition. The women and men in the *barrio* are in agreement that infants should be breastfed for as long as is deemed necessary. In the postpartum period the health and nutrition focus of care is important in that the quality of milk is checked regularly by elder female relatives and *parteras*. It is common for women to maintain or improve the quality of milk by the mother drinking oat milk or *atole*. Different herbs such as fennel, spearmint, pine and eucalyptus, either consumed as infusions or inhaled through steam baths, are used to increase the flow of milk. The use of herbs and foods to help the milk supply continues throughout the breastfeeding lifecycle but is most intense during the initial postpartum period. The forty-day confinement, though often interrupted for various reasons, provides the opportunity for mother and baby to remain relatively protected from external (outside family) influences. It serves to retain or recoup the bond that began in utero. The confinement and intense support is evidenced to have a positive effect on breastfeeding retention and on the mental and physical wellbeing of the mother. At the same time, the efforts made to ensure a peaceful and protected environment for mother and infant, and the use of herbs, do suggest that mothers' milk is not always deemed of a sufficient quality and strength for a healthy baby. In this sense it is impossible to decipher whether this is a gradual impact of medicalized attitudes towards mothers' milk, particular in terms of strength and quality, though it is unlikely to be so simple.

The comments from women about the quantity and quality of milk – that it is not enough to fill the baby or it is too watery – do mirror the types of things that medical professionals tell women, who are encouraged to supplement with formula milk. It is a case of bolstering pre-existing beliefs as opposed to creating new ones. The environmental protection afforded to a new mother and her infant demonstrates the importance of emotional connection and mutual reliance in the process of recuperation. In this way breastfeeding and the flow of milk are part of a comprehensive system of beliefs that is deeply entrenched in sensory awareness. Thermal dynamics (notions of hot and cold), vulnerability and risk play an intrinsic role in how the senses shape and inform action in local postpartum practices. Overall, in the context of this chapter the postpartum practices show that though susceptible to contamination, mothers' milk can be made pure again. The emphasis in the home postpartum practices is on the bodily and sensual connection between mother and infant via breast, mouth and milk being paramount for the wellbeing of both.

Clinical and state attitudes to breastmilk and maternal bodies appear contradictory and disjointed at best. The strength of the Mexican state's efforts to project modernity through maternal bodies meets with techno-scientific models of risk so that responsibility and blame lay squarely at the feet of mothers. Medicalized reproductive care is part of the state apparatus for achieving modernity and as part of this medical authority is perceived as legitimate, privileged and consequential (Smith-Oka 2012). Other ways of knowing are therefore often dismissed and/or delegitimized (Jordan 1993; Sesia 1996). The narratives in this chapter show how local ways of knowing are not simply dismissed but manipulated to legitimize physicians' interventions in postpartum and feeding practices. This is, however, challenged by women's authoritative knowledge which lies within more comprehensive and holistic maternal belief systems. The decision to interrupt semi-exclusive feeding or to cease and replace with formula depends upon the wider social network of the mother. Continuation of breastfeeding is strongly connected to the strength of family networks and whether aspects of women's reproductive health and caregiving are deemed to be outside the realms of medicine.

The Mother as Novice

In la Orilla the *cuarenta días* postpartum quarantine comes into being through close family ties, spiritual beliefs, traditions and reconnection to the natal home (in most cases). It is also a place where external medical influence, empirical midwifery, modernity and economy interweave in a similar way to the out-of-hospital births discussed in Chapter two. The *cuarenta días* is practised whether a birth takes place at home or in a clinic and regardless of how a woman gives birth. It is often interrupted for working women and lone mothers who lack family networks for support and therefore its practice is closely linked to political and labour economies. The *cuarenta días* provides an important focus for the study of local maternities because it is a point of postpartum convergence for all types of birth outcomes. Analytically, it is a way of bringing together women who share the same moral culture but who within this take various paths into giving birth. It is a space where internal and external life entangles to create a particular sensory learning experience for the new mother. It is quite clear in the *cuarenta días* environment who are the experts in postpartum health and mothering. Older female relatives and the *partera* pull rank in their duties to the new mother and baby while a particular kind of passive behaviour is expected from the mother. Under closer inspection the performance of passivity in the new mother makes her complicit in the construction of a maternal identity that works to strengthen the social value of dependency on others. Although the two narratives chosen here are from first-time mothers, similar postpartum routines and compliance are required of women having second, third or fourth babies where established support networks are available. This means that women of low- to middle socio-economic status who live in multi-generational households are well placed to reproduce this form of postpartum care routine. Great emphasis is placed by senior family members such as Doña Carla or Doña Reina on the importance of the *cuarenta días* as an essential period of protection. These women understand the *cuarenta días* as an opportunity for experienced mothers, knowing what hardships lie ahead, to provide a further gestation period for the mother-baby unit and a time for the new mother to gather strength.

Aside from the health implications, there is the supposition that the new mother is still very much a novice and not ready to take on sole responsibility for her child. In this sense the *cuarenta días* is a temporal breathing space between pregnancy and actual motherhood. It provides an opportunity for a woman to learn the basics of childcare behind closed doors and with an abundance of advice. For women with strong family networks, they will rarely be left alone with their child as it develops up to school age. Often in the joint care of grandmothers, aunts, siblings, cousins or hired domestic help for many hours during the day, mothering comes under the definition of communal practice in *barrios* like la Orilla. As demonstrated in Lupita's narrative, this can create tension between social and individual values on care giving. In many ways the *cuarenta días* introduces the new mother to the reality that birth itself does not denote passage into experienced motherhood. She will remain very much a novice in maternal matters until she produces further children or even becomes a grandmother herself.

The shared belief that mothering is not a solitary practice became very apparent to me during my residence in la Orilla due to the daily concern expressed by my friends and neighbours in regards to the absence of my husband. I often explained that he was away working and looking after my son in England, to which they expressed further concern until I added that my own mother was taking care of them. My neighbours always conveyed a sense of relief when my mother-in-law and other female relatives or friends came to visit. Doña Reina in particular was always commenting, 'Your daughters are company, but a mother shouldn't be on her own'.

These postpartum and nurture practices focus on 'mothering the mother', as much as caring for the newborn baby. There are interlinking elements of care, protectiveness and control that reproduce ways of mothering through generations. Taking the mother and baby back into the maternal home environment for birth and postpartum care reinforces that a woman is still very much a daughter who has not been abandoned by her own family. Or in the case of my neighbours Lila, Magali and Josefina, who all moved into their mother-in-law's households when pregnant and stayed on postpartum, it demonstrated that they were accepted as daughters by their new families.[3] In such a tight knit community like la Orilla I did not witness any mothers living alone and unable to complete the *cuarenta días*. There were of course lone mothers in the sense of the fathers being absent but in the *barrio* they lived amongst family. In the wider city there were many women, usually rural migrants, who alone in the city received no postpartum care other than the post-birth hours in hospital and who were often back at work within days of giving birth. These women are generally viewed as outsiders and are pitied by the local women and midwives and abused by hospital staff as irresponsible mothers. The *cuarenta días*, understood as a distinct set of learning practices, reveals how dependency on others remains an important social value for *barrio* families. In this way new mothers embody a collective resistance to a state modernity project that promotes independence from family and community as a core socio-economic value.

Many women I spoke to about the *cuarenta días* defended it as necessary and were grateful for the time to recover and bond with their child. For others, like Lupita, it was a stifling and frustrating experience that led to them locking themselves away to be alone with their babies. Recognizing the role of emotion is essential to understanding the meshwork of interactions and relationships at play during the *cuarenta días*. Learning and embodying the language of mother love is implicit to the creation of the maternal subject in the early days of motherhood (and beyond). Lupita and Carlita understand the social necessity of becoming a good mother and that this is, in part, displayed through a language of emotion.

Mexican society stereotypes motherhood as a natural desire in women. Society places emphasis on belief in a maternal instinct and love that guide women towards being good mothers. There is a collective consensus that a woman feels her way through motherhood using the child as her guide. I attempted on numerous occasions in groups of mothers to pose the question (in various forms), 'How do you know how to mother?' In group conversations I always received a unanimous answer in regard to 'instinct'. Focus on postpartum care, however, reveals that the training in the basics of feeding, bathing, clothing and comforting that takes place in the *cuarenta días* demonstrates transference of core social values via bodily practices which are expressed as natural (instinct) when they are clearly culturally constituted. Here new mothers have an embodied sensibility to social norms and exhibit awareness and social control in their modes of attention to others (Rouse 2004).

Aside from the benefits of creating the mother-baby bond and getting to grips with the basic caregiving skills, the *cuarenta días* is positively associated with reducing stress in the new mother. A *crisis posparto*, as in the clinical diagnosis of postpartum depression, is not a phenomenon recognized by most women in the *barrio*. The existence of postpartum stress or 'baby blues' is mentioned occasionally and is understood to happen as a result of not adhering to the rest period or not receiving enough social support. This indicates that those who practise the *cuarenta días* rest period see it as making an important contribution to the overall wellbeing of the new mother and her transition into motherhood. This attitude mirrors existing studies that associate the *cuarenta días* with establishing milk supply and confidence in breastfeeding, and with decreasing chances of postpartum depression (Waugh 2011; Martinez-Schallmoser et al. 2005; Niska 1999). Lack of recognition of postpartum depression or other postnatal mental health problems does not equate to their non-existence (as Bety's narrative demonstrated in Chapter Two). Collective silence on a subject can just as well indicate that it is a social taboo as opposed to it simply not existing. Children and pregnancy (or the foetus that results from the pregnancy) are socially described as being a blessing from God – meaning there are few culturally appropriate spaces for women to express unhappiness or inability to cope. The coming together of close female relatives to take care of the new mother and support her in making a connection to her baby can be read as a way of acknowledging her vulnerability to stress without having to openly speak of it.

Negotiating Relationships

The *cuarenta días* is very much a women's space where relationships between mothers or close female kin and daughters are central. The presence of close and extended female family members forms a further protective barrier around the mother and baby. The exclusion of fathers from this period is often further underpinned by the temporary return to the maternal home. In postpartum care a woman is meant to abstain from sexual intercourse for the duration of the *cuarenta días* as her cold body is susceptible to illness. Indigenous thermal dynamics understand penetrative sex and mixture of bodily fluids, characterized as heat, as a potential risk to the woman's health, resulting in dryness and diarrhoea (Katz 1996: 103). In Indigenous cosmology sperm is thought to carry a bad risk to the quality of milk. Though I did not hear this type of reasoning whilst I lived in the *barrio*, the adherence to some form of quarantine period for most new mothers, which involves a physical separation from partners, suggests that sexual activity in this period is something to be avoided. It also implies that a woman is not always able to negotiate abstaining from sex due to established gender power differentials. The absence of male relatives and partners from the postpartum environment and presence of senior female relatives ensures that a new mother remains protected from sexual advances. Though it was rare that I spoke about sex with women in their postpartum period, the way in which the new mothers were cocooned during the *cuarenta días* suggested that measures were in place to protect them from intimate contact with anyone apart from the baby.

Though I witnessed few complaints from men during this time I was only privileged to very brief discussions with new fathers, and so was unable to gain any real insight into their opinions on the matter. It was possible, however, from conversations with women to see that many new young fathers turned to their own mothers during the postpartum period in search of some mothering for themselves. A shift in interpersonal boundaries and personal space during the *cuarenta días* had to be further negotiated when the couple returned to the marital home or bedroom (if living within the parental family home). These new boundaries often continued with the mother tending to co-sleep with the baby during the first six months to a year or more. It is impossible to say whether the rules for abstinence and isolation during the *cuarenta días* have any significant impact on couples' relationships in the long term. The introduction of children in itself brings changes to any relationship and defined roles are just as likely to help in such situations as they may hinder. Women place emphasis on how the maternal body contributes to the survival of a baby in the first few weeks of life. Within this context paternal bodies, after the donation of sperm, are effectively defunct and during the postpartum period a man's sexual energy can put the baby at risk (Waugh 2011), hence the need for protective boundaries in the quarantine. Such bodily practices act to reaffirm set caring roles from the outset. Matthew Gutmann (1996) describes parenting in a low-income *barrio* in Mexico City as an ideological concern intimately connected to a practical one:

> A system of constraints is perceived by many such that infant care is routinely equated to maternal care ... For example, in a baby's first year, breastfeeding is more common ... This requires the mother's rather constant presence and establishes a fairly rigid division of labor from early on ... The body – in this case the man's inability to lactate – influences but does not in any sense dictate culture, yet the body is routinely used to justify and explain cultural forms. (1996: 75–76)

For young men caught between generations of paternal role defining and the contemporary image often portrayed in the media of the hands-on father as opposed to the distant macho stereotype, what they were actually supposed to do as fathers was a matter of some confusion. Whether their exclusion from the *cuarenta días* practices provides the opportunity to avoid caring responsibilities from the outset or whether it creates tension in the couple's relationship is a matter for further exploration. According to Lupita, 'It certainly didn't help a problem that already existed'.

Thinking about the senses, emotions and transformation in direct relation to environment and practices has wider implications for the understanding of embodiment in the context of maternity and learned bodily practice. The families' commitment to completing and maintaining the *cuarenta días* in la Orilla is a sign that it continues to form a significant part of shaping the early experience of motherhood. The local importance of adhering to the *cuarenta días*, whether in part or full, highlights a shared social value as well as an individual corporeal process of postpartum recuperation. Although not exempt from outside influence, the *cuarenta días* is an important part of the reproductive life cycle which has yet to come under the control of the state or be seriously modified via medical intervention. It is reliant on strong family networks, the need to protect mother and baby, and respect for knowledge of thermal dynamics. Within this external womb-like environment, state notions of modernity are contested and local maternities are reproduced. For young women it is a space where they are mothered and experience a gradual transition of self that is implicit in the maintenance of local maternal ideologies – and within which a form of collective agency occurs. This does not, however, translate to an individual freedom in the remaking of self. Instead, it results in a transition to motherhood that adheres to the norms and beliefs of what makes a good or good enough mother within the constraints of local ways of being.

Notes

1. Elements of Carlita's postpartum narrative derive from a previously published article: J. Murray de López, 'Maintaining the Flow: Medical Challenges to Breastfeeding and "Risky" Bodies in Mexico', *Medical Anthropology Quarterly* 33 (2019): 403–19.
2. For example, the writing on environment by Ingold (1998) and sensory embodiment by Csordas (1993), Sack (2005) and Rouse (2004). I find Ingold and Csordas a good juxtaposition due to Csordas' commitment to embodiment and Ingold's questioning of it along with his critique on agency.
3. In the cases of Lila, Magali and Josefina both households were dominated by men due to their mothers-in-law (Doña Perla and Doña Frida) only having sons. In these male-dominated households it is very common for the daughters-in-law to be welcomed (and protected) as daughters, as they are an essential help to the female head of household.

Chapter 6

SARA, BANIA AND LILA
GOOD ENOUGH MOTHERS

In short, to love a child is like being permitted to rise amongst the clouds of incense, until one reaches the pinnacle of self-sacrifice.

—Rosario Castellanos (Mexican poet),
'La abnegación: una virtud loca'

The good-enough mother ... starts off with an almost complete adaptation to her infant's needs, and as time proceeds she adapts less and less completely, gradually, according to the infant's growing ability to deal with her failure. Her failure to adapt to every need of the child helps them adapt to external realities.

—Donald Winnicott (British paediatrician), 'Mirror-Role of the Mother and Family in Child Development'

Being a mother is the most beautiful thing in this life because it is a blessing from God.

—Angela, 36 (mother, la Orilla)

In this second chapter on nurture, I am concerned with the wider social and political economic issues that shape motherhood for women in la Orilla. From the women's stories and my discussion of them, two related topics emerge. Firstly, I focus on the strength and limitation of women's individual agency when developing their maternal practices, their identity and the pressure to conform to established gender roles. Inspired by Nancy Scheper-Hughes' (1993) call for a pragmatics of motherhood and in its broadest sense Winnicott's (1967) notion of the good enough mother, I think about how new mothers 'create their own culture, but they do not create it just as they please or under circumstances chosen by themselves' (Scheper-Hughes 1993: 342). Secondly, I explore how women's agency and capacity for social and individual change are challenged in hierarchal societies where motherhood is valued as the most desirable attribute, and where a direct link is made between the capacity to bear and the capacity to rear. This ideological glorification of motherhood results in a state and societal rhetoric that ultimately maintains social hierarchies and restricts women's capacity to drive change. However, as I have demonstrated in previous chapters, the contradictions brought about by everyday practices as part of competing discourses can also open up ways for women to contest accepted norms and drive social change on more subtle levels.

A political economy of emotions and the trope of mother love that is universally applied to all women regardless of social status, age or ethnicity are woven into the fabric of this chapter. How women speak about being mothers, and moreover how they describe their relationships with their children and partners, is bound by a code that is shaped by inherited habits of thought and social imagination. The tropes of mother love are intricately connected with a form of divine status that mothers have traditionally been given in Mexican society, which places responsibility firmly in the hands of maternal subjects as moral regulators of children and partners alike. In this chapter the pragmatics and practicalities of mothering beyond babyhood show a more complex intersection and friction between maternal and female subjectivities that develop throughout the life course.

Amongst my neighbours in la Orilla there are two specific and common domestic situations that arise in terms of the lives of new mothers and which are directly related to the average age that women become mothers: firstly, women who move into their partner's parental home (living with the *suegra* – mother-in-law); and secondly *madres solteras* (lone mothers) who had remained in the family home or, less frequently, those who lived alone while remaining close by to family. These two categories differ in a practical sense and they are worth looking at separately with a focus on how transition is experienced, and how maternal subjectivity can be reconceived and individually constructed as both separate and simultaneously part of a continuously developing female subjectivity. Whereas Stone (2012a) asserts that we must not lose sight of what is specific about maternity, I would extend this argument to say that in the identification of maternal subjectivity, as distinct from female subjectivity, we must not lose sight of what is peculiar about the circumstances within which motherhood and nurture occur. In this sense my discussion in this chapter will situate the process of becoming a mother firmly in relation to the environment with a focus on types of separation which occur within it.

Though they also differ in their family and educational background, the women in this chapter are linked by the fact they all had unplanned pregnancies when they were under twenty-five. Unplanned pregnancies were common amongst the younger mothers I met in la Orilla and this reflects much about how relationships are conducted and the void between reproductive rights rhetoric, social values and everyday realities. Becoming pregnant in this way was a defining factor in their transition to early motherhood. For all the women emotional work had to be done to accept that their pregnancy was part of 'God's plan' and that it was something they wanted. As will become evident, they use the language and feeling rules of mother love as rooted in the divine to explain this transition to acceptance.

Madres Solteras

Unless they are closely linked through family connections, young couples tend to develop relationships away from the prying eyes of parents and older relatives. They manage this with the collusion of younger siblings and cousins who they are charged with looking after. An unplanned pregnancy is often what brings fledging relationships out into the open and a young couple under the spotlight. Of course, not all women become *madres solteras* at the reveal of the pregnancy test; many relationships are supported through the process and survive (as will be seen further on), and many other women find themselves abandoned, divorced or widowed much later in their maternal lives, resulting in a very different kind of experience. As my focus in this chapter is on the transition to early motherhood, I have decided to let the narratives of Sara and Bania guide the discussion on lone mothers. They faced pregnancy and motherhood without their partners, one due to abandonment and the other by choice. Their narratives reveal much about women struggling with expected and established gender roles, intersecting projects of modernity and daily economic survival. Exploring the conditions of lone motherhood 'questions the need for the stable married couple and the good mother ideology that champions the fulltime mother' (Bringas et al. 2004: 68; my translation) in the Mexican social imagination. These two women, albeit with very different tales to tell, were also significant in the fact they left the family home soon after their first children had been born. In la Orilla, as with other *barrios* in San Cristóbal, it would be difficult for both financial and cultural reasons for a lone mother (of any age) to leave the family home, yet occasionally women like Bania feel like they have no choice, or in the case of Sara the decision is made for them. Bania and Sarah provide a challenge to local ideas of mothering as communal practice, and in doing so they also gain a liberty of movement as women, that can come at a cost.

Sara and Bania were not friends; I often thought they should have been as they had a lot in common. They were both lone mothers, in their late twenties who were working hard to bring up their daughters in ways that challenged local convention. They knew of each other, as everyone in the *barrio* did, but they lived at different ends of the *barrio*, their families were not connected like most through blood or marriage, and so their worlds were apart. Sara was my immediate neighbour and the person I could hide nothing from. Our small yards were connected, and her two-storey house loomed over mine where she was privy to most of my everyday routines of mothering, laundry, mealtimes, occasional visitors and evening television viewing. She shared her house with her cousin Ruby, also a lone mother to ten-year-old Iván, but was mostly there alone with her youngest daughter Valeria as Ruby often worked away. Besides the obvious visual insight into my daily home life, Sara and I maintained an 'over the garden fence' friendship which generally consisted of *barrio* and town gossip and the ups and downs of parenting. I liked Sara on a personal level; she struck me straight away as being unusually candid about her family life and feelings about being a mother. Like other lone mothers I met living outside of their family home, she was very proud of the challenges she had faced and the way she was able to maintain her small family unit in the face of all the odds.

The metaphorical garden fence between her yard boundary and mine gradually served as a daily confessional from which she recounted her life and the difficult choices she had to make from the time of her first pregnancy. One morning as we stood watching over the girls playing, Sara told me about her eldest daughter Ana who lived with her mother at the lower end of the *barrio*. I was a little confused at first as she had never mentioned her before and I had assumed that Valeria was her only child. I asked her why she and Ana lived apart and she told me how she first got pregnant in her late teens and at that time had remained living at home with her mother, older brother and aunt:

> I got pregnant at nineteen and like always when you say you are pregnant they [the men] disappear and I was left alone ... It was a beautiful pregnancy, I lived with my mum and she had student lodgers at the time, they all looked after me a lot. After I gave birth things became more complicated because then I was a lone mother and my family are very strict.
>
> When Ana was about two years old I met Valeria's father and the problems started. I wasn't allowed to go out or have a life of my own because I had a child, but I mean I was twentysomething, about twenty-two years old which is still young. After a while I met someone else and I wanted to move in with him, they [her mother and aunt] took my daughter off me, my mum hit me and threw me out and because my mum had cancer at the time I didn't wanted to fight with her. I went to live with Valeria's father and his mother ...

Sara highlighted the social transition to mother that took her from one identity to another. Though she had given birth she remained unseparated from her baby in the sense that she must be seen to live only for the child. Leaving home in order to pursue a new relationship meant losing the right to parent her first child in any meaningful and emotional sense. In this situation as a young woman Sara was powerless against her own mother, who in this one act temporarily stripped her of her mothering status. Sara explained to me that her mother, a devout Catholic and embodiment of the abandoned *mujer abnegada* (self-sacrificing woman), held the belief that 'I shouldn't go out or speak to anybody, I shouldn't have a life'. Sara's father had left the home when she was a young child and like most women of her generation her mum had devoted her life to bringing up her children. It had not been an easy childhood and Sara was often left alone in the house whilst her mother ran errands or worked. 'She left me with this person, with that person. My dad was busy with his women and my mum with my brother. I remember or lots of people have told me that [when I was little] my food would be left by the door, one leg would be tied to the bed and the television switched on'. She told me that her mother refused to acknowledge that this had been the case and instead spoke of the sacrifices she had made for her children, as any good mother should.

Sara's mother's beliefs of what constituted a good mother led her to the drastic action she took by removing Ana from her. Sara described that time in her life as 'unbearable and suffocating' yet she often spoke about it pragmatic terms: 'Since she was born, she was with me, she came to work with me, she bathed with me, I would breastfeed her and she would sleep with me, that's why it was so sad'. In order to resist a traditional submissive mother role and defend her right to 'have a life' as a young woman, Sara was made to temporarily relinquish parental responsibility and redefine her role as a mother to Ana. Other grandmothers and aunts I knew who had taken or been given (unofficial) custody of children explained it within the rhetoric of self-sacrifice. Children were seen as 'better off' with grandmothers or aunts and young mothers were being 'given the chance' to pursue a career or marriage by being released from the obligation of mother work.

This early transition from a protected pregnancy period to a difficult and unstable early motherhood shaped how Sara understood herself as both a woman and a mother in modern-day Mexico. Although Sara had eventually split up with Valeria's father after he had an affair, and she had worked hard to rebuild the relationship with her own mother, she had never regained full custody of Ana. She had settled with moving back to the *barrio* in order to be close to Ana and attempted to parent her in the more practical aspects of her life she was able to control, but this was not without complication:

> I am the one who supports her [financially], her uniforms, school, between her father and I, but for example if I want to take her out, I get 'No, the girl is not coming'! It is my mum's sister, my aunt they call her *niña vieja* [old maid] like she's never married or had any children and she doesn't want to let go of my daughter. So, she really is the problem, but with my mum I don't get angry because well, where will it end? I try to remain calm...

Part of Sara accepting her role as 'absent mother' to Ana was to do with love and a protective need to 'do what's best for her' no matter how she may be viewed by other women as abandoning her child for a man. In resistance to her mother's maternal ideology, Sara wanted to parent her daughters differently in the hope that when she was older Ana would understand her actions and come to live with her: '[My mother and aunt] blackmail her emotionally and she feels bad, but I won't play that game, she needs to know I'm not that way'. She felt that by taking a different approach to lone motherhood she could show her daughters that her love allowed them to live more freely and that having children did not mean your life as a woman came to an end. The desire to parent differently from previous generations was a common theme arising in conversations I had with new mothers. This was not exclusive to women who felt estranged from their families and highlights the tensions within meanings of modernity and gender discourse. For many women, there was a conflict in the early transition to motherhood between wanting to 'do things differently' and being aware that in trying to do so they often unintentionally mirrored their own mothers.

The category of *madre soltera* comes into question as problematic when women's lives are placed under greater scrutiny beyond that of social and political rhetoric. Women in la Orilla rarely mother completely alone and despite the efforts of their own mothers and aunts they often continue to maintain on-off relationships with the fathers of their children and also find new partners. The label *madre soltera* takes on a false permanency that assumes a woman will always remain the sole principal carer of her child no matter how her personal relationships develop. It performs the act of stripping women of their sexuality and reinforces the ideal that the maternal role is defined by a level of self-sacrifice in a similar way that the title of widow does to other women. It fails to adequately represent the women I met and grates against the description they give of their own lives and relationships.

My friend Lupita's cousin Bania is a poignant example of this oversimplification of women's maternal lives. I saw Bania often when I went to visit Lupita on my supposed downtime from fieldwork. She was providing valuable emotional and practical support to Lupita during her separation and subsequent divorce from Diego. Educated in the capital alongside her cousin, Bania was outspoken and analytical about her position in society and role as a mother. One morning I was dropping my daughter off with Lupita while I went to record some interviews. Bania had stayed over the night before because Diego had taken to dropping by the house on his way home from the cantina. 'If she's on her own she'll just let him in', she said nodding towards Lupita, 'she never learns'. Lupita grimaced and shook her head: 'it's not like that, I just don't want to end up alone, it's alright for you, you chose to go it alone'. I asked Bania what she meant by choosing. She told me how she had left her partner soon after her first baby had been born and had lived alone as a *madre soltera* for four years until recently reuniting with him: 'I think I fell into some kind of depression. I split from my partner and went to live alone with my daughter. I wanted to show myself that I could do it alone, I think really I was just following what my own mother had done, I was stubborn'. Comparable to Sara's childhood, Bania often spoke of a lack of expression of love in her childhood as something she hoped to remedy with her own children:

> ...my mum tells me that when we were young she held us, kissed us, she showed us love, but I hardly remember, I just remember my mum shouting ... because my dad was absent, they fought a lot so my mum left with us, and then later she fell into alcoholism. Can you imagine? I said I would never be like that.

When she talked about becoming a mother, Bania often reflected upon how the breakdown of her relationship with her own mother and subsequently living her teenage years with her father had shaped her identity as a young woman and her ideas about mothering practices:

> We live in a patriarchal system where men rule and I was brought up to be more like a man than a woman ... when I started my periods it was my male friends who taught me what was happening, no woman ever explained it to me, that's why I felt closer to men than women. I knew that a man would look after me better than a woman. But then I became a mother and thank God because now I understand that as a woman, as a mother I can look after my children.

Bania interested me as a woman and as a mother who challenged convention in a social world where staying in an unhappy marriage was preferable to not being in a marriage at all. It was an everyday story to hear of a man leaving his wife for another woman, but Bania was the only woman I knew during my time in the *barrio* who had voluntarily left her partner to live alone with her daughter. This was made all the more significant by her partner coming from a 'good family' and being described (by other women) as a man who knew how to be a 'good man' in that he worked, did not drink and was not violent or abusive. Lupita once described her as *una loca* for giving it all up. Bania created a categorical distinction between object (child) and experience (motherhood) when she spoke about the negative impact of her unplanned pregnancy. She often wanted to stress that the 'trauma' she lived through during her initial unwillingness to accept motherhood was separate to how she felt towards her daughter. Using the vocabulary of mother love, she was able to describe how being unexpectedly thrown into motherhood had challenged everything she knew about herself and her world. She also spoke about how for her, it is her daughter as opposed to society or self who confirms her legitimacy as a good mother:

> I don't consider my daughter to be a mistake, because everything happens for a reason, I don't know if it was a message from God, from life or destiny but it happened for a reason. So, my experience with Lua caused drastic change in my life because at the time I was enjoying being free. I was twenty-one, young, independent and then suddenly I was a mother... it was the emotional change, the change to say whether or not I could or couldn't do things, thinking about what people would say about me, whether I should get married or not.
>
> All of this and also the physical changes that I just didn't feel ready for... It took a long time to accept the first baby, even after she was born I still didn't feel like a mother I felt estranged, I would stay looking at her for hours when she slept and think is this mine, did I make that, now what do I do? I would keep touching her to see if she was breathing. I think it was a combination of many things no? Obviously, my age, immaturity, well actually I think we are all immature with our first ... When I see her laugh or when she calls me mamá, when she hugs me and says I'm the best mum in the world, not because I tell her to say it but because there's an honesty, a sincerity in her words. Or sometimes there's no words and just hugs. This is when I know I'm doing okay that I'm becoming a mother.

Bania's self-imposed isolation from her partner, in-laws and family resulted in her feeling more in control of her maternal practices and she measured her successes (and failures) by her daughter's actions. When mother love was reciprocated it often validated the women's sense of 'motherness' and made them feel that they were making the separation they desired from their own experiences of childhood. Similarly, Sara was keen to construct relationships with her daughters that were very different from her relationship with her own mother. She once told me 'I like to be a child with her we watch cartoons, tell jokes and laugh. I am her mother, but we can also be friends'. Here is an example of how the constructed notion of unconditional maternal love is anything but; Sara shows she has a strategy in place. For her the giving of love is an exchange for the recognition that she is a good mother and capable of effecting change. By defining for herself (albeit from within a popular maternal discourse) what mother love is and should be used for, she is enforcing a particular ideal on her daughter. She is shaping how she will come to understand maternal love in the future.

Conflict and disciplining their children also served to validate who they were as women and as mothers. In his ethnography on Mexican fatherhood, Gutmann (1996) describes how mothers are the principal disciplinarians and instigators of physical punishments against children. This was often the case in the families I knew more intimately in la Orilla, though not in every home. When the *madres solteras* in the *barrio* spoke of disciplining their children, it was with little difference to how co-habiting mothers acted. The difference with the *madres solteras* who lived alone was that they were left to regulate their own actions away from the eyes of other family members. I found that younger mothers were more reflective in how they dealt with the consequences of lashing out. This resonated with media representations of modern families and a fashion for experts in the attachment theory, pop psychology approach to parenting that often appeared on daytime television. Both Bania and Sara spoke about how they unconsciously repeated the actions of their own mothers, particularly when they referred to the stress of parenting. But they also sought to remedy this by self-regulating and developing coping strategies to avoid lashing out. Lutz (1990) refers to this as rhetoric of emotional control common to hierarchal societies. She argues that to speak about controlling emotions is to engender the view of emotions as dangerous, irrational and in need of regulating. This then transfers onto gendered bodies who acquire the same attributes and forms of regulation. Sara was aware that being alone with Valeria could often lead to a conflict of emotions that spilled out into her maternal practices:

> ... Sometimes I notice that I'm sad and then she is sad, it's like your mood affects theirs, how you feel is how they feel. So, I try to stay calm so that she is calm ... I do hit Valeria, I don't hit her all the time, because neither is it the case I'm walking about with a stick, but yes sometimes she does some things ... I put her in her room and slam the door, I will be on one side crying and she will be on the other side crying as well. After she had calms down, I say, 'Ya te pasó?' and she will come out and say 'it's because I'm angry because my dad hasn't come'... We've started to talk a lot like that, if she feels angry about her dad then she tells me, and we talk ...

When Bania spoke about arguing or losing her temper with her daughter, she described a split in identity between her own self as a woman and her social role as a mother that helped her to justify her actions:

Practically you forget who you are as a woman and you just dedicate yourself to being a mum. But just the fact of being a mother, that doesn't mean you lose who you are completely but in terms of feelings, it hurts when you have to scold them, or hit them on the behind, but you have to do it as a mum, you have to guide them. I am a mother and okay sometimes I say or do something and I say to myself 'hey calm down, think about what you're doing because you're not acting with your heart', if I'm chasing after her with my shoe or something I think, 'Ay calm down!' Although I know that there must be a reason why the child is acting up and that it's better to talk than start hitting them but sometimes, perhaps I have some inner demons or something horrible and I start being like that …

It is self-explanatory that *madres solteras* who live alone will spend more time in isolation with their children. In many respects this made the initial transition to motherhood a very intense period for these women and they used an equally emotive language in which to describe the mother-child relationships that develop as a result. I had a fleeting conversation with Bania one rainy afternoon as we sheltered in a doorway waiting for our *combis*. I dutifully jotted our conversation down soon after as I always did. It was only months later that I looked at the notes again and saw that in a few comments she had managed to encapsulate the emotion work that takes place in the ongoing transition to motherhood:

What I've lived through has been worth it, becoming a mother to Lua. When I arrived home late from work and she would say 'Come on mum let's play a little' and I would be like okay just for a while. But in those five or six minutes I would be rolling around the floor laughing, it's that simple. It's so nice just for those ten minutes or so not to be worried about the next day or anything else. You have to live for the moment. Every night I try to give her many kisses and hugs and tell her how much I love her. If we argue about five minutes after I say let's talk about it, I don't want to feel bad because it hasn't been sorted. I feel empty [after we argue] like I've lost the connection with my daughter and I have to sort it out.

Living with the *Suegra*

In the *barrio*, tradition dictates that in the case of unplanned pregnancy or when a relationship becomes serious, a young woman moves in with her partner's family. Over the months I spent in the *barrio* I began to unpick the family networks between my neighbouring households and work out who was who in terms of blood and non-blood relation. I eventually came to understand that every household on my block housed two to three generations of son plus daughter-in-law family units. I became more curious about why this was and what it said about the continuation of established gender roles and family life in modern Chiapas. There is a gender bias associated with this subject in that attention is generally placed upon *la suegra* as opposed to *los suegros* (the in-laws). This relates historically to legal definitions of marital homes, as discussed in Chapter one, where the home and domestic labour were enshrined in family law as pertaining to 'one, and only one woman' per household (Varley 2000: 244). The underlying message insinuates that it is women who dominate the running of the home and who maintain the family structure. The presence of daughters-in-law in households was not new to me; it has long been a popular representation of urban Mexican families in both real life and fiction (see Franco 1989).

Outside of these representations I had never really thought about it from the point of view of the young couple and the young woman who becomes a mother under these circumstances. The negative gendered stereotype propagated in classic literature and popular media is of the daughter-in-law as a concubine in *la casa de la suegra* (the mother-in-law's house) where she constantly fights for her husband's affections and secretly desires to separate him from his mother. My midwife Cristina often commented on the problems that women had when preparing for motherhood: 'They don't say it as such but many of my clients insinuate in *consultas* that they wish their mothers-in-law would stop "sleeping with their sons", they say their husbands won't do anything in their defence'. Despite often hearing attitudes like this, and mindful of oedipal insinuations, I wondered if the mother-son (and daughter) relationships I had previously allowed myself to see were really as they appeared. Was there more to the over-bearing behaviour of women towards their sons and their partners?

As with most gendered stereotypes – *madre soltera*, widow, *la mujer abnegada, el macho* – there were expected behaviours attached that serve to perpetuate and embody myths. But such a reductionist view of a fixed identity bears little relation to everyday lives and relationships in la Orilla. The classic representation of the *suegra* (as with the *mujer abnegada*) is harmful to Mexican female identity and glosses over the complexities, similarities and differences of women and their intimate family relationships. Mother-son relationships depend far more on specific family history and individual personalities than on any overriding cultural imperatives. In my earlier naivety I had been seduced by the myth of the *suegra* and failed to see the wider significance for gender politics and power relations. When I got to know the families in my block on a more intimate level, I began to see how the situation worked for the family on distinct levels, most importantly economic, interpersonal relationships and shaping maternal practices. If the relationship was a good one the move into the partner's family home can be a positive one and provide a transitional experience with support. If the relationship is poor or abusive then there were problems, as Cristina had noted in her *consultas*. A good arrangement will provide a young woman with security, protection in her relationship and training in motherhood that may differ from her own or act to confirm what she already knows.

The young women who lived with their in-laws on my block appeared content and were loved by their new families. It is possible that their arrangements were successful because where there were children, they were dedicated to mother work (whether they were mothers or not) and contributed greatly to domestic labour within homes. 'I don't know what I would do without them', Doña Perla said when I called by her shop one morning, 'I was on my own with all men until they moved in, now with the extra help I can run the business and the house is seen to'. For my neighbours Doña Perla and Dona Frida, their daughters-in-law provided welcome female company and a gender balance to previously male-dominated households. It was not difficult to see the benefits for the *suegra* in having extra pairs of hands around the house, but I wanted to know more about how the young women experienced living outside of their own families as they became mothers for the first time.

As we saw in the last chapter, married women tended to return to the maternal home for the duration of the postpartum quarantine and this period was as much to do with the protection and bonding of female kin as it was to do with risk of illness and learning for new mothers. The scrutiny over new mothers' abilities was particularly intense during this period, with everything from maternal practices to bodily transformation overseen by more experienced women. Many of the younger women on my block had come to live with their boyfriends due to the outcome of unplanned pregnancies, and unlike the married women they did not return to their family home for postpartum recuperation. Their forty-day convalescence had been overseen instead by their *suegra* and sisters-in-law, with their own mothers visiting regularly. Ultimately, these women had arrived at a decision to stay with their in-laws during this period, they were certainly not sequestered against their will, and so questions arise as to how their transition to motherhood was shaped by the experience. Were they able to exert more agency in how the baby was cared for? Did they achieve a more adult status in the household, or did they remain still very much in girl status within the household gender hierarchy? And in relation to paternal practices, were the fathers better included in the initial transition to parenthood?

One September afternoon after around seven months living in the *barrio*, I was finally able to speak to Lila. She is the daughter-in-law of Doña Frida and mother to the much doted upon baby Estrella. Doña Frida and her family lived in a large house made up of several extensions built up over the years. The plot of land originally belonged to Frida's father Don Juan and different sections have been given to his children as the family has grown. Don Juan and Doña Rosa still lived in the main part of the house with Frida's brother Hernán, his wife and their two children. Doña Frida, her husband Don Rogelio, four sons, two daughters-in-law and granddaughter live in the right-hand annex of the original concrete and adobe house. With so many young residents, it was the most *alegre* (happy) household on the block, with the sounds of *musica ranchera* or thumping *cumbia*, family debate and laughter floating out through windows and spilling out into the air from early morning to late evening.

Doña Frida ran numerous enterprises from the side entrance to her house and she was the 'go to' woman whenever you ran out of cheese, eggs or sweetbread. In the late afternoons and evenings, she set up stall at the front of her house selling corn on the cob dripping with mayonnaise, chilli and grated cheese, *chayote* boiled to within an inch of its life and, much to my daughter's delight, popcorn and chilli sweets. It was on these afternoons that the smell of the corn and *chayote* would lure me out of my cabin, and I would sit chatting with Doña Frida and her family until the evening temperature dropped and she scolded me for having the baby outside so late. It was also on these occasions that I was able to chat with the men and get some idea of the part they played in family life.

Lila was common-law wife to Doña Frida's second eldest son Roger, and they had been seeing each other for about a year when

Lila fell pregnant. At the time she was nineteen and working in a hotel in the city centre. Early on in her pregnancy she moved from her parent's house to live with Roger and his family. I very rarely saw Lila alone outside the house and only occasionally saw her in the sole capacity as mother to Estrella. Being aware of family hierarchies, I approached Doña Frida to ask permission to speak alone with her daughter-in-law. She agreed without hesitation: 'I'll send her over when she's finished feeding the baby', she responded. About an hour later when Lila knocked on my door I felt very conscious that she had arrived under duress but she was quick to reassure me that she was happy to talk. I wanted to find out what it was like to become a mother in such a lively household far away from her own family home. In order to find some clarification and deeper perspective on relationship dynamics, I began by asking her why so many women left their families and moved in with their in-laws: 'Here they say that when a man wants to be responsible he should take the woman home to live in his house. That's why I came to live here'. Hearing this opened up a new way of thinking about young couples and what moving in with the in-laws symbolized to the nearby community. It highlighted that in many cases it was a necessary move to make if the reputation of the young man and woman (and therefore their families) were to remain intact. I asked her to tell me more about when she found out she was pregnant and what she felt about it:

> When I found out I was pregnant it was difficult because I saw when my sisters got married very young that it was a lot of work, that they were really still young and I felt the same when I got pregnant. I thought 'what am I going to do'? I didn't know how I was going to face up to it alone but then I told my partner and he said that he would support me. My mum was really angry with me when I told her but my *suegra* welcomed me in she treats me very well. I felt horrible because I didn't feel very secure in myself as it wasn't planned, but everything happens for a reason though at first, I was very scared. When I first went to get the pregnancy test the doctor asked me if I wanted to [have an abortion] she said that she would charge me so much and well I did think about it. I did think that maybe it was for the best if I didn't go through with the pregnancy but then I thought that I couldn't, that I would have the baby. My husband helped me see that it was a blessing from God, and it had happened for a reason. So, I started to enjoy the experience like any other pregnant woman, I started to dream about being a mother. I was ready to meet her I was very excited ... [The doctors] told me if I

didn't look after myself I would miscarry so I focused a lot on that and looked forward to meeting her ...

Like all families in the *barrio* Lila's family and her in-laws are practising Catholics and although she did not find being offered an abortion a problem in terms of recognizing it as a right to choose, the dominant shared belief that children are a blessing from God influenced her final decision to stay pregnant. I asked her how her pregnancy had been and how she had been supported during this period and when she went into labour:

> I had prenatal care in the local free clinic from around four months until nine months and my *suegra* took me to see the *partera* every month to make sure everything was okay. My *suegra* said I should give birth with the *partera*, but I was too scared to do it at home, I was scared so I wanted to give birth in the local clinic but they kept sending me home, they said I wasn't ready yet. My *suegra* gave me the option to go to a private clinic where they could check *mis dolores* [contractions] give me something and have the baby there. We spoke to my *suegro* and he said they would take me if that's what I wanted and so I went to the private clinic ...

Though it is clear from Lila's narrative that Doña Frida oversaw the antenatal care decisions, it does appear she was acting out of care rather than control. Doña Frida took Lila's fears and feelings into account and she was able to decide to give birth wherever she felt safest. The act of providing her with access to a private clinic is significant as it involves a much higher cost than the local *partera* or the public clinic. That her in-laws were willing to do this without question demonstrates the level of affection and responsibility they felt towards her. After giving birth Lila returned to Doña Frida's house where she completed her forty-day quarantine and was given the same care and attention that mothers and grandmothers give to their own daughters in the postpartum period. The postpartum period was as challenging for Lila as for any new mother with struggles and doubts over her abilities and niggles concerning the changes to her body:

> After the birth I suffered a lot, I had a lot of tears and I had stitches, but they came apart. The stitches hurt a lot and I suffered. But everything else was fine, here [at home] I was able to recuperate with support. I didn't have a lot of milk in the first days. I felt that my baby wasn't getting enough, she cried a lot and so I knew I didn't have a lot. There was milk but it was very watery. I used formula and they said that I

should take *noche buena* [hibiscus], I took some and my milk came but I felt very dizzy. It was a woman who lives here nearby who told me. So I took it and got very dizzy, coconut water helped as well and also oat milk. But I never had lots of milk it's like water still, it's not white like milk. My *suegra* said that it has to be really white to be any good ... When I came home after the birth they bathed me in herbs to close up the body and bound me. My *suegra* used a *faja* made from cotton. I wore it for about two months, for the whole forty days at least but I still have a tummy and lots of stretch marks. To be honest I'm not happy with my body, I feel chubby, I look down at my stomach and I don't like it. After the birth I felt awful, I felt really fat and I didn't like it. My husband says that I'm fine, that I'm not fat. He says I look better now. My *suegra* says that it is not a game having children and that your body changes. Even my periods aren't the same, I haven't had a proper period since I gave birth six months ago but my *suegra* she says that it's normal.

Undoing Fixed Identities

With my use of the narratives in this chapter I have sought to undo the notion of a fixed maternal identity. In doing so I hope to draw attention to specific questions surrounding childrearing as a practice charged with great social significance that is yet paradoxically experienced subjectively. Historically, in Mexico the idea that good motherhood and good womanhood are synonymous has dominated cultural representation and social thought (Sanders 2009). In the following paragraphs I will consider the ways in which these ideas prevail and also how they are challenged through the production of local modernities. By relating my ethnographic material to combined theories of maternal transition and emotion, I will return to the arguments I raised in the introduction concerning the pragmatics of motherhood and women's agency and capacity for social and individual change. To provide an analytical framework from which to develop my argument of the aforementioned, I will use the following three observations made from Oakley's work on the institution of motherhood and transition to motherhood in industrialized societies (1979, 1980):

1. The idealization of motherhood and its ramifications constitute the greatest problem for women in industrialized societies.

2. The institution of motherhood demands that women mother by instinct and their mothering be a selfless act

relating to the creation of others. In industrial society the notion of instinct has been naturalized and promotes a widespread belief that it qualifies women for childbearing and childrearing alike.

3. There is a pervasive ambivalence that motherhood is expressed in the combination of ideological glorification and actual socio-economic discrimination. Encompassed within this there is a falsehood in gender equality perpetuated by the state (via rights discourse and legislation) that acts as a smokescreen for the everyday lives of women.

Though Oakley's work is based upon a sociological ethnography and analysis of transition to motherhood in 1970s UK, I find that many of her arguments resonate with my own observations in la Orilla, and with Mexican feminist discourse on maternity, womanhood and modernity (Castellanos 1992; Lamas 2001; Palomar 2004; Bringas et al. 2004; Guerrero Menses 2004; Gonzalez Ávila 2005). Though I draw from cross-cultural feminist perspectives throughout this book the application of local feminist thought (which is in itself hybrid) can advance a wider understanding of transition to motherhood in Mexico and offer a critique of maternalist social policy from within a cultural context. Jolly (1998) writes how Asian and Pacific feminists have embraced the maternal subject position, in part to distance themselves from what are perceived as anti-family tendencies in Western feminism. Castellanos echoes this standpoint, arguing 'if we propose to create an authentic feminism that is above all effective, we have to move away from the position of others' (1992: 288; my translation).

Mexican feminism has wrestled with the maternal subject in its efforts to challenge the state, institutional and medical constructs, whilst trying to move the focus onto reproductive health politics, gender, class and ethnic distinctions, and on deconstructing the meaning of motherhood in contemporary Mexico. Mexican feminist thought uses the maternal subject as a referent object that goes beyond individual bodies to permeate gender relations in every aspect of Mexican society – therefore giving questions of maternal identity and practices a broader scope beyond the mother-woman dichotomy. Some Mexican feminists have presented the argument that the question of maternal policy is better approached as a gender issue to make policy more effective and to highlight more efficiently continuing inequalities (Gonzalez Ávila 2005; Palomar

2004). Highlighting the transition to motherhood for lone mothers and new mothers living in matrilocal, multigenerational homes contributes to Mexican feminist debate in a way that juxtaposes distinctly female bodies with a politics of parenting that is inherently gendered.

The way that mothering is understood as communal practice in la Orilla (without demoting the actual mother to a secondary role) demonstrates a challenge to patriarchal social and political frameworks which value autonomy. Communal parenting within close family networks suggests that autonomy and independence are negative characteristics in the local imagination and not conducive to good mothering practices. In a mother-centric society where the 'mother-infant fusion' is encouraged for a longer duration into early motherhood, the developmental preference for separateness and independence is challenged as a desired position. If we think of this in terms of the wider neoliberal political economy which has promoted individuality and personal responsibility through adherence to state values, we can see how local maternal practices – as gendered behaviour – that value dependency and bodily intimacy go against state ideals and projects of modernity which are shaped by neoliberalism.

Constructs of (M)other Love and Becoming through Ideas of Separation

> Love is love. It is without a category, without description, without title and without labels. It is just love. Love is free from judgement, it does not question, or restrict, it doesn't damage or hurt, love is pure and unconditional. It is because of this love that we are able to live; it is why we exist. When we start to put labels on it or attempt to justify it, it is then we become prejudiced and limited and then we don't love. We respond and act out what we are shown is love, we act according to custom, according to taboos and general cultural rules ... You see true pure love in your children, even though you may scold them they come back to you, they just love you they don't ask why you scolded them. If we restrict this right to love we become limited as people. (Bania, during a group Facebook conversation on how the women define a mother's love, August 2013)

In her eloquent words above, Bania highlights the tension and contradictions integral to the political economy of mother love where discourse of nature and awareness of social construction intersect.

This perception of love as a disembodied and divine force that is at once internally produced and externally manipulated provides a symbolic vehicle by which the 'problem and maintenance of social order can be voiced' (Lutz 1990: 72). The construct of maternal love in Mexico requires a psychophysical essence that is tied to an emic notion of instinct assumed to be unmanageable and problematic on the one hand and something to be manipulated as a force for good on the other. When these mothers act out of love their embodied actions employ emotional discourses as communicative performance (see Lutz and Abu-Lughod 1990) based upon their judgements of the world around them. In this way they utilize mother love not as a vehicle of expression but as a way of negotiating power relations embroiled within maternal ideologies and subjective experience. The vocabulary of mother love indicates that these women are striving to adhere to the good-mother paradigm much perpetuated by Mexican modernity discourses that promote a particular view of women's roles. Lone mothers and unmarried young mothers come within the cultural definition of bad mothers (Smith-Oka 2012) and as such their strategic use of mother love reclaims their right to be regarded as moral women and valued citizens.

I understand the transition to motherhood to be at once inseparable and separated from the biological process of childbearing, in the sense that the biological activities of conceiving, gestating, giving birth and lactating are culturally organized and given meaning in a context of dynamic social interactions and relationships (Arendell 2000). The way in which the women in this chapter speak of their transition to motherhood adheres to this notion of inseparability when they talk about maternal emotion, bodies and relationships in the context of their personal and social interactions and their physical environment. The women in the *barrio* place their maternal identity and practice in a context of family relationships, social networks and the embodied experience of being in the world. They make connections between the biological activity of childbearing and childbirth and learning to care for and love their children; however, they separate these events through their feelings. They also relate their identity and practice to their life histories and adherence to maternal feeling and performance rules. The overlapping and inseparability of biological from social avoids imposing a false nature/nurture position whilst at the same time acknowledging that there are elements of psychobiological experience that are impenetrable and limited by description.

My route to understanding what external forces shape women's transition to motherhood in Chiapas lies in the concept and vocabulary of mother love and how it is interpreted, utilized and embodied in relation to the wider political economy. Feminist literature on the political economy of emotions has proved useful for thinking through how mothers in the *barrio* (and wider society) speak of mother love in the context of global and local modernities. It demonstrates a widespread ideological framing of motherhood as a particular form of self-sacrifice which is prevalent in many societies – one which does not take into account intersecting structural factors which create the conditions for the ideology to exist in the first place and penetrate across cultural contexts. Following Lutz and Abu-Lughod's assertion that 'emotion talk must be interpreted as in and about social life rather than as veridically referential to some internalistic state' (1990: 11), I understand mother love to be emotion as discourse which incorporates speech as an expression of sensation and an indicator of social feeling rules. In this way emotion is embodied and shaped through social interaction and is historically constituted in the learning of maternal practices.

Women express learnt maternal feeling rules and emotions through bodily posture, gestures and facial expressions that are a result of being reared under similar physical and social conditions. A woman embodies and reproduces the social position and role of her mother and her grandmother before her in the way she carries, feeds and sleeps with her baby. For example, in the *barrios* of San Cristóbal infants are carried on the front, side or back of women using a *rebozo*. This enables the women to do their work, feed whilst walking, standing or travelling and ensures the safety and warmth of the infant. Using the *rebozo* and breastfeeding in various moving and sitting positions while carrying out other tasks inevitably shapes the posture of the woman to reproducing that of a good mother (in a particular social and political context).

The significance of carrying and holding infants is often expressed in general conversation with mothers. When I asked my hairdresser Angela how she felt about her relationship with her son, she replied 'I carried him on my back all the time and he behaved himself. Now he doesn't because he is growing and he wants to play with his cousin, so he goes off playing and forgets about me. Imagine, he's six years old and he's already off having his own life, in his own world'. Here she is evoking the emotional language of loss and the emotional physicality of carrying her son to refer to the mother work she did in order to show she could keep him safe and monitored. Angela's words demonstrate how emotions are 'tied to tropes of interiority and granted ultimate facticity by being located in the natural body' (Lutz and Abu-Lughod 1990: 1). Ideas about emotion and embodiment that are located in the natural body are inherently gendered and as such vulnerable to misinterpretation and ethnocentrism.

The women's narratives in this chapter provide the vocabulary that represents the maternal feeling rules characteristic of local values and they also demonstrate the limits of language in the expression of the bodily sensation incorporated in becoming a mother. My use of the concept and vocabulary of mother love arises from an attempt to show how the meanings and symbolism attached to emotion are used by mothers to navigate their way between subjective experience and social expectation. In her study of negative maternal emotion, Donath (2015) observed how women negotiate with systems of power in ways that indicate the intensity of social and cultural mechanisms that institutionalize good motherhood and womanhood. She uses Hochschild's concept of emotional regulation (Hochschild 1990) to show how mother love relates not only to local maternal ideals but also to the cultural thinking of children as innocents. The giving of love to a child is entrenched in the meshwork of the relations between social conditions and forms of power.

The emotion work that women undertake is significant in shaping who they are as mothers and the experiences of those around them. In her writing on love as political action, Ahmed (2004) contends that acting in the name of love enforces a particular ideal on others by requiring that they live up to that ideal. For the daughters of Bania and Sara, this meant they were required to recognize their mothers' actions and reciprocate accordingly with praise, appreciation and love. In relation to this, Oakley writes how the apparent self-sacrificing love a mother feels for her child has different gendered outcomes. She argues that, from this, daughters have unrealistic expectations of maternity (from which they then suffer as a result) and that sons' attribution of maternal love to women ultimately sustains the idealization of motherhood that is central to hierarchal capitalist societies (Oakley 1979). Yet, as Bania and Sara strove to distance themselves from how they had been mothered, it can be argued that they attempted to shape their expectations to meet the reality of their situation. According to Oakley, what happens to women as they become mothers reflects what has already happened to them as they become women. In other words, they find themselves being fitted into an existing role that is shaped by an element of biological universality and which evades any type of cultural hybridity. This leads to unrealistic expectations and prevailing disjunctures 'between the ideologies of mothering and motherhood, and the experiences of real women' (Arendell 2000: 1196).

Sara, Bania and Lila are evidently dealing with preconceived notions of what a good mother is and how the other women around them impact on how they mother. Yet, they are also conscious of how and who they want to be – incorporating rather than perpetuating ideology in their ongoing transition to motherhood to produce new, historically, culturally and socially determined ways of 'being modern' (Hryciuk 2010). They are contesting the imposition of a fixed identity by using their life experiences and a hybrid of local and global influences to think about who they are as women and as new maternal subjects. Abu-Lughod (1990) writes that in the case of Bedouin women, although individuals may desire and embrace aspects of modernity (such as cosmetics or alternative styles of dress) because they signify resistance to historically dominant gender ideals, these individuals make themselves subject to new forms of power that accompany and inform modernist projects. Amongst my informants in la Orilla, the new forms of power that emerge as a result of rejecting both aspects of tradition and modernity are less obvious and perhaps, as such, provide greater scope for collective agency to bring about a different kind of social change in the long term.

The narratives demonstrate how maternal subjectivity can be understood as developing out of the mother's separation from the other, whether it be the child at birth or by other means. This way of re-centring the mother provides scope to reimagine the concept of maternal subjectivity in its own right – in a way that is not reliant on the presence of a child. The way that the mother role, in the urban Mexican context, reunites the maternal subject directly with the female bodily form gives rise to a new kind of subject who generates meaning and acquires agency from her place in maternal body relations (as argued by Stone 2012a: 3). These ideas about separation which arise from the narratives of lone motherhood warrant further exploration from the position of the maternal subject and her experience in its own right. Here, philosopher Stanley Cavell's standpoint that 'the "proof" of the others' existence is a problem not of establishing connection with the other, but of achieving, or suffering, separation from the other' (2005: 146) provides the key to maintaining the maternal subject as central. Separation in Cavell's terms provides proof of existence from the experience of the mother in her own right, without denying that this individuation is in 'respect to the one upon whom [her] nature is staked' (Cavell 2005: 146).

The 'unbearable certainty of separation' for Cavell marks the 'moment of being known', or alternatively a remaking of self and a recognition of transformation. These perspectives resonate profoundly with the way in which women spoke to me of their experiences and how they had lived through significant changes in their lifecycle. This moment of being known through separation points towards the notion that the child does not have to be physically present for a type of maternal subjectivity to emerge. This provides a way to think about mothers who are separated from their children either for long periods or permanently. As Sara clearly demonstrates, women do not cease to feel like a mother in the absence of a child – they become a mother of their own making albeit in circumstances not chosen for themselves.

The women in la Orilla share the idea that on the one hand, maternal instinct and love are a divine notion granted by the appearance of a child – a blessing from God – but on the other, good (competent) motherhood is not something that comes pre-programmed or naturally. In the way they express themselves verbally, they are clear that motherhood requires hard work and is something that requires guidance from others. On a macro-level, however, it is arguably still the case that representations of motherhood are 'expressed in the combination of ideological glorification and actual socio-economic discrimination' (Oakley 1980: 285). There remains a falsehood in notions of gender equality perpetuated by the state (via rights discourse and legislation) that acts as a smokescreen for the inequalities in the everyday lives of women on domestic and localized grounds. Yet, these inequalities remain in a system that purports to eradicate them through a project of modernization that places the (good) mother role as central to its success. The women in la Orilla appear to comply with this when they speak of their roles as mothers as being central to their existence in relation to others, but not central to their selves as women. For them, being a woman and mother are not synonymous, yet neither does one identity exist without the other. In this way they reflect the arguments made by Mexican feminists that in their position as mother, they gain a certain social and political standing that other women are denied, and they do not accept that liberation comes from having to reject motherhood completely. Their maternal identity is central to them at the time that it most serves a purpose, but this does not define who they are in every aspect of their lives.

Though the themes of agency, established gender roles, modernity and change are prevalent throughout all their narratives, they manifest in different ways and according to different priorities. Transition to motherhood takes place in a complicated web of global and local processes and individual expectations where women come to embody the understanding that they have shifted from one context to another. These narratives show that the process of becoming a mother happens differently for women depending upon their own social worlds. Knowing they have made the transformation to mother is intrinsically linked to the recognition of their maternal practices by others, which in turn informs their thinking and perceptions of their world and their role within it.

For Bania, the actions and presence of her daughter confirm her maternal identity and for her act as a measure of how well she is doing. Sara, however, did not stop being a mother to Ana when she left home to live with a new partner. Her role as a mother did not cease to exist, it merely changed course. Lila's maternal identity is reinforced by the presence of her baby and family unit around her. Her transition to motherhood is validated by her *suegra* who oversees her practice but who is at the same time careful not to deprive Lila of her own maternal status. All of these women are immersed in the production of modernities, where modernity is an attitude rather than a process: where women are expected to adjust to the needs of the modern state, which are mediated and transformed in local socio-cultural contexts by the activities and opinions of individuals differing in positionality. New mothers are negotiating with systems of power that govern maternal feelings and that indicate the social and cultural mechanisms of institutionalized motherhood within the confines of local social relations.

Conclusion
Translating a Local-Global Maternal Health

I began this book by asking the following questions: how is global health as praxis gendered? In what ways is gender (when reduced to a binary) prioritized over other inequality indicators and social categories, and to what cost? And whilst universal concepts of gender, wellbeing and health are applied on top of local contexts, does anthropology have an appropriate framework that allows us to question these terms from an epistemological perspective?

To address these questions, I set out in the chapters to map out different stages of maternal and nurture transition for a particular group of women in a certain time and space in Southeast Mexico. These women are arguably geographically and systemically on the periphery of Mexican society. Their navigation between public and private healthcare services demonstrates a collective agency ignored by policy-makers and overseers of global maternal health. The women's use of *parteras* and non-allopathic remedies evades the metrics of maternal health profiling and puts them at less risk of institutionalized violence. It does little, however, to improve respect for the essential role that midwifery plays in improving not only maternal but also sexual, reproductive and women's health overall.

Another distinct point of learning from my research has been the importance of postpartum care practices and early nurture work as intergenerational expertise. I am certain that the women in la Orilla and Luna Maya would agree that their postpartum lives are woefully neglected by the state and its healthcare systems. To take infant feeding practices and mothers' health as an example, little data exists on infant feeding in an urban context yet health promotion and policies on the subject abound. So, on what evidence are these interventions based upon if there is little insight into the nurture practices behind closed doors? Relying on universalized best practice is of little use if it does not relate to localized lives in the everyday and in relation to socio-cultural politics. In addition, whilst there is a lack of nuance in the intersection of class, ethnicity, age and sexuality dynamics of populations under the SDG umbrella term of gender equality, health services remain inevitably inequitable.

Throughout the years of data collection in Chiapas I have struggled with the disconnect between the ethnographic data, the 'empty category' of 'colonized women' and the macro worldview of global health. I have gradually concluded that although in the field I saw every moment through the analysis of localized and intersecting gender, ethnicity and class dynamics, when I came to turn the same analytical lens to the theory and practice of globalized health, there was a lacuna. Whilst global health bodies may claim to focus on and target gender, they do little to acknowledge the ways in which their approach is inherently gendered.

Despite the shift to a 'grassroots, all-inclusive agenda', the global health praxis itself remains bereft of a contextualized intersectional analysis, and therefore its politics (gendered or otherwise) are obscured. Furthermore, there is a disconnect between the universal ideology of 'equity and justice' and how people live in the ordinariness of the everyday. Gender equality (SDG5) has been singled out as an essential element to 'ensure healthy lives and promote wellbeing at all ages' (SDG3) by 2030. SDG3 broadens the scope of global health beyond non-communicable diseases (NCDs) and maternal-infant mortality, which should in theory work to address the prior essentializing of women's health as synonymous with maternal and reproductive health. Yet, in countries like Mexico, who were committed and failed (like most) to achieve the mortality rates set in 2000 under MDG5, the funnelling of women's health resources into maternal health and mortality-related programmes only appears to have increased under the SDGs.

Whilst the need for high-quality maternal health care is undeniable, women's access to health care as determined by their reproductive capacity continues to miss the point on what constitutes good health across the gendered life course. Global health discourse as gender neutral tends to view local struggles as being less significant than global ones. Hence, in Chiapas we have a maternal health system shaped by a global concern with MMR, that fails to deal with a toxic combination of Mexican misogyny and structural violence in the medical system.

The chapters in this book have confronted this lack of gender analysis in global health praxis by demonstrating the subtle ways in which indirect consequences of health policy and coloniality of motherhood impact on the lives of low- to middle-income women. These women's lives are simultaneously interdependent and in tension with the state precisely because of their maternal status and what that symbolizes in Mexican society in the twenty-first century. In this way, the ethnographic material moves beyond borders to speak to a transnational feminist critique of globalization and neoliberalism that, amongst other things, argues that perspectives of global ideology tend to overlook local variations in the causal processes of inequalities and, as such, fail to deal with root causes and effect change (Abu-Lughod 2006; Chant and Craske 2003; Lugones 2010; Lutz 1995; Mohanty 2013; Nash 2007; Tsing 2002: Viveros Vigoya 2018).

In the case of Mexico, the universal and interchangeable notions of sex and gender in global health discourse often results in a continuing emphasis on women as naturalized carers. This issue is further complicated by a blurring of the lines between maternal health (concerned with sexed female bodies) and reproductive health (concerned with gendered bodies). Though they may intersect under the umbrella of gender policy/equality, treating maternal and reproductive health as one and the same perpetuates social inequalities in a way that mostly impacts on maternal subjects. The maternalization of reproductive health (and rights) actively excludes men and women who do not wish to be mothers from being incorporated into policies directed at family planning, and reproductive and sexual health behaviours. It reinforces dominant attitudes about the nature of gender relations and fails to challenge wider societal inequalities in Mexican society. The non-recognition of local gender dynamics in reproductive and maternal health policies also fails to represent the everyday diversity in the distribution of household labour and family structure and dynamics. Men's own nurture work goes unrecognized and their position beyond wage earner and sperm donor is unclear in the state's image of the family. Maternal and reproductive health policies, framed in global health discourse, promote universal ideologies of gender equality but they fail to include all people within the gender spectrum. As such, on a macro level, they seek to make fundamental social change but fail to challenge historical patterns of state-society interaction.

In Mexico maternal and reproductive health policies are framed by a rhetoric of rights which are interdiscursive with concerns over maternal and infant mortality. For the state, the right of mother and infant to survive birth takes precedence over local beliefs and knowledge about maternity as a process within the wider life cycle, one option out of many for the sexual lives of women. The choices that new mothers make in managing the various stages of caregiving are clearly influenced by political and social ideas of what it means to be a good mother, yet these women are content to be good enough mothers. Taking this into account, we can locate nurture practice and decision-making in broader questions of what it means to be Mexican, and a Mexican woman, in the twenty-first century. Where we understand the local and global contexts to be inseparable and enmeshed, a situation arises in which instituted interventions intersect with political cultures, medical institutions, domestic norms and individual strategies to generate lived transformative experience. Although these interconnecting factors retain their own agendas in shaping women as mothers, it is the unintended consequences of their intersection that demonstrate how external forces become implicated in the ordering of gender relations in any given society.

Appendix

On Doing Fieldwork with Children

Since my research and career as an anthropologist centres so frequently on the intimate family lives of others, I wanted to take a moment to consider my own positionality in the field as a parent and that of the dependents who accompany me. There is an eerie adult silence in the (metaphorical) halls of academia; it is an environment where children are rarely seen and even less heard. This is only something that came apparent to me when I began to have children and started my research career concurrently. When childcare and babies become your world, you very quickly start to wonder about your place in spaces that appear child and family bereft. When I conduct fieldwork in Chiapas I do so as both a parent and a scholar. Yet, the presence of dependents is gradually erased from the published accounts and along with them essential learning on the precarious balance between family and academic career commitments.

Early career researchers feel isolated at the best of times. Those navigating the identity politics of being Black or minority ethnic, non-cis queer, female, working class, a first-generation scholar or having a disability of any kind alongside their early career status feel that isolation tenfold. The idea that you also have dependents or may one day plan to is only ever brought up in the context of 'not letting it get in the way' of your career or 'deep thinking'. Over the last decade I have observed gradual change in attitudes to family life in academia; I have worked in institutions where colleagues combine early career parenting more openly with early career contracts and degree life. In departments where I have worked, family making is increasingly acknowledged in classrooms and meeting rooms, for childbearing cishet women at least. The global COVID-19 pandemic beginning in 2020, when I was completing the final edits of this book, brought academics' family life into the online classroom and faculty meeting as parents struggled to balance career and homeschooling. If ever there were a time to reflect upon family, nurture work and scholarship practice it is now.

Despite this, I continue to sit in meetings where I hear a student's pregnancy discussed as 'a problem', hear younger colleagues lament over never being able to imagine how they would 'fit a baby' in without damaging their career progression, watch new parents struggle to maintain full-time hours and temporary contracts, and I have yet to be able to include childcare costs in a funding bid externally or internally. These observations indicate that parenthood and academia remain an ill fit and the idea that research can learn from parenthood in the field remains a subject untouched. To continue with this silence in print, in a book about good enough parenting, would be woefully un-feminist of me and simply reproduce the same problem.

Anthropology is methodologically more privileged than most in that it requires researchers to spend extended periods of time living alongside communities and developing intimate relationships. The ethnographic method and output require reflection on positionality and a narrative style that provides space for mention of who you were with in the field. The visibility of the researcher (and therefore their dependents) is intrinsic to ethnographic analysis and rigour. Anthropologists work hard to include themselves in their process whilst concentrating on the subject and population under study. Despite this, there remains a practice of skimming over the presence of children in most ethnographic texts or media and this often leaves the early career scholar unable to imagine themselves doing the same. At the beginning of my PhD research (which coincided with starting a family) I was comforted by the fleeting mentions of parenting in the field in a handful of ethnographies (notably Nancy Scheper-Hughes' *Death Without Weeping*, 1993, and Mathew Guttman's study on fatherhood in Mexico City, *The Meanings of Macho*, 1996). Yet even in these brief accounts, the authors never spoke of separation from children, financial and childcare issues, and the various dilemmas involved in navigating small children in and out of fieldsites where poverty and violence were prevalent – all things that I have had to confront throughout my career to sustain myself in my chosen discipline.

Having dependents with you in the field influences the fieldsite and places limits on your movements. I was alone in the field and heavily pregnant, for all intents and purposes I was a lone parent. This positive move to a place where other families were on our doorstep and with a kindergarten place arranged drastically smoothed over the initial settling-in period. As homelife settled down I began to realize that everything I needed to know about family dynamics and motherhood was on my doorstep. Having to take the school day into account I was left with a short period of five hours each day to focus on data collection and this gave me structure. The fact that I was a pregnant mother, living alone, drew a lot of attention in a small neighbourhood defined by intergenerational households sharing the burden of childrearing. There was a communal desire amongst neighbours to simultaneously judge me as a mother and protect me from any immediate dangers. I was heavily scrutinized by my neighbours, which I later reflected on as just desserts considering that was exactly what I had set out to do to them. The daily interrogations I received on birth and parenting choices told me much more about social rules than my poorly worded questions ever could.

Whenever I read through my diaries or publications, I am met with the memory of emotion as well as the knowledge commitment I put into these initial years of fieldwork and family making. I can clearly map the pregnancy, birth and postpartum stage of data collection and analysis and have a raw example of how our emotions and relationships shape the core of our learning in the field. I must acknowledge the level of privilege that allowed me to meet the challenge of childbearing and childrearing whilst researching in Mexico. There were particular factors that made this possible and kept us relatively safe in a precarious field environment. I had full-time employment in one university whilst completing my part-time doctoral studies in another. This enabled me to combine fieldwork with maternity leave and therefore to self-fund for a year in the field, whilst also financing a house and care for my son back in the UK. I was returning to a familiar fieldsite where I had established connections (though no fixed site) and friends and family close by. I had a healthy pregnancy and a trouble-free birth which enabled me to continue without pause throughout the year. Above all I had a supportive family back home who took on the burden of care for my son in my absence.

By bringing my children into the field I learnt about my own culture's attitude to parenting and working mothers. I often floated questions on social media asking for advice or comments from academics with families. A consensus amongst many respondents was the idea that fieldwork should only be done for short periods and that finding time to parent well would be too difficult. This did make me reflect on the perspective of my children and how appropriate it was to have them with me. Yet, this was consistently outweighed by my commitment to my discipline and my desire to complete an in-depth ethnographic study. When I was considering the viability of cutting my stay short, a UK colleague commented that it was probably the right thing to do as I had 'compromised my family enough already'. I could not help but wonder at the time if they would be saying the same to a male colleague.

On a final note, by bringing the researcher's family out from the shadows we break from the idea that the personal and professional must remain separate. The practice of field research becomes more egalitarian because the private life of the researcher is forced out into the open, in the way they expect the lives of their participants to be revealed to them. Ultimately, this can lead to a better understanding and more thorough social science as dynamics are more reciprocal, and that is something we should all be striving towards. As we conduct ethnography and participate in academia, we should not need to pretend to be other than what and who we are.

References

Abu-Lughod, Lila. 1990. 'The Romance of Resistance: Tracing Transformations of Power Through Bedouin Women', *American Ethnologist* 17(1): 41–55. doi: 10.2307/645251.

_____. 2006. 'Writing Against Culture', in Ellen Lewin (ed.), *Feminist Anthropology: A Reader*. Oxford: Wiley Blackwell, pp. 153–69.

ACHPR. 2016. 'Joint Statement by UN Human Rights Experts, the Rapporteur on the Rights of Women of the Inter-American Commission on Human Rights and the Special Rapporteurs on the Rights of Women and Human Rights Defenders of the African Commission on Human and Peoples' Rights'. Accessed September 2016, http://www.achpr.org/news/2015/09/d192/.

Adams, Vincanne, Nancy J. Burke and Ian Whitmarsh. 2014. 'Slow Research: Thoughts for a Movement in Global Health', *Medical Anthropology* 33(3): 179–97. doi: 10.1080/01459740.2013.8583

Adams, Vincanne and Stacy Leigh Pigg. 2005. *Sex in Development: Science, Sexuality, and Morality in Global Perspective*. Durham, NC and London: Duke University Press.

Addisu, D., A. Asres, G. Gedefaw and S. Asmer. 2018. 'Prevalence of Meconium Stained Amniotic Fluid and its Associated Factors Among Women Who Gave Birth at Term in Felege Hiwot Comprehensive Specialized Referral Hospital, North West Ethiopia: a Facility Based Cross-sectional Study', *BMC Pregnancy Childbirth* 18(1): 429. doi: 10.1186/s12884-018-2056-y.

Ahmed, Sara. 2004. *The Cultural Politics of Emotion*. Edinburgh: Edinburgh University Press.

_____. 2016. *Living a Feminist Life*. Chicago: Duke University Press.

Alonso, Cristina, Alison Danch, Jenna Murray de López and Janell Tryon. 2018. 'Lessons from Chiapas: Caring for Indigenous Women Through a Femifocal Model of Care', in David A. Schwartz (ed.), *Maternal Death and Pregnancy-Related Morbidity Among Indigenous Women of Mexico and Central America*. Springer Nature, pp. 369–84. doi:10.1007/978-3-319-71538-4.

Alonso, Cristina and Jenna Murray de López. 2017. 'Casas de Parto: una estrategia de prevención contra la violencia obstétrica'. Primer Congreso

sobre Violencias de Género contra las Mujeres, Mexico. http://dx.do1 .org/10,22201/crim.UNAM000001c.2017.c5.
Arendell, Terry. 2000. 'Conceiving and Investigating Motherhood: The Decade's Scholarship', *Journal of Marriage and Family* 62(4): 1192–07. doi: 10.2307/1566731.
Auyero, Javier. 2012. *Patients of the State: The Politics of Waiting in Argentina.* Durham, NC: Duke University Press.
Ayuntamiento San Cristóbal de Las Casas [SCLC]. 2013. 'El Plan Municipal de Desarrollo de San Cristóbal de las Casas 2012-2015'. Accessed September 2015, http://sancristobal.gob.mx/plande-desarrollo-municipal-2012-2015/.
Berer, Marge. 2013. 'A New Development Paradigm Post-2015: A Comprehensive Goal for Health that Includes Sexual and Reproductive Health and Rights, and Another for Gender Equality', *Reproductive Health Matters* 21(42): 4–12. doi: 10.1016/S0968-8080(13)42750-7.
Berry, Nicole S. 2010. *Unsafe Motherhood: Mayan Maternal Mortality and Subjectivity in Post-war Guatemala.* New York: Berghahn Books.
Biehl, João. 2013. *Vita: Life in a Zone of Social Abandonment.* Berkeley: University of California Press.
Biehl, João and Vincanne Adams. 'The Work of Evidence in Critical Global Health', *Medicine Anthropology Theory* 3(2) (2016).
Biehl, João Guilherme and Adriana Petryna. 2013. 'Critical Global Health', in João Guilherme Biehl and Adriana Petryna (eds), *When People Come First: Critical Studies in Global Health.* Princeton, NJ: Princeton University Press, pp. 1–22.
Braff, Lara. 2009. 'Assisted Reproduction and Population Politics: Creating "Modern" Families in Mexico City', *Anthropology News* 50(2): 5–6. doi: 10.1111/j.1556-3502.2009.50205.x.
Bringas, Ángeles Sánchez, Sara Espinosa, Sara Espinosa Islas, Claudia Ezcurdia and Edna Torres. 2004. 'Nuevas maternidades o la desconstrucción de la maternidad en México', *Debate Feminista* 30 (October): 55–86. doi: 10.2307/42624831.
Castellanos, Rosario. 1971 [1992]. 'La abnegación: una virtud loca', *Debate Feminista* 6 (September 1992): 287–92.
Castro, Arachu, Angela Heimburger Ana Langer. 2003. *Iatrogenic Epidemic: How Health Care Professionals Contribute to the High Proportion of Cesarean Sections in Mexico.* Cambridge, MA: David Rockefeller Center for Latin American Studies.
Castro, Roberto and Joaquina Erviti. 2015. '25 años de investigación sobre violencia obstétrica en México', *Revista CONAMED* 19(1).
Castro, Roberto and Sonia M. Frías. 2019. 'Obstetric Violence in Mexico: Results From a 2016 National Household Survey', *Violence Against Women* 26(6–7): 555–72. doi: 10.1177/1077801219836732.
Cavell, Stanley. 2005. *Philosophy the Day After Tomorrow.* Cambridge, MA: Belknap Press of Harvard University Press.
Centro de Investigaciones Economicas y Politicas de Accion Comunitaria CIEPAC. 2007. La lucha por la reubicación de la torre de Telefonía

Celular en el Barrio de La Garita *Boletines*. Accessed 13 August 2013, http://www.ciepac.org/boletines/chiapasaldia.php?id=533.

Chant, Sylvia and Nikki Craske (eds). 2003. *Gender in Latin America*. London: Latin America Bureau.

Cheyney, Melissa, Marit Bovbjerg, Courtney Everson et al. 2014. 'Outcomes of Care for 16,924 Planned Home Births in the United States: The Midwives Alliance of North America Statistics Project, 2004 to 2009', *Journal of Midwifery & Women's Health* 59(1): 17–27.

Classen, C. 2005. 'McLuhan in the Rainforest: The Sensory Worlds of Oral Cultures', in David Howes (ed.), *Empire of the Senses: The Sensual Cultural Reader*. Oxford: Berg, pp.147–163.

Cosans, Chris. 2004. 'The Meaning of Natural Childbirth', *Perspectives in Biology and Medicine* 47(2): 266–72.

Csordas, Thomas J. 1993. 'Somatic Modes of Attention', *Cultural Anthropology* 8(2): 135–56. doi: 10.2307/656467.

Dalsgaard, Anne Line. 2004. *Matters of Life and Longing: Female Sterilisation in Northeast Brazil*. Copenhagen: Museum Tusculanum Press, University of Copenhagen.

Davis-Floyd, Robbie. 2001. 'The Technocratic, Humanistic, and Holistic Models of Birth', *International Journal of Gynecology & Obstetrics* 75 (Supplement 1): S5–S23.

_____. 2003a. *Birth as an American Rite of Passage*, 2nd edition. Berkeley: University of California Press.

_____. 2003b. 'Home Birth Emergencies in the U.S. and Mexico: The Trouble with Transport', *Social Science and Medicine* 569: 1913–931.

Deka, Prasanta Kumar, Sachchithanatham Kanagasabai and Laxminarayan Karanth. 2010. 'Caesarean Section Incision in Abdomen Revisited', *Internet Journal of Gynecology and Obstetrics* 14(1). https://print.ispub.com/api/0/ispub-article/4829.

Donath, Orna. 2015. 'Regretting Motherhood: A Sociopolitical Analysis', *Signs* 40(2): 343–67. doi: 10.1086/678145.

Douglas, Mary. 1990. 'Risk as a Forensic Resource', *Daedalus* 119(4): 1–16. doi: 10.2307/20025335.doi:10.2307/20025335.

El Kotni, Mounia. 2019. 'Regulating Traditional Mexican Midwifery: Practices of Control, Strategies of Resistance', *Medical Anthropology* 38(2): 137–51. doi: 10.1080/01459740.2018.1539974.

El-Kotni, M. and A. Ramírez-Pérez. 2017. 'Actas que reconocen, Actas que Vigilan: Las constancias de alumbramiento y el control de la parteria en Chiapas', *Liminar* 152. doi:http://dx.doi.org/10.2536/liminar.v15i2.533.

ENSANUT (Encuesta Nacional de Salud y Nutricion). 2012. Accessed 3 March 2013, http://ensanut.insp.mx/informes/ENSANUT2012Resultados Nacionales.pdf.

Fassin, Didier. 2012. 'That Obscure Object of Global Health', in M.C. Inhorn and Emily A. Wentzell (eds), *Medical Anthropology at the Intersections: Histories, Activisms, Futures*. Durham, NC: Duke University Press, pp. 95–115.

Franco, Jean. 1989. *Plotting Women: Gender and Representation in Mexico*. New York: The Columbia University-New York University Consortium.
Freeman, Carla. 2001. 'Is Local: Global as Feminine: Masculine? Rethinking the Gender of Globalization', *Signs* 264: 1007–37. doi:10.2307/3175355.
Freyermuth, Graciela. 2010. 'Desiguales en la vida, desiguales para morir. La mortalidad materna en Chiapas: un análisis desde la inequidad', in *Informe sobre Desarrollo Humano en Chiapas*. Programa de las Naciones Unidas para el Desarrollo: CIESAS-sureste.
_____. 2015. 'La Voz de la Coalición: El Programa de Salud Materna y Perinatal 2013-2018', *Cimacnoticias* (24 February). http://cimacnoticias.com.mx/node/68890.
_____ (ed.). 2018. *Los caminos para parir en México en el siglo XXI:experiencias de investigación, vinculación, formación y comunicación*. Mexico: CIESAS-ciudad de Mexico.
Freyermuth, María Graciela, José Alberto Muños and María del Pilar Ochoa. 2017. 'From Therapeutic to Elective Cesarean Deliveries: Factors Associated With the Increase in Cesarean Deliveries in Chiapas', *International Journal for Equity in Health* 16: 88. doi: 10.1186/s12939-017-0582-2.
Freyermuth, G. and P. Sesia (eds). 2009. La muerte materna. Acciones y estrategias hacia una maternidad segura. Serie evidencias y experiencias en salud sexual y reproductiva. Mujeres y hombres en el siglo XXI. *Comité Promotor por una Maternidad sin Riesgos en México, Centro de Investigaciones y Estudios Superiores en Antropología Social, México*. http://elrostrodelamortalidadmaterna.cimac.org.mx/sites/default/files/La_Muerte_Materna_2_Acciones_y_Estrategias_hacia_una_maternidad_Segura.pdf.
Garita Edelen, A., B. Flores Perez and A. Ruiz Tovar. 2016. *Embarazo y Maternidad en la Adolescencia: Estado de madres en Mexico*. Mexico: Save the Children.
Gibbons, Luz, José M. Belizán, Jeremy A. Lauer, Ana P. Betrán, Mario Merialdi and Fernando Althabe. 2010. *The Global Numbers and Costs of Additionally Needed and Unnecessary Caesarean Sections Performed per Year: Overuse as a Barrier to Universal Coverage*. World Health Organisation. http://www.who.int/healthsystems/topics/financing/healthreport/30C-sectioncosts.pdf.
González de Cosío, Teresita, Leticia Escobar-Zaragoza, Luz Dinorah González-Castell and Juan Ángel Rivera-Dommarco. 2013. 'Prácticas de alimentación infantil y deterioro de la lactancia materna en México'. *Salud Pública de México* 55, S170–S179.
Gonzalez Ávila, Yanina. 2005. 'Mujeres Frente a los Espejos de la Maternidad: las que eligen no ser madres', *Descatos* 17(1): 107–26.
Groark, K.P. 1997. 'To Warm the Blood, to Warm the Flesh: The Role of the Steambath in Highland Maya (Tzeltal-Tzotzil) Ethnomedicine', *Journal of Latin American Lore* 20(1): 3–96.

Grupo de Informacion en Reproduccion Elegida (GIRE). 2015. *Violencia Obstetrica un enfoque de derechos humanos*. Mexico: GIRE. https://gire.org.mx/wp-content/uploads/2016/07/informeviolenciaobstetrica2015.pdf.

Guerrero Meneses, Maria de los Angeles. 2004. 'Maternidad, Reproductividad y Trabajo', in María Ileana García Gossio (ed.), *Mujeres y Sociedad en el Mexico contemporaneo: nombrar lo innombrable*. Mexico: Cámara de Tecnológico de Monterrey, M.A. Porrúa, pp. 101–24.

Gutiérrez, Natividad. 1999. *Nationalist Myths and Ethnic Identities: Indigenous Intellectuals and the Mexican State*. London: University of Nebraska Press.

Gutmann, Matthew C. 1996. *The Meanings of Macho: Being a Man in Mexico City*. London: University of California Press.

———. 2007. *Fixing Men: Sex, Birth Control and Aids in Mexico*. Berkeley: University of California Press.

———. 2009. 'Planning Men Out of Family Planning', *Sexualidad, Salud y Sociedad* (1): 104–24.

Herrera, C. 2013. 'Protesta por invasión a la Reserva Gertrude Duby', *La Foja Coleta* (4 January). Accessed September 2013, http://lafoja.com/151/notprin151.htm.

Hochschild, Arlie Russell. 1990. 'Ideology and Emotion Management: A Perspective and Path for Future Research', in Theodore D. Kamper (ed.), *Research Agendas in the Sociology of Emotions*. Albany, NY: SUNY Press, pp. 117–42.

Hryciuk, Renata E. 2010. '(Re)constructing Motherhood in Contemporary Mexico: Discourses, Ideologies and Everyday Practices', *Polish Sociological Review* 4(172): 487–502. doi: 10.2307/41275176.

INEGI (Instituto Nacional de Estadística y Geografía). 2010. *Censo de Población y Vivienda 2010*. Mexico: INEGI.

———. 2015. *México en cifras*. Mexico: INEGI.

Ingold, Tim. 1998. 'From Complementarity to Obviation: On Dissolving the Boundaries Between Social and Biological Anthropology, Archaeology and Psychology', *Zeitschrift für Ethnologie* 123(1): 21–52. doi: 10.2307/25842543.

———. 2011. *Being Alive: Essays on Movement, Knowledge and Description*. London: Routledge.

Instituto para el Federalismo y el Desarrollo Municipal (INAFED). 2010. *Enciclopedia de Los Municipios y Delegaciones de México Estado de Chiapas*. Mexico: INAFED.

Jolly, Margaret. 1998. 'Introduction', in Kalpana Ram and Margaret Jolly (eds), *Maternities and Modernities: Colonial and Postcolonial Experiences in Asia*. Cambridge: University of Cambridge Press, pp. 1–25.

Jordan, Brigitte. 1993. *Birth in Four Cultures: A Crosscultural Investigation of Childbirth in Yucatan, Holland, Sweden, and the United States*, 4th edition, revised and expanded by Robbie Davis-Floyd. Prospect Heights, IL: Waveland Press.

Katz, E. 1996. 'Recovering After Childbirth in the Mixtec Highlands', in E. Schroeder, G. Balansard, P. Cabalion, J. Fleurentin and G. Mazars (eds), *Medicines and Foods: The Ethnopharmacological Approach*. Paris: CIFOR, pp. 97–109.

Kim-Godwin. 2003. 'Postpartum Beliefs and Practices Among Non-Western Cultures', *American Journal of Maternal Child Nursing* 28(2): 74–78.

Kitzinger, S. 1997. 'Authoritative Touch in Childbirth: A Cross-Cultural Approach', in R. Davis-Floyd and C. Sargent (eds), *Childbirth and Authoritative Knowledge*. Berkeley: University of California Press, pp. 209–231.

Kleinman, Arthur. 1997. *Writing at the Margin: Discourse Between Anthropology and Medicine*. Berkeley: University of California Press.

Laako, Hanna. 2016. 'Los derechos humanos en los movimientos sociales: el caso de las parteras autónomas en México', *Revista Mexicana de Ciencias Políticas y Sociales* 227: 167–94.

Lamas, Marta. 2001. *Política y reproducción: aborto, la frontera del derecho a decidir*. Barcelona: Plaza & Janés.

Lazos Álvarez, C.A. 2013. *El Plan Municipal de Desarrollo de San Cristóbal de las Casas 2012-2015*. Chiapas: H. Ayuntamiento de San Cristóbal de las Casas, Chiapas.

Lock, Margaret. 1993. *Encounters with Aging: Mythologies of Menopause in Japan and North America*. London: University of California Press.

Lugo, Alejandro. 2008. *Fragmented Lives, Assembled Parts: Culture, Capitalism, and Conquest at the U.S. - Mexico Border*. Austin: University of Texas Press.

Lugones, Maria. 2003. *Pilgrimages/Peregrinajes: Theorizing Coalition Against Multiple Oppressions*. Washington, DC: Rowman & Littlefield Publishers.

———. 2010. 'Toward a Decolonial Feminism', *Hypatia* 25(4): 742–59. doi: https://doi.org/10.1111/j.1527-2001.2010.01137.x.

———. 2016. 'The Coloniality of Gender', in W. Harcourt (ed.), *The Palgrave Handbook of Gender and Development: Critical Engagements in Feminist Theory and Practice*. London: Palgrave Macmillan UK, pp. 13–33.

Luiselli, Valeria. 2012. *Faces in the Crowd*. United Kingdom: Granta Publications.

Luna, Monica Adriana, Georgina Sanchez and Juan Carlos Velasco. 2015. 'Parteras Institucionalizadas en San Cristóbal de Las Casas: Su Labor a Lo Largo de Tres Décadas', in Georgina Sanchez (ed.), *Imagin Instantanea de la Partería*. Mexico: El Colegio de la Frontera sur, pp. 49–84.

Lutz, Catherine A. 1990. 'Engendered Emotion: Gender, Power, and Rhetoric of Emotional Control in American Discourse', in Catherine A. Lutz and Lila Abu-Lughod (eds), *Language and the Politics of Emotion*. Cambridge: Cambridge University Press, pp. 69–91.

———. 1995. 'The Gender of Theory', in Ruth Behar and Deborah A. Gordon (eds), *Women Writing Culture*. Berkeley: University of California Press, pp. 249–66.

Lutz, C.A. and L. Abu-Lughod. 1990. *Language and the Politics of Emotion*. Cambridge: Cambridge University Press.
MacKenzie Bryers, Helen and Edwin van Teijlingen. 2010. 'Risk, Theory, Social and Medical Models: A Critical Analysis of the Concept of Risk in Maternity Care', *Midwifery* 26(5): 488–96. doi: http://dx.doi.org/10.1016/j.midw.2010.07.003.
Martinez-Schallmoser, Lucy, Nancy J. MacMullen and Sharon Telleen. 2005. 'Social Support in Mexican American Childbearing Women', *Journal of Obstetric, Gynecologic, & Neonatal Nursing* 34(6): 755–60. doi: 10.1177/0884217505281856.
Mills, Lisa Nicole. 2017. *The Limits of Trust: The Millennium Development Goals, Maternal Health, and Health Policy in Mexico, McGill-Queen's Studies in Gender, Sexuality, and Social Justice in the Global South*. Montreal: MQUP.
Mohanty, Chandra Talpade. 2013. 'Transnational Feminist Crossings: On Neoliberalism and Radical Critique', *Signs* 384: 967–91. doi: 10.1086/669576.
Molina, Rose L., Suha J. Patel 4, Jennifer Scott, Julianna Schantz-Dunn and Nawal M. Nour. 2016. 'Striving for Respectful Maternity Care Everywhere'. *Maternal and Child Health Journal* 20(9): 1769–73. doi:10.1007/s10995-016-2004-2.
Morgan, Lynn M. and Elizabeth F.S. Roberts. 2009. 'Rights and Reproduction in Latin America' *Anthropology News* 50(3): 12–16. doi: 10.1111/j.1556-3502.2009.50312.x.
Murray de Lopez, Jenna. 2015. 'Conflict and Reproductive Health in Urban Chiapas: Disappearing the Partera Empírica', *Anthropology Matters* 16(1). doi: https://doi.org/10.22582/am.v16i1.339.
———. 2017. 'Mala leche: interpretación de los riesgos y desafíos médicos de la lactancia materna en la zona urbana de Chiapas México', *Dilemata* 25: 13.
———. 2019. 'Maintaining the Flow: Medical Challenges to Breastfeeding and "Risky" Bodies in Mexico', *Medical Anthropology Quarterly* 33(3): 403–19. doi:10.1111/maq.12511.
Murray de López, Jenna and Cristina Alonso. 2018. 'Riesgo o Aliento: El caso de una Casa de Partos', in Graciela Freyermuth (ed.), *Los caminos para parir en México en el siglo XXI Experiencias de investigación, vinculación, formación y comunicación*. Mexico: CIESAS, pp. 142–49.
Nash, June C. 2007. *Practicing Ethnography in a Globalizing World: An Anthropological Odyssey*. Lanham, MD: AltaMira Press.
Nazar, A.B., B.I. Salvatierra and E.M. Zapata. 2007. 'Atención del Parto, Migración Rural-Urbana y Políticas Publicas de Salud Reproductiva En Poblaciòn Indígena de Chiapas, Mexico', *Ra Ximhau Revista de Sociedad Cultura y Desarrollo Sustenable* 763–79.
Niska, K. 1999. 'Family Nursing Interventions: Mexican American Early Family Formation', *Nursing Science Quarterly* 124: 335–40.

Oakley, Ann. 1979. *Becoming a Mother*. New York: Schoken Books.
_____. 1980. *Women Confined: Towards a Sociology of Childbirth*. Oxford: Martin Robertson.
Observatorio de Mortalidad Materna en Mexico (OMM). 2014. *Indicadores de mortalidad materna*. Mexico: OMM.
OECD. 2015. Measuring Wellbeing in Mexican States: Executive Summary [Online], 3 November. http://www.oecd.org/gov/regional-policy/Mexican-States-HighlightsEnglish.pdf.
Palazuelos, Daniel and Linnea Capps. 2013. 'Mexico', in Margo J. Krasnoff (ed.), *Building Partnerships in the Americas*. Dartmouth: Dartmouth College Press, pp. 1–41.
Palomar, Cristina Verea. 2004. '"Malas madres": la construcción social de la maternidad', *Debate Feminista* 30: 12–34. doi: 10.2307/42624829.
Paris Pombo, M. 2000. 'Identidades excluyentes en San Cristóbal de las Casas', *Nueva Antropología* XVII: 89-100.
Pigg, Stacy Leigh. 2005. 'Globalizing the Facts of Life', in Vincanne Adams and Stacy Leigh Pigg (eds), *Sex in Development: Science, Sexuality, and Morality and Global Perspective*. Durham, NC: Duke University Press, pp. 39–66.
_____. 2013. 'On Sitting and Doing: Ethnography as Action in Global Health', *Social Science & Medicine* 99: 127–34. doi:http://dx.doi.org/10.1016/j.socscimed.2013.07.018.
Quijano, Ana. 2000. 'Colonialidad del poder, eurocentrismo y America latina', in *Colonialidad del Saber, Eurocentrismo y Ciencias Sociales*. Buenos Aires Argentina: CLACSO-UNESCO, pp. 201–46.
Rivera Cusicanqui, Silvia. 2012. 'Ch'ixinakax utxiwa: A Reflection on the Practices and Discourses of Decolonization', *South Atlantic Quarterly* 1111: 95–109. doi:10.1215/00382876-1472612.
_____. 2018. *Un Mundo Ch'xi es Posible: Ensayos desde un presente en crisis*. Buenos Aires: Tinta Limón.
Resau, L. 2002. '"Cooking the Body" in a Changing World: Postpartum Practices in the Mixteca'. Dissertation, University of Arizona. https://arizona.openrepository.com/arizona/bitstream/10150/278781/1/azu_td_1409150_sip1_m.pdf.
Roberts, Elizabeth F.S. 2012. 'Scars of Nation: Surgical Penetration and the Ecuadorian State', *The Journal of Latin American and Caribbean Anthropology* 17(2): 215–37. doi: 10.1111/j.1935-4940.2012.01223.x.
Romano, Mattea, Alessandra Cacciatore, Rosalba Giordano and Beatrice La Rosa. 2010. 'Postpartum Period: Three Distinct but Continuous Phases', *Journal of Prenatal Medicine* 4(2): 22–25.
Rouse, Carolyn. 2004. '"If She's a Vegetable, We'll Be Her Garden": Embodiment, Transcendence, and Citations of Competing Cultural Metaphors in the Case of a Dying Child', *American Ethnologist* 31(4): 514–29. doi: 10.2307/4098866.

Sacks, Oliver. 2005. 'The Mind's Eye: What the blind See', in David Howes (ed.), *Empire of the Senses: A Sensual Cultural Reader*. Oxford: Berg, pp. 25–42.
Sánchez Ramirez, Georgina (ed.). 2015. *Imagen Instantánea de la Partería*. Mexico: EcoSur-Asociación Mexicana de Partería.
_____. 2016. *Espacios para parir diferente: Un acercamiento a Casas de Parto en México*. Mexico: ECOSUR.
Sanders, Nichole. 2009. 'Mothering Mexico: The Historiography of Mothers and Motherhood in 20th-Century Mexico', *History Compass* 7(6): 1542–53. doi: 10.1111/j.1478-0542.2009.00650.x.
Say, Lale, Doris Chou, Alison Gemmill, Özge Tunçalp, Ann-Beth Moller, Jane Daniels, A. Metin Gülmezoglu, Marleen Temmerman and Leontine Alkema. 2014. 'Global Causes of Maternal Death: a WHO Systematic Analysis', *The Lancet Global Health* 2(6): e323-e333. doi: 10.1016/S2214-109X(14)70227-X.
Scheper-Hughes, Nancy. 1993. *Death Without Weeping: The Violence of Everyday Life in Brazil*. Berkeley: University of California Press.
Scheper-Hughes, Nancy and Carolyn Sargent. 1998. *Small Wars: The Cultural Politics of Childhood*. Berkeley: University of California Press.
Secretaría de Salud. 1993. *Norma Oficial Mexicana NOM-007-SSA2-2016*. Mexico.
Sesia, Paola. 1996. 'Women Come Here on Their Own When They Need to': Prenatal Care, Authoritative Knowledge, and Maternal Health in Oaxaca', *Medical Anthropology Quarterly* 10(2): 121–40.
SINAIS. 2009. *Sistema Nacional de Información en Salud: Bases de Datos*. Mexico.
Smith-Oka, V. 2012. 'They Don't Know Anything: How Medical Authority Constructs Perceptions of Reproductive Risk Among Low-Income Mothers in Mexico', in Lauren Fordyce and Aminata Maraesa (eds), *Risk, Reproduction, and Narratives of Experience*. Nashville: Vanderbilt University Press, pp. 103–42.
_____. 2013. *Shaping the Motherhood of Indigenous Mexico*. Nashville: Vanderbilt University Press.
Soto Laveaga, Gabriela. 2007. '"Let's Become Fewer": Soap Operas, Contraception, and Nationalizing the Mexican Family in an Overpopulated World', *Sexuality Research & Social Policy* 4(3): 19–33. doi: 10.1525/srsp.2007.4.3.19.
Speed, Shannon. 2008. *Rights in Rebellion: Indigenous Struggle and Human Rights in Chiapas*. Stanford, CA: Stanford University Press.
Stone, Alison. 2012a. *Feminism, Psychoanalysis, and Maternal Subjectivity*. New York: Routledge.
_____. 2012b. 'Psychoanalytic Feminism and the Dynamics of Mothering a Daughter', in Sheila Lintott and Maureen Sander-Staudt (eds), *Philosphical Inquiries into Pregnancy, Childbirth, and Mothering*. Oxford: Routledge, pp. 126–37.

Tsing, Anna Lowenhaupt. 2002. 'Conclusion: The Global Situation', in J.X. Inda (ed.), *The Anthropology of Globalization: A Reader*. Oxford: Blackwell, pp. 485–86.

Tuiran, Rodolfo, Virgilio Partida, Octavio Mojarro and Elena Zuniga. 2009. 'Fertility in Mexico: Trends and Forecast', in *Completing the Fertility Transition*. https://www.un.org/development/desa/pd/sites/www.un.org.development.desa.pd/files/unpd_egm_200203_countrypapers_fertility_in_mexico_tuiran_partida_mojarro_zuniga.pdf.

Unnithan-Kumar, Maya. 2001. 'Emotion, Agency and Access to Healthcare: Women's Experiences of Reproduction in Jaipur', in Soraya Tremayne (ed.), *Managing Reproductive Life: Cross-Cultural Themes in Fertility and Sexuality*. Oxford: Berghahn Books, pp. 27–51.

Uribe-Leitz, Tarsicio, Alejandra Barrero-Castillero, Arturo Cervantes-Trejo, Jose Manuel Santos, Alberto de la Rosa-Rabago, Stuart R. Lipsitz, Maria Antonia Basavilvazo-Rodriguez, Neel Shah and Rose L. Molina. 2019. 'Trends of Caesarean Delivery from 2008 to 2017, Mexico', *Bulletin of the World Health Organization* 97(7): 502–12. doi: 10.2471/BLT.18.224303.

Valdez-Santiago, R., E. Hidalgo and M. Mojarro. 2013. 'Nueva evidencia a un viejo problema: el abuso de las mujeres en las salas de parto'. *Revista CONAMED* 18(1): 14–20.

van Teijlingen, Edwin, Vanora Hundley, Zoe Matthews, Gwyneth Lewis, Wendy J. Graham, James Campbell, Petra ten Hoope-Bender, Zoe A. Sheppard and Louise Hulton. 2014. 'Millennium Development Goals: All Good Things Must Come to an End, So What Next?', *Midwifery* 30(1): 1–2. doi: 10.1016/j.midw.2013.10.022.

Varley, Ann. 2000. 'Women and the Home in Mexican Family Law', in Elizabeth Dore and Maxine Molyneux (eds), *Hidden Histories of Gender and the State in Latin America*. Durham, NC: Duke University Press, pp. 238–61.

Vega, Rosalynn. Adeline. 2018. *No Alternative: Childbirth, Citizenship, and Indigenous Culture in Mexico*. Austin: University of Texas Press.

Villanueva-Egan, Luis Alberto. 2010. 'El maltrato en las salas de parto: reflexiones de un gineco-obstetra Mistreat in the labor rooms: gynecologist reflections', *Revista Conamed* 15(3): 148–51

Viveros Vigoya, Mara. 2018. 'Entre la extraversión y las epistemologías "nuestramericanas": el lugar de la producción antropológica con enfoque de género', *18° Congresso Mundial IUAES*. Florianopolis, Brazil, 16–19 July.

Waugh, Lisa Johnson. 2011. 'Beliefs Associated with Mexican Immigrant Families' Practice of La Cuarentena during Postpartum Recovery', *Journal of Obstetric, Gynecologic, & Neonatal Nursing* 40(6): 732–41. doi: 10.1111/j.1552-6909.2011.01298.x.

Wendland, Claire L. 2007. 'The Vanishing Mother: Cesarean Section and "Evidence-Based Obstetrics"', *Medical Anthropology Quarterly* 21(2): 218–33. doi: 10.1525/maq.2007.21.2.218.

———. 2016. 'Estimating Death: A Close Reading of Mortality Metrics in Malawi', in Vincanne Adams (ed.), *Metrics: What Counts in Global Health*. Durham, NC: Duke University Press, pp. 57–81.

Winnicott Donald. 1967. 'Mirror-Role of the Mother and Family in Child Development', in P. Lomas (ed.), *The Predicament of the Family: A Psychoanalytical Symposium*. London: Hogarth Press, pp. 26–33.

Wong, S.F., K.M. Chow and L.C. Ho. 2002. 'The Relative Risk of "Fetal Distress" in Pregnancy Associated with Meconium-stained Liquor at Different Gestation', *Journal of Obstetrics and Gynaecology* 22(6): 594–99. doi: 10.1080/0144361021000020333.

World Health Organization, Unicef, UNFPA, World Bank Group & Division, U.N.P. 2015. *Trends in Maternal Mortality: 1990-2015*. Geneva: WHO.

Ziarek, Ewa. 1992. 'At the Limits of Discourse: Heterogeneity, Alterity, and the Maternal Body in Kristeva's Thought', *Hypatia* 7(2): 91–108.

INDEX

A

Abu-Lughod, Lila, 58, 76, 162–164, 171
abuse
  of alcohol, 19–20, 98, 150
  of children, 147–148
  medical abuse and mistreatment, 35, 53, 94
  See also violence
abortion, 28, 51, 75, 92, 98, 157–158
advice
  on breastfeeding, 125
  medical, 41, 58, 101, 121, 125
  mothers and aunts, 79, 137
  unsolicited, 1
Ahmed, Sara, 33, 164
Alonso, Cristina, ix, 13, 23, 87–92, 95–96, 103–104, 107–109, 112n5, 154–155
antenatal care, 69, 75–77, 92, 99–102, 158
anthropology
  anthropological fieldwork (*see* ethnographic fieldwork)
  anthropological studies on maternal health, 83n4
  of global health, 7, 169
  medical anthropology, 8
anti-state citizenship, 4
atole, 3, 118, 135
aunts, 69, 128–129, 147–148
authoritative knowledge, 45, 80, 110, 136
Auyero, Javier, 3

B

babyhood, 1
barrio
  barrio la Orilla, 8, 13–20, 119, 126, 134, 138–140, 146–148, 152–158, 162–163
  barrio midwifery, 63–82 (*see also barrio parteras*)
  barrio parteras, 63–82, 85–86, 89–90, 93, 97, 99, 113n15
  barrio popular, 1–8
  ethnography of low-income *barrios*, 141
  San Cristóbal de Las Casas *barrios* and *colonias*, 21–23, 132
Berry, Nicole, 83n7
Biehl, Joao, 'zones of social abandonment', 113n13
binding, 131–133. *See also faja*
birth, 42
  certificate, 72, 121, 124
  homebirth, 63–67, 73–75, 105, 112n1, 124
  hospital birth, 42–54, 90
  humanized birth, 67, 97, 106, 111
  labour and, 26, 42–49, 51–52, 58–59, 69–73, 76–81, 86, 90, 92, 94–97, 100, 103–107, 120–121, 127, 158
  men's presence at, 118, 121
  model, 63 (*see also* midwifery model of care)
  natural, 38, 46, 101, 104, 111
  practices, 60, 66, 124

out-of-hospital, 61n3, 69, 85–88,
93–97, 112n1, 112n3, 136
technocratic model of, 42, 44, 60,
75, 111
vaginal, 78, 93, 133 (*see also*
caesarean section: vaginal birth
after)
violence during, 52, 42–54 (*see
also* obstetric violence)
See also caesarean section
birth centre, 8, 19, 37–38, 61n3,
84–110, 112n1, 112n3, 112n5,
113n6, 113n10, 113n15
and the law, 72, 96, 112n2,
113n6
See also Luna Maya
birth control, 51. *See also*
contraception
birthing bodies, 46
biomedical, 76, 119, 125, 134
biosocial, 6, 8, 111
bodily autonomy, 50, 95, 110
bodily integrity, 29, 45, 57–59
bodily knowledge, 41–42
bodily practices, 29, 130, 139, 141
body
Indigenous women's bodies and medical racism, 78
as a source of contamination, 125
breastfeeding
and alcohol, 123
after caesarean section, 46, 128–129
difficulties with, 55, 134
interruptions to, 124, 136
and postpartum health, 139
practices, 117, 134–135, 163, 169–170
in public, 2, 122, 163
retention, 135, 141
and socio-economic class, 46
social significance of, 134, 136
breast milk, 135
contamination, 124–125, 134, 140–141
establishing supply, 119, 123, 128–129, 135, 139
flow, 135
quantity, 122, 158–159
See also mothers' milk
breech birth, 89, 93, 95, 98
bureaucracy, 3, 6, 109–110

C

caesarean section, 26, 41, 52, 57
and avoidance, 73, 78, 95
and breech babies, 94, 98
and coercion, 47–48, 60 (*see also* obstetric violence)
elected and programmed, 121
emergency caesarean, 42–46, 48, 107–108, 128
incision types and scars, 54, 62n5–6
national rates of, 35, 53, 92
and postpartum healing, 55, 128, 133
vaginal birth after (VBAC), 93–95
See also cesárea
care
midwifery model of, 76, 88, 91, 100, 104 (*see also* femifocal model)
caregivers and caregiving, 4–5, 19, 111, 125, 136, 139, 172
Castellanos, Rosario, 143, 160
Castro, Arachu, 61n2
Catholic families, 118–119, 126
Catholic mother figures, 22, 147.
See also mujer abnegada
Catholicism, 22, 37–38
Cavell, Stanley, 166. *See also* separation
census, 16, 21, 24
cesárea, 111. *See also* caesarean section
Chiapas
and Indigenous populations, 21, 23, 118, 132
low intensity conflict in, 9n3, 23, 49
and colonialism, 21–22
and coloniality of motherhood, 24–26, 28, 163, 170

and socio-economic inequalities, 33–35
childbearing, 35–36, 41, 48, 57, 72
  institutionalized, 58, 60, 67
  'natural', 110–112
  and *parteras*, 72, 75–76
  pathologizing of, 75, 100–101
  See also pregnancy
children, 14, 17, 19, 72, 117
  fieldwork with, 173–176
  infant mortality, 24, 49, 96, 112, 172
  and lone mothers, 144–150, 152–153
  and mother love, 161–162, 164
Cho'l, 97
coletas, 13, 16, 22–24, 64, 67, 72, 102, 105
colitis, 124–125, 127
collective agency, 64, 74, 97, 141, 165, 169
colonial city, 20, 22. *See also* San Cristóbal de Las Casas
colonialism, 21
coloniality
  coletas and, 27–24
  of gender, 4–5, 7, 60 (*see also* Lugones, Maria)
  of knowledge, x, 83n4
  of motherhood, 5, 24–30, 171
  of violence, 6
Comandanta Ramona, 6, 9n3
combis, 1–3, 14, 17, 20, 153
competing cultural metaphors, 64, 76, 119, 131, 134, 144
compliance (with doctors), 50, 52, 57, 60, 121, 137
conditions of emergency, 48, 51–52, 54
contraception, 28, 50. *See also* family planning
Cosans, Chris, 111
cousins, 6, 14, 137, 145–146, 149, 163
critical global health, 7–8, 25
Csordas, Thomas J, 142n2
cuarenta dias, 117–125, 128–141
curandera, 76–77

D
Dalsgaard, Anne Line, 18
daughter-in-law, 26, 68, 73, 88, 142n3, 154–157
Davis-Floyd, Robbie, x, 70. *See also* birth: technocratic model of
death
  fear of, 41–42, 48, 52, 60
  of infant (*see* infant mortality)
  of mother (*see* maternal mortality)
decentralization, 33–34
de-colonize and de-canonize ethnography, 83
discrimination, 22, 24–25, 78, 160, 166
divorce, 149
doctors, 40–41, 46–49, 52–53, 56–60, 68–72, 75, 98, 107–108, 123–125
  and *parteras*, 77–79, 83n7–8, 89, 96, 102, 110, 134
  See also iatrogenic trauma; obstetric violence
domestic
  consumption, 15
  labour, 17, 23, 30n2, 128, 137, 154–155
  norms, 172
Donath, Orna, 164
Douglas, Mary, 52

E
early motherhood, 5, 14, 28–29, 38, 54, 57, 104, 145, 148, 161
education
  children, schools and schooling, 16–17, 137, 148
  girls', 24, 44
  health promotion and, 86, 88–90, 99–101
  medical, 70
  midwife, 66, 71–71, 92
Ejercito Zapatista de Liberación Nacional (EZLN), 9. *See also* Zapatistas
embodiment, 130–132, 141–142n2, 147, 164

emergency
  conditions of, 48, 51–52, 54
  treatment, 25–26
  See also caesarean section: emergency
emotion
  and language, 163
  maternal, 159, 162–164
  and postpartum care, 134–135
  and touch during labour, 80
epidural, 34, 111
episiotomy, 34, 53, 104, 111
ethnicity
  Indigenous ethnicity by language spoken, 21
  and intersections with social class, gender and age, 23–26, 36, 49, 54, 62n6, 78, 82n1, 170
  mixed, 16, 22
  social construct of Mexican, 6, 9n2, 22
ethnographic fieldwork, 173–176. *See also* children: fieldwork with
ethnographic perspective, 24, 63, 87, 111, 171
ethnography of parenthood, 152, 160, 174
European women, 101, 113

F
faja, 123, 128, 133, 159. *See also* binding
family networks, 76, 79, 136, 141, 154, 161
family planning, 27–29, 50, 171
family size, 27
Fassin, Didier, 7
fathers, 19–20, 38–39, 58, 121, 150
  absent, 44, 138, 147–148
  exclusion of, 140
  fatherhood, 152, 156, 174 (*see also* Gutmann Mathew)
  new, 140–141
femifocal model, 90–92, 95, 103, 105, 110–112, 113n8
fennel tea, 122–123, 135
fertility
  problems, 75
  rates, 27, 29
foetus, 35, 42, 52, 79, 139
  foetal abnormality, 94–95
  foetal distress, 106–107
formula, 46, 124–125, 135–136, 158. *See also* breastfeeding
Freyermuth, Graciela, 113n7

G
gender
  based violence, 53, 92 (*see also* obstetric violence; violence)
  as a category of analysis, 36, 48, 171
  and global health, 50, 70, 169–171
  politics, 51, 155, 160, 166
  power, 50, 53, 140
  relations, 160, 171
  roles, 133, 144, 146, 154, 156, 167
  See also coloniality: of gender
global health, 5, 7–8, 25, 29–30, 50, 66, 76, 92, 95, 107, 196–171. *See also* critical global health
Global South, 7
God, 40–41, 150–151, 157–158
  blessing from, 139, 143, 166
Godmother, 127
grandchildren, 68
granddaughters, 2–3, 26, 67–68, 156
grandmothers, 19, 64, 133, 137, 148, 158
Gutmann, Matthew, 51, 141, 152
gynaecologist, 47
gynaecology
  gyno-obstetrics, 75, 83n9, 127
  natural, 89

H
healthcare
  and maternal health policy, 34, 65
  and medicalization of childbearing, 65, 76, 90, 95
  midwifery-led, 63–65, 88, 99, 109

mixed economy of, 65, 77, 101
providers, 49, 101, 110
and public health insurance, 33–34, 77, 169
system, 6, 33, 169
and violence, 52–54, 60 (*see also* obstetric violence)
healthcare services, 15, 24–28, 33–34, 41–42, 64, 59, 75–77, 88, 98, 169–170
herbal medicine, 73, 79, 99, 120, 132
highlands, 2, 13, 25, 79, 118
history
of *barrio*, 18, 72–73
colonial, 7, 21, 24
of Luna Maya, 89–90
of midwifery in Chiapas, 64–67
Hochschild, Arlie Russell, 164
hogar comunitario (women's hostel), 98
homebirth
and family pressure, 87
and law, 66, 72, 112n2
and midwives, 63–69, 73, 75, 102, 105, 112n1
registering, 124
and risk discourse, 110, 113n11, 130
and socio-economic class, 64–65, 67
See also birth
hospital
private, 38, 108, 123–124
public, 35, 38, 42, 49, 64, 73, 75, 78, 95, 103, 105, 108, 123
transfer, 49, 71, 90, 92, 93–95, 98, 103–105, 107–110, 112n2
household
gender inequality, 20, 68, 171
intergenerational, 6, 142n3, 154, 156–157
labour, 17, 171
humanized birth model, 67, 97, 102, 106, 111. *See also* birth

I
iatrogenic trauma, 36, 41, 54, 61, 95

illness
beliefs, 73, 83n9, 131–134, 140, 155
perinatal, 40, 123–125, 131
IMSS, 33–34
IMSS-BIENESTAR 2, 9n1
income, 16–17, 24
and healthcare, 17, 45, 49, 54, 64–65, 67, 72, 119
Indigenous
cosmology, 140
girls and women, 6, 25–26, 31n2, 49, 78, 98
identity, 16, 21–24
languages, 21, 25
midwives (*see* midwives)
people and colonialism in Chiapas, 22–23
politics (*see* Zapatistas)
women and birth, 35, 44–45, 66, 86
women and maternal mortality, 25 (*see also* maternal mortality)
infant mortality, 24, 29, 49, 96, 112n2, 172
institutions, 7, 44, 50–51, 53–54, 72, 79, 172–173. *See also* hospital
ISSTE, 34, 77
IUD (intrauterine device), 48, 51–52, 56–58

J
Jolly, Margaret, 160

K
kin (female), 63, 73, 139, 155
Kitzinger, Sheila, 80
Kleinman, Arthur, 9n4

L
la Orilla. *See barrio* la Orilla
labour
economic, 18, 136
gendered, 171
household/domestic, 17, 23, 30n2, 154–155
lactation. *See* breastfeeding

life-course, 5, 30, 54, 73, 75, 91–92, 95, 144, 170
local biologies, 24, 30, 76, 131–133
Lock, Margaret, 30n3
lone mothers, 118, 136, 138, 144–146, 161–162
Lugo, Alejandro, 21
Lugones, Maria, 4–7
Luna Maya. *See* birth centre

M
MANA Stats, 92, 94–95
maternal mortality, 24–25, 49–50, 83n7, 86–90, 95
maternal transformation, 4, 101, 103–104, 130–132, 141, 155, 166, 167
maternal transition, 49, 64, 73, 159
Maternidades Sin Riesgos, 87, 89
masculinity, 19
Maya. *See* Indigenous
Maya cosmologies, 24, 132, 140
men, 4–6, 14, 17, 19–20, 22–23, 29, 39, 51, 118, 121, 134, 140–141, 142n3, 147, 150, 155–156, 171. *See also* fathers
metrics, 7, 169
Mexican state, 4, 29, 58
midwifery model of care, 59, 76, 88, 90–95, 97, 100, 104, 109, 112n1
midwives
  autonomous, 86–92, 96–110
  barrio/empirical, 63–83
  professional, 37, 61n3, 99, 112n5
  traditional, 65, 66, 82n1, 98
  See also partera
Millennium Development Goals (MDGs), 25, 71
Mills, Lisa Nicole, 64, 75
mistreatment, 35, 53, 61n2, 94. *See also* obstetric violence
mother love, 138, 144–145, 150–151, 161–164
mother-in-law, 6, 26, 121, 137–138, 144, 154. *See also suegra*
mothers' milk. *See* breastfeeding
moral economy, 81–82

mujer abnegada, 147, 154
Murray de López, Jenna, 61n1
Muslims, 21, 37

N
National Survey of Health and Nutrition (ENSANUT), 35
natural childbearing (construction of), 110–112
natural childbirth, 111
nature, 134, 161–162, 166, 171
Nazar, Austreberta, 113n7
NGOs, 6, 15, 54, 70, 96
NOM-007-SSA2-2016, 34, 112
non-Indigenous Mexican women, 6, 78
non-Indigenous *partera*, 65–66
novice (mother as), 118, 136–139
nurture, 5, 14, 37, 54–58, 143–145, 162, 169, 172
nurture work, 7–8, 115–142, 169–170, 174
nurses, 49, 51–53, 57, 67, 98, 107, 125, 128. *See also* obstetric nurses
nutrition, 9n1, 35, 134

O
Oakley, Ann, 164, 166
obstetric nurses, 43–46
obstetric transition, 34, 53
obstetric violence, 52–54, 61n1–3, 93–95, 107, 111
obstetricians, 59, 61n3, 71–72, 78, 82, 86, 107, 111
OECD, 25
OPORTUNIDADES. *See* IMSS-BIENESTAR
oxytocin. *See* Pitocin

P
parenthood, 26–27, 29, 156, 174
partera
  barrio partera, 65–68, 71, 73, 76, 81, 93
  empírica, 65–66
  profesional, 65, 86
  técnica, 65
  tradicional, 65–66

See also midwives
personhood (and coloniality), 5, 14
Pitocin, 34
placenta, 48
Plan Nacional del Desarrollo 2013–2018, 34
political economy, 3, 8, 96, 161–163
  of emotions, 144, 161
population
  Chiapas, 24–25, 33–34
  Indigenous, 21, 23, 25
  Mexican (fertility and mortality), 27–29, 50
  San Cristóbal de Las Casas, 20–23, 78
positionality (author's), 173–174
postpartum
  beliefs, 117–119, 130–138, 140–141
  care after caesarean birth, 128–129
  care following home birth, 120–125
  depression, 38, 55, 139, 150
  at home, 130–142 (*see also cuarenta días*)
  and illness, 123–125
poverty
  anti-poverty programmes, 2–3, 9n1
  in Chiapas, 24–25, 35, 49
power relations
  between state and society, 5–6, 58
  and breastfeeding, 130–134, 140
  and childbearing, 36, 42, 48, 50–53, 58–59, 71, 73, 78–79, 109–111
  colonial, 4, 21
  gender and, 55, 162, 164–165, 167
pregnancy
  adolescent, 26, 28–29, 44
  in the *barrio*, 68–70, 73–78, 81–82, 120–122, 126–127, 130, 137, 139, 153, 157–158
  and birth centre women, 97, 101–103, 105–110
  during fieldwork, 175
  and illness, 39–42, 57–58, 61n4
  institutional management of, 49, 52, 56, 113n11
  and lone mothers, 145–148, 150
  obstetric violence during, 37–42, 58–59
  and state health programmes, 34
prenatal care, 25, 39–45, 51, 68–69, 82, 89, 92, 125, 127, 158. *See also* antental care
primary health care, 24, 76, 82
Programa de Acción Específico para la Atención (PAE) a la Salud Materna y Perinatal (SMP) 2013–2018, 34

Q
Quijano, Ana, 4, 6

R
rebozo, 98, 122, 163
religion, 21, 36. *See also* Catholicism
reproductive health, 4, 27–28, 53, 70, 86, 91, 119, 136, 160, 170–172
risk
  and childbearing, 39–42, 50, 52, 60, 77, 119, 12
  competing cultural metaphors of, 64, 76, 119, 131, 134, 144
  and conditions of emergency, 48, 54
  gender and, 49, 58
  and midwifery, 64, 70–73, 76, 78, 81, 86, 92–93, 95, 105, 109–110, 113n11
Roberts, Elizabeth F.S., 62n6
Romano, Mattea et al., 2010

S
Safe Motherhood Initiative, 25, 82n2, 83n7
San Cristóbal de Las Casas, 20–27, 35–39, 42, 44, 49–50, 64, 111
  history of midwifery in, 66–69, 77–79, 83n5, 87–88, 99, 112n1

postpartum practices in (see postpartum)
Sanchez-Ramirez, Georgina, 113n7
Save the Children Mexico, 28
Scheper-Hughes, Nancy, 144, 174
Seguro Popular, 27, 33–34
self-sacrifice. See *mujer abnegada*
separation
   mother-child, 151, 161, 165–166, 175
   from partners, 149
sex, 140
sexuality, 8, 149
Skilled Birth Attendant (SBA), 66, 83n2, 85, 112n2
social media, 27, 86, 119, 176
Soto Laveaga, Gabriela, 27
Stone, Alison, 145
suegra. See mother-in-law

T
technocratic model. See birth: technocratic model of
teenage pregnancy, 6, 28, 49, 143, 147, 150–151
telenovelas, 6, 14, 27, 126
temazcal, 132
thermal dynamics, 131–132, 135, 140–141
Traditional Birth Attendant (TBA), 66
transfer
   during labour, 70–71, 90, 92–95, 103–105, 107–110, 112n2
transformation. See maternal transformation
trauma
   birth, 36–37, 57, 59, 95, 104–105, 107–108, 110
   iatrogenic, 36, 54, 61n2, 95

trust
   limits of, 38, 64–65 (see also Mills, Lisa Nicole)
   and midwives, 65, 70–73, 81, 89, 101, 103, 106, 109
tubal ligation, 51–52
Tuxtla Gutiérrez, 35, 44, 46, 77–79, 99, 126–128
Tzeltal, 21, 24–25, 44, 97
Tzotzil, 21, 24–25, 83n9, 97, 132

U
ultrasound, 39–40, 42, 46, 75, 82
Unnithan-Kumar, Maya, x

V
vaginal birth. See birth
vasectomy, 51
VBAC. See birth
violence
   gender based, 26, 92
   intersecting forms of, 49, 60, 61n2, 62n7, 90, 98
   obstetric (see obstetric violence)
   structural, 6, 24–25, 83n2, 169, 171, 174
Viveros Vigoya, Mara, x, 4, 6

W
Wendland, Claire, 42
Winnicot, Donald, 143
womb, 35, 118, 123, 133–134, 141
women's hostel. See *hogar comunitario*

Z
Zapatistas, 6, 9n3, 23–24. See also Ejercito Zapatista de Liberación Nacional (EZLN)

www.ingramcontent.com/pod-product-compliance
Lightning Source LLC
Chambersburg PA
CBHW051544020426
42333CB00016B/2091